Also by Frank Walker

Maralinga

'An amazing tale – utterly gripping, it reads like a thriller' *Jon Faine, ABC Radio Melbourne*

'The story reaches out and grabs you by the throat' *Dr Clare Wright, historian*

'Shocking revelations ...' *Margaret Throsby, Midday Interview, ABC Classic FM*

'An extraordinary story – there are things here that would make your hair stand on end.' *Philip Clark, ABC Radio Canberra*

'This account ... sparks a rage in the reader that human beings could be treated with such contempt, such cold-blooded, Nazi-like calculated evilness.' *Law Society Journal*

The Tiger Man of Vietnam

'One of those great untold stories ... Walker tells it with verve and excitement and with meticulous attention to detail.' *Sydney Morning Herald*

Ghost Platoon

'Walker and others like him are doing their country a great service by bringing both the good and bad deeds of Aussie diggers out of the shadows and into the open.' *Sunday Age*

Commandos

'Amazing stories' *Mark Colvin, ABC Radio PM*

'A cracking read ... forget those thriller novels, this is the real thing and the stories are incredible' *Scott Levi, ABC Central Coast*

'Incredible stories ... a great book' *Miranda Devine, 2GB*

Frank Walker has been an Australian journalist and foreign correspondent in Germany and the United States for forty years, covering wars and coups, floods and fires, terrorist attacks and political brawls, movie stars and street crime.

This is his fifth non-fiction book. His first two bestselling books – *The Tiger Man of Vietnam* and *Ghost Platoon* – revealed uncomfortable truths about Australia's actions in the Vietnam War. His third bestselling book, *Maralinga*, lifted the veil of secrecy thrown over the British atomic bomb tests in the outback and shocking human experiments in Australia in the 1950s and 1960s. His fourth book, *Commandos*, examined the most daring secret raids behind enemy lines by Australians and New Zealanders in World War II.

He can be contacted through his website
www.frankwalker.com.au

TRAITORS

FRANK WALKER

hachette
AUSTRALIA

hachette
AUSTRALIA

Published in Australia and New Zealand in 2017
by Hachette Australia
(an imprint of Hachette Australia Pty Limited)
Level 17, 207 Kent Street, Sydney NSW 2000
www.hachette.com.au

10 9 8 7 6 5 4 3 2 1

National Library of Australia
Cataloguing-in-Publication data

Traitors : how Australia and its allies betrayed our Anzacs and let Nazi and Japanese war criminals go
free / Frank Walker.

978 0 7336 3717 9 (paperback)

Social justice. World War, 1939–1945–Collaborationists–Recruiting.
War criminals–German–Moral and ethical aspects.
War criminals–Japan–Moral and ethical aspects.
Atrocities–Law and legislation.
Combined operations (Military science)–History–20th century.

Cover design by Christabella Designs
Cover photograph courtesy of the National Archives and Records Administration (United States)
Text design by Bookhouse, Sydney
Typeset in 12/17.2pt Simoncini Garamond Std by Bookhouse, Sydney
Printed and bound in Australia by McPherson's Printing Group

This book is dedicated to all the victims of war crimes,
and those who fought to bring the perpetrators to justice.

CONTENTS

CONTENTS

INTRODUCTION

History is alive. It will tell us much we need to know, if we can watch, listen and learn. Walking the long, grid pattern gravel paths of the Buchenwald concentration camp, peering into the crematorium and touching the furnaces where tens of thousands of bodies were obliterated in flames, gazing into the cells where innocent men and women were tortured before they were murdered, seeing the uniforms and personal items of those who were killed in this terrible place, brings home that the consequences of history are still living with us today.

Buchenwald is a place of silence. Words are inadequate in this place. But that silence speaks volumes. German schoolchildren have to visit these camps to learn about the atrocities their forefathers committed, an education program aimed at ensuring this never happens again. They walk in shock at what they see. *Was my grandfather here? What did he do in the war?*

On the furnace in the camp's crematorium is a brass plate proudly proclaiming the manufacturer's name. It raises the question, did the manufacturers know what they were building? How could they design such an efficient machine for obliterating the victims of the Nazi regime? Later, digging in dusty wartime files to find out the answers and what happened to those factory owners, the Topf family, it is shocking to discover that they went unpunished, and, even worse, did very well for themselves after the war. How could they not face justice?

Once you start digging, it is horrifying to learn the Topf story is just the tip of the iceberg. Further investigations uncover evidence of so many more horrific deeds and treacherous deals done by industrialists and Allied leaders during and after the war. Many of these corporations are household names today. They are revealed in this book. Their success is neither admirable nor justifiable.

It wasn't meant to be this way. During the war, when a million Australian volunteers joined the Allied fight against the evils of Nazi Germany and imperialist Japan, Allied leaders proclaimed loudly how the perpetrators of the atrocities would eventually face justice.

In October 1943, as Allied fortunes in the war were starting to turn, foreign ministers representing Winston Churchill, Franklin D Roosevelt and Josef Stalin met in Moscow to discuss their progress against Hitler's Nazi Germany. For the first time, there were some hopeful signs that an Allied victory was possible. They knew of the horrors being committed by their enemy – mass murder of civilians, systematic genocide, human experiments, executions of prisoners of war: the list of war crimes was already long.

Churchill and Roosevelt added to their list the war crimes committed by their enemy Japan. Stalin wasn't to join the fight against Japan until 1945. By then, the Soviet leader had his own list of Japanese outrages. After the Moscow meeting, Churchill, Stalin and Roosevelt signed what became known as the Moscow Declaration on Atrocities. It was largely drafted by Churchill, and made a solemn pact that once their enemies were defeated they would 'pursue them to the uttermost ends of the earth and will deliver them to their accusers in order that justice may be done'.[1]

It was a powerful declaration, one they undoubtedly intended to carry out at the time they signed the pact. Initially, at war's end, it seemed the pact would be honoured. The Allies captured hundreds of Nazi and Japanese war criminals and brought them to justice at Nuremberg and Tokyo, and in other lesser-known military trials. Many war criminals were executed; many more received lengthy jail terms.

A large proportion, however, later had their sentences commuted or reduced. This wasn't justice, but sadly the Allies had already fractured. They were at each other's throats in a new war – the Cold War – that would be fought in the shadows. The pact and its promise to pursue war criminals to the 'ends of the earth' was blown away in the new threat of an atomic war that could end all life on Earth.

The scale of war crimes in World War II was unimaginable. Perpetrators numbered in the tens of thousands, even hundreds of thousands. While it was impossible for all of them to be put before a court and tried, it would turn out that far too many were deliberately allowed to walk free.

This book investigates why these people were allowed to escape justice, and shines a spotlight on what many in power would prefer was ignored and forgotten. Why did governments turn a blind eye to war criminals? Why were so many companies allowed to profit from their evil practices? What was behind the decisions by those in power to permit the evil to go unpunished?

Though today the war criminals are nearly all dead, there are some who are still alive and are still being hunted. As walking those silent windswept paths of the Buchenwald concentration camp teaches us, we should never turn our back on the lessons history reveals to us. While Japan has mostly chosen to ignore its dark past of terrible war crimes, Germany, as mentioned earlier, insists its children know every detail of the country's Nazi past. German courts are still convicting men in their nineties for being part of the Nazi genocide. No longer do prosecutors have to prove an accused concentration camp guard actually committed murder himself; under German law, it is now enough to have been part of the horror and have done nothing to stop it.

We learn nothing if we don't confront the failings of our past. And our governments are emboldened to hide truths if they have done so before without consequences. The investigations revealed in *Traitors* detail the ugly side of war and power, and the many betrayals of our own ANZACs who sacrificed so much in their battle for freedom from tyranny. After reading this book you won't help but wonder, what else did they hide?

'The world is a dangerous place, not because of those who do evil, but because of those who look on and do nothing.'

— *Albert Einstein*

1

ANZAC GUINEA PIGS

'There were 40,000 doctors like Meythaler who were all polite and respected citizens but who did experiments on humans they couldn't do in peacetime.'

The young Australian digger listened intently to the heavy footsteps coming down the corridor. He turned his head and saw the Nazi doctor in the long white lab coat take a salute from the German army guard as he entered the hospital ward.

'Not again,' he cried to himself. 'No more, I can't take any more.' He was just twenty-one years old, a nuggety sheetmetal worker from Melbourne. Now he was a lab rat for mad Nazi doctors. He'd been held for weeks in this hospital ward with three other Australian prisoners of war.

He wanted to get up and fight, to defend the other Australian soldiers who had also been forced to undergo the never-ending series of injections, blood tests and bouts of severe sickness that followed.

He was a lance corporal, the only non-commissioned officer (NCO) among the digger POWs. He felt the responsibility of the stripe. He should be leading the men out of this terror. But he couldn't raise himself off the bed. He was too sick from all the injections, and weak from the blood taken from his body. He could only watch in growing dread as the doctor came towards him, holding a syringe filled with blood he had just taken from a sick German soldier.

The young digger struggled to get away. The doctor ordered the guards to hold him down, then, without a word, inserted the needle in the Australian's arm. The Nazi doctor pressed the plunger, forcing the blood infected with God knows what into the digger's bloodstream. The 21-year-old knew that within a short period of time he would once again break out in a vicious fever, sweat pouring out of his body, until he was delirious, vomiting and utterly helpless . . .

•

Lance Corporal George Alan Savage was a typical young Aussie digger. Just months after war was declared, he gave up a good job in Melbourne as a sheetmetal worker to volunteer for the army at Heidelberg barracks. The young larrikin almost immediately found himself in trouble with military authority: shortly after his unit, the 2/5th Battalion, arrived in Palestine for training, he was fined the sum of two pounds and lost ten days' pay for being in Haifa without a pass and swearing at military police.

Swearing at military police is a praiseworthy act among most soldiers, and Savage caught the eye of his superiors. He was recognised as a scrappy young leader who didn't like to be pushed around. Two days before Christmas 1940, the wiry

172 centimetre tall (five foot eight inch) soldier was promoted to lance corporal. A few days later, the 2/5th Battalion and the 6th Division were thrown into battle against the Italians in eastern Libya.

It was the first taste of battle for the Australian troops and, after three days of fighting, they took the fortress of Bardia and captured 40,000 Italian troops. It was a tremendous achievement for the raw troops from Down Under. They advanced west, taking the coastal town of Tobruk on 22 January 1941 and another 25,000 Italian prisoners. Three weeks later, Australia's 6th Division entered Benghazi, weeks ahead of schedule.

The Italians were on the run. North Africa seemed destined to fall to the Allies. Australians had entered the war and immediately made a huge impact. British military writer Len Deighton declared in his history of World War II: 'Australians were widely regarded as the most effective combat infantry on either side in the war'.[1]

But immediately after the Aussie Diggers' hard-earned victories in North Africa, their political leaders stabbed them in the back. British Prime Minister Winston Churchill wanted the Australians and New Zealanders who were in North Africa reassigned to Greece to bolster the defence against the German juggernaut's rapid advance south through the Balkans. Churchill had been impressed by the Greeks' fierce resistance to Mussolini at a time when Nazis and fascists were rolling their armies across Western Europe. The Greeks had forced Italian invaders back to the coast of Albania. Churchill also wanted to demonstrate to the United States that he was taking the fight to the Germans. He was defending the ancient cradle of democracy in the hope that the spectacle would encourage the United States to enter the war against Nazi Germany.

Australian Prime Minister Robert Menzies was in London and Churchill had wooed him to the extent that the Anglophile Menzies was all aflutter. Churchill granted Menzies a weekend stay at Chequers, a rare honour for the leader of a mere dominion nation. Menzies wrote breathlessly back to his cabinet in Canberra that Churchill had confided to him that 'Australia is Dominion No. 1'.[2] Menzies had travelled to England to try to persuade Churchill to send more British forces to defend Australia against the advancing Japanese, but Churchill played Menzies like a violin. He had no intention of sending more British forces to the other end of the world to defend Australia. For Churchill, the war had to be won in Europe first. Germany was the enemy and all energies had to be directed to defeat Hitler.

Instead of getting British reinforcements, Menzies agreed to divert the Australian 6th and 7th Divisions from North Africa to lead Churchill's ill-considered campaign to defend Greece. Perhaps Menzies had forgotten that it was Churchill as First Lord of the Admiralty in World War I who engineered the disastrous campaign to defeat Germany by invading Turkey, which resulted in the bumbled Gallipoli landing. Then again, Menzies did not serve in the Great War, choosing instead to pursue his law career at home, so the similarities with Gallipoli probably didn't occur to him.

Churchill's Greek campaign was a disaster. British war historian Antony Beevor described it as 'the most unnecessary defeat of all in that initial period of Allied humiliation at the hands of Hitler's Wehrmacht'.[3] Beevor said Churchill diverted 60,000 Anzac and British troops at a critical moment in the

North Africa campaign just to save 'British honour'. Military historian Correlli Barnett said Churchill's decision on Greece 'prolonged the war in Africa by two years'.[4]

Anzac troopers like George Savage were totally overwhelmed by the far superior German army that raced through Bulgaria, Yugoslavia and into Greece. The debacle lasted just three weeks. The Anzac and British forces were outgunned, outnumbered and outmanoeuvred by a better-equipped and better-trained German force. The Anzacs fought with great bravery against greater odds, and like the 300 Spartans in 480 BC, made a stand at the historic Pass at Thermopylae. Churchill loved the historic resonance. 'The intervening ages fell away ... why not one more undying feat of arms?' he wrote.[5] Once again Churchill was prepared to fight to the last Anzac. Australian Brigadier George Vasey told his men: 'Here you bloody well are and here you bloody well stay. And if any bloody German gets between your post and the next, turn your bloody Bren around and shoot him up the arse.'[6]

Fighting words, but we know what happened to King Leonidas and his 300 Spartans – and they didn't have to face Stukas, Messerschmitts, howitzers and Panzer tanks. Nevertheless Churchill urged a policy of no retreat, no surrender.[7] Once the Greek government collapsed, the Anzacs were forced to fall back, and on Anzac Day 1941, 50,000 Allied troops were evacuated by the Royal Navy. It was an Anzac Dunkirk, with all the confusion and stuff-ups that go with a hurried withdrawal by sea. Most evacuated troops sailed for Egypt, but Churchill had a new place for the Anzacs and British troops to dig in – the island of Crete.

Left behind in Greece were 320 dead Aussie diggers, 500 wounded and 2030 prisoners. New Zealand's casualties were 300 dead, 600 wounded and 1600 prisoners – a far greater loss given the small population of the country. Britain's count was 150 dead, 100 wounded and 6500 prisoners. Sixteen thousand Greeks lay dead.[8]

Menzies feared the Greece fiasco would be criticised by his opponents back in Australia, and warned Australian Labor leaders that 'it would be a pity for a few politicians to impair our high reputation in Britain . . . our losses are very small concerned with those of, say, Scotland'.[9] That would, no doubt, be little comfort to the families of those who were killed in this politicians' game of corpses.

Meanwhile Germany's Desert Fox, General Erwin Rommel, took advantage of the weaker Allied force in North Africa to advance. The Afrika Korps retook Benghazi and Bardia, and laid siege to Australians and British forces desperately holding on in Tobruk.

Australian war correspondent Kenneth Slessor (also one of the country's leading poets) was furious after he heard Churchill proclaim on radio that the Greek campaign had won the world's respect and was a 'glorious episode in the history of Britain'.[10] Slessor wrote in his diary: 'Either the British or Australian government or both were prepared callously and cynically to sacrifice a comparatively small force of Australian fighting men for the sake of a political gesture – that is to gamble with Australian lives on a wild chance, wilder than Gallipoli'.[11] The Australian commander in the Middle East, General Thomas Blamey, confided to Slessor that the Greek operation had been doomed from the start. Slessor wrote in his diary that Blamey told him: 'I am thinking of the men I sent on the mountains of Greece – what is a gesture to the politicians is death to us.'[12] The truth Slessor wanted to tell the Australian public about the Greece fiasco was buried by the censors and remained hidden for forty years.

Lance Corporal George Savage knew nothing of these games played by politicians – games that sacrificed diggers just as they'd been sacrificed at Gallipoli. All Savage knew was that he had been lucky to get out of Greece alive. While most of his 2/5th Battalion were shipped to Egypt, Savage and a couple of dozen 2/5th men were landed on Crete. If mainland Greece had been tough, for Savage and his mates things were about to get even tougher. Many troops had lost their weapons along with supplies in the evacuation. They were thrust into makeshift combined ANZAC units. The Allied force of 40,000 on Crete was led by the New Zealand Division with remnants of Australian, British and Greek forces evacuated from Greece.

Churchill ordered this ramshackle and under-equipped force to hold Crete at all costs. The order to stand in Crete served no military purpose. It was just pride and bluster from Churchill, a sacrifice he could once again show off to the Americans. Two weeks later German warplanes bombed and strafed Allied positions. On 20 May 1941, German paratroopers shocked the defenders with the first mass aerial parachute drop of the war. In the most ferocious fighting seen since the start of the war, 4000 Germans were dead within days of dropping in. They were killed not only by the Allies, but also by the tough Cretan partisan resistance. German paratroopers managed to capture a vital airfield, however, and transport planes immediately flew in reinforcements. It was fierce hand-to-hand fighting, with New

Zealand Maoris in the thick of it uttering their terrifying war cries. But the defenders of Crete were vastly outnumbered. It was all over in just eleven days. In the final days of the fighting, thousands of Anzacs were pulled off Crete by the Royal Navy and by Australian destroyers *Napier* and *Nizam*, and evacuated to Alexandria. Left behind on Crete were 1692 New Zealanders and 3102 Australian prisoners of war – among them Lance Corporal Savage. Buried in Cretan graves lay 274 Australians and 671 New Zealanders. Also buried were hopes that Britain would come to the Pacific in sufficient numbers to help stave off the Japanese advance. The defeats in Greece and Crete, along with setbacks in North Africa, left Menzies unable to convince Churchill to send more British troops and aircraft to defend Australia. The defence of Britain was now paramount for Churchill. The Anzac sacrifices in Greece and Crete were in vain.[13]

After the long, bitter fight, and with the sight of paratroopers still hanging dead from trees, the German victors were in no mood to make life comfortable for their prisoners. German troops carried out deadly reprisals against anyone who resisted. In some villages, all Cretan men were executed to stop attacks by partisan resistance fighters.

Lance Corporal Savage was captured on Crete on the last day of the Allied fighting, 1 June 1941, and marched into a POW camp. Savage and his fellow non-commissioned officer prisoners were put to work repairing damaged airfields and roads. To comply with the Geneva Convention, which stipulates POWs can't be used as slave labour, they were told they would be paid ten drachmas a day for their work, but they never saw any money. Five weeks later, Savage and two other POWs escaped, hiding in the hills with Cretan resistance fighters. They were recaptured and sentenced to hard labour, working ten hours a day building defence works around an aerodrome and laying wire entanglements on the beaches.

Conditions were hard. Savage later recollected: 'One meal only a day was provided consisting of a handful of cooked beans and one slice of Greek bread at midday. About half a pint of drinking water was provided in the morning and in the evening, but nothing to drink was allowed with the midday meal. In consequence of this treatment I lost nearly three stone in weight.'[14]

Savage and fellow POWs were set to work mixing concrete at Rethymno Hospital on the north coast of Crete. Savage had been there just a few hours when a doctor arrived and stood watching the POWs work. After a while the doctor walked over and, with guards watching, approached Savage. The doctor told him to stand still, then examined his eyes, turning up his eyelids. The next day the same doctor returned and ordered Savage to go inside the hospital. The doctor then gave Savage a thorough medical examination, X-rayed his chest, tested his urine and took blood samples.

The doctor told Savage he was ill and took him to a ward where several German soldiers lay sick in rows of beds. He ordered Savage into one of five empty beds that had been sectioned off in the ward. Over the course of the day, four other Australian POWs who had been working with Savage were ushered into the ward and ordered into the empty beds. Savage identified them as Private Douglas Cheeseman, twenty-three, a grocer from Hawthorn, Private Stanley Williams, thirty-three, a married labourer from Hobart (both with the 2/5th Battalion), Private James Devlin, twenty-three, from Manly in

Sydney, and Private William Lindley, twenty-nine, a cook with a wife back in Dulwich Hill in Sydney's inner-west (both with the 2/3rd Battalion). The doctor examined these new arrivals as he had Savage, poking and prodding and taking blood and urine samples. At this stage it seemed a good deal for Savage and the four diggers. Although weak, they weren't sick, they had a comfortable bed, and apart from sharing a ward with sick German soldiers, they could relax in relative comfort.

The next morning the doctor once again examined the Australian POWs, taking temperatures, pulse readings and blood and urine tests. The doctor returned in the afternoon and Savage saw him use a six-inch (fifteen-centimetre) long syringe to draw half a syringeful of blood from one of the nearby sick German patients. The doctor then walked over to Savage, applied a tourniquet to his arm and promptly injected the syringe of blood straight into a vein. Savage was no doctor, but he knew this wasn't normal medical procedure.

The guards were standing next to his bed and Savage was too weak to protest. He watched as the doctor did exactly the same to the four other Australian POWs. Savage had no idea what was going on, and the doctor said nothing to them. The next day the doctor came back and conducted the same methodical tests of their temperature, pulse, blood and urine, jotting everything down on a clipboard. The doctor then injected Savage and the four other Australians in the arm with a clear fluid. Again, the doctor said nothing.

Within hours Savage felt terrible. He was sweating, felt faint, his head was swirling, his heart was racing and his innards were churning. He was extremely sick, vomiting up what little he had in his stomach. The doctor took notes but offered no explanation, no medicine to help, not even aspirin. Instead, every morning he marched into the ward and diligently took temperature, pulse, blood and urine tests, checked eyes, then prodded and poked the five Aussies in various parts of their bodies to see if they cried out in pain. He took detailed notes on his clipboard and left.

The doctor did this every day for the next ten days. It was the same routine every time. Still no explanation or medicine was offered. Savage thought the doctor looked disappointed when he examined the colour of his urine. He didn't know if the doctor was disappointed because the colour wasn't bad enough, or because he was getting better; the doctor didn't say.

By the tenth day the pain and fever had subsided somewhat. The doctor then gave the Australian POWs a second injection of blood taken from someone else. Savage couldn't be sure if it was taken from one of the sick German troops. By this time he was too weak and exhausted to notice. Two hours later the Australians all fell very sick again. They had the same symptoms as the first attack. But this time their reaction was much stronger.

In the morning the doctor returned and injected the Australian prisoners with a clear fluid. Over the next eight days the doctor examined the POWs every morning, taking detailed notes on their temperatures, aches and pains, and taking blood and urine samples. Through his pain and fever, Savage could see on neighbouring beds that at least two of his Aussie mates had a tube inserted into their stomachs through their throats. It wasn't clear to Savage whether the Germans were forcing something into their stomach or taking stuff out. Again, no medicine was administered, but the doctor frequently examined the Australians' eyes, taking detailed notes on what he found.

Savage saw that the sick German soldiers in the ward received regular doses of medicine. He didn't know the nature of their illness but could see that they were shaking and sweating from fever and their skin was markedly yellow. One patient was close enough for Savage to see his eyes, and he was shocked to see that even his eyes were yellow.

By the eighteenth day Savage and his fellow POWs were starting to recover. He feared the doctor would see their improved condition and try to inflict another bout of injections and tests on them. When the doctor came in that morning with a collection of needles, Savage knew he had to make a stand. He only had one stripe as a lance corporal, but he was the senior soldier in that horror ward and he felt a tremendous responsibility for the four privates with him. By this stage they all knew they were being used as guinea pigs for Nazi medical experiments. Despite their frail condition, the POWs were determined to fight back. During the night the five had whispered to each other so the guards could not hear, and agreed they would not let themselves be injected again.

As the doctor approached, Savage struggled and lashed out at him, shouting as hard as he could that he would not be injected again. He thrashed around, making it difficult for the doctor to get a grip. The four other diggers started shouting too, telling the doctor in good Aussie vernacular to leave Savage alone.

In the stiff, dry words of a military report typed up years later, when Savage reported to Australian army authorities what had happened at the hospital: 'I protested (in which the other four joined in) against the treatment we were receiving. I stated that we all knew that we were being used for experimental purposes and objected.'[15]

Three German guards leapt on Savage, dragging him from the bed where he'd been confined for the past eighteen days. They laid into him, kicking and punching him on the ground and beating him with the truncheons they always had ready to enforce discipline. Savage had been a POW long enough to recognise the bruisers who were beating him – a warrant officer and two sergeants; ranks well above the brutes who normally enforced authority in a POW camp. The doctor must have been influential to have those relatively senior NCOs assigned to act as his enforcers.

Savage doesn't recount the reaction of the doctor to this act of brutality, but says that after the beating they were all told to get dressed in their army uniforms and were taken back to the POW camp.

'No explanation as to our treatment was given by the doctor or the hospital authorities,' Savage later reported.[16]

As soon as the hospital guards dumped Savage and the others back into the POW camp, the German army camp commandant called them into his office. He demanded to know why they had been in the hospital for almost three weeks. Savage told the commandant what had happened, and that they had been used for illegal medical experiments. This breached all conventions of war and violated the Geneva Convention on the treatment of prisoners of war. Savage said the commandant was outraged. He'd been told the five Australians had fallen sick while working and required hospital treatment.

'He appeared to recognise that we had been wrongfully used for experimental purposes and, apparently feeling his responsibility for us, he was very indignant at the action of the hospital doctor,' Savage reported.[17]

The commandant gave them a week off work and ordered they be given a solid meal. Savage believed the food was drawn from the commandant's own personal rations.

'He was sympathetic towards us and stated we would not again be sent to work near the Rethymno Hospital.'[18]

The commandant was true to his word. A week after resting in the POW camp, Savage and the four diggers were sent to work at the aerodrome. Savage scouted for a chance to escape. It was difficult – they were on an island swarming with Germans – but determined Cretan partisans were still conducting guerilla ambushes in the rugged hills, and Savage heard they were prepared to help escaped Allied prisoners. It seems the German tactic of inflicting terrible punishment on Cretan villagers in retaliation for resistance wasn't working too well.

At the end of a day's work, when prisoners were being rounded up to return to the POW camp, Savage hid among the building equipment. A couple of prisoners created a diversion and Savage slipped away, running into the mountains. Alone and lost, he slept in snow for days and fell ill. He found an isolated shepherd's hut high in the mountains and staggered inside to hide from German patrols. Cretan partisans found him there, barely conscious. For ten days they smuggled food to Savage as he slowly regained his strength.

The Cretan resistance were in touch with British special operations agents who were smuggled on and off the island by submarine. When Savage recovered enough to move, he was brought down from the mountain, hidden on a fishing boat and eventually made it to a Royal Navy vessel off the coast. Savage was one of many Anzac and British POW escapees who were spirited off Crete by the incredibly brave partisans, who continued their fight against German occupiers throughout the war.

The four privates who'd gone through the experiments with Savage were later transferred to a notorious POW camp in Germany called Stalag VIII-B (renamed Stalag 344 in 1943). It was located deep inside German territory near the Silesian town of Lamsdorf (now in Poland and called Lambinowice) and there was little chance of a successful escape. It was one of the largest POW camp complexes in Germany, occupied by more than 100,000 British, Australian, Canadian, New Zealand, Greek and French POW enlisted men who were forced to work in nearby mines and factories.[19] Cheeseman, Williams and Devlin survived the war and were liberated by Soviet forces in 1945. Private William Lindley, the cook with a wife waiting for him in Dulwich Hill, was listed in camp records as being shot while trying to escape from a work camp on 30 May 1942. He is buried at Krakow Commonwealth War Cemetery.[20]

The underground escape route eventually got George Savage to Syria, where he rejoined the Australian forces. Four weeks after leaving Crete he came down with fever and severe sickness. Australian army doctors were mystified. They wrote it down as 'an interesting pyrexia which we have investigated without success'.[21] Over the course of a week he slowly recovered, and was returned to Australia where he fell ill once again, with symptoms including high fever and body pains, especially in the back, and cramps in the legs. Savage was fine for a while, then nine months later, on 9 September 1942, he again became seriously ill and was admitted to Seymour Camp Hospital in Victoria. He had a high pulse rate and aches and pains. He was diagnosed with mild anxiety neurosis.

Weak and underweight, Savage was transferred to a salvage unit where his skills as a sheetmetal worker could be utilised. It was while talking to Australian military doctors that he revealed what had been done to him while he was a prisoner of war on Crete. The doctors concluded from his symptoms and recovery patterns that the German doctor had been injecting him with blood taken from patients suffering typhoid or malaria. The Australian army doctors were shocked at this human experimentation conducted on POWs and reported their concerns to senior officers. In April 1943 Savage sat down with Australian military intelligence officers and finally told his story.

His account was recorded in the usual dry military manner, but the contents were shocking. It was classified 'Secret' and filed away. Copies were sent to Australian military authorities in London to be passed on to British authorities 'for any action deemed necessary'. So far as is known, the file disappeared into the dusty war archives and nothing was done.[22]

Savage's file is the only known documented account of Australian prisoners of war being used in Nazi medical experiments. Perhaps other Australians were used, but none made it home to tell their story.

The file gathered dust until 2016 when it was found in the Australian National Archives. Australian surgeon and academic George Weisz examined the file and, using his medical knowledge, tracked down the identity of the Nazi doctor who had conducted the illegal experiments on the Australian POWs. Weisz identified the doctor as SS physician Dr Friedrich Meythaler, a renowned German bacteriologist who was trying to establish how infectious hepatitis was transmitted from one human to another. Before the war Meythaler had written numerous well-regarded papers on liver dysfunction and infectious disease. At a young age he had risen through the academic ranks at Erlangen University.

Weisz wrote in a 2015 academic paper[23] that Meythaler was a Nazi Party member who went the extra step of joining the SA, the notorious Nazi paramilitary Sturmabteilung Brownshirt thugs. Membership of the Nazi Party probably helped Meythaler advance to the position of professor. When war broke out he became a military physician with the SS. Weisz said Meythaler's impressive record of medical papers on infectious diseases enabled him to join German invasion forces in Crete, where soldiers on both sides were severely affected by jaundice. Meythaler wanted to research the transmission of hepatitis, and the POWs gave him the human guinea pigs he needed.

Meythaler made no secret of what he did in Crete. In 1942 he had a paper published in the prestigious German medical journal *Wiener Klinische Wochenschrift* openly stating that he experimented on humans. 'I carried out on Crete transmission experiments from person to person through transfer of blood in pre-Icterian condition,' Meythaler wrote. He said he had 'singular success' in three of the 'experimental subjects'.[24] Weisz said Meythaler managed to achieve results from his human experiments on transferring disease that have not yet been confirmed in a laboratory.

'These Australian prisoners had been used in a non-consented forced experimentation, probably in an ad hoc unscientific, ill-prepared attempt to diagnose the German soldiers' infection,' Weisz concluded. 'Ignoring their Hippocratic obligations, physicians of the Third Reich committed war crimes and crimes against humanity as defined by the Geneva Convention to which Germany was a signatory.'[25]

Historians generally agree that thousands of German doctors committed war crimes and crimes against humanity, conducting forced medical experiments on prisoners from all nations and ethnic groups. Savage's revelation demonstrates it also included healthy Australian POWs.

Meythaler was suspended from academic life and working in medicine from 1946 to 1947 for his membership of the Nazi Party and the SS, as part of the de-Nazification process. But within two years of the war's end, Meythaler was in prestigious and respected positions as Director of Medicine at Nuremberg Hospital and Professor of Internal Medicine at Erlangen University.

World-renowned Nazi hunter Professor Konrad Kwiet of Sydney's Macquarie University and resident historian at the Sydney Jewish Museum said there were hundreds of thousands of medical experiments on prisoners of war from all nations conducted by German military doctors.

'Meythaler injected the Australian prisoners with hepatitis, but he went on to conduct many more experiments on prisoners, injecting them with malaria and other war-related infections and diseases that affected German soldiers,' Kwiet said during an interview in the research centre of Sydney's Jewish Museum, surrounded by Holocaust files, documents, photos and maps.[26] He explained that barbaric and bizarre medical experiments on prisoners in concentration camps and mental asylums, like those done by the notorious Dr Josef Mengele, needed the personal approval of Gestapo and SS chief Heinrich Himmler. But military doctors doing human experiments on POWs, like those done by Meythaler, needed no permission. Each doctor operated under his own code and initiative.

'There were about fifty Mengele-type doctors out of 40,000 doctors – like Meythaler – who were all polite and respected citizens but who did experiments on humans they couldn't do in peacetime. They conducted experiments on prisoners of war to pursue their own professional research,' said Kwiet.

Meythaler went on to enjoy a distinguished medical career, winning accolades for his research into infectious diseases. No mention was made of how he forced Australian POWs to act as human guinea pigs for his experiments. The report filed by Australian military authorities from George Savage's revelation was forgotten. Australian and British authorities simply weren't interested in pursuing the Nazi doctor.

Savage suffered health problems for the rest of his life. He'd survived the ordeal of Nazi medical experiments on POWs. He'd risked his life to escape Crete and tell his alarming story to army intelligence, only to have the shocking revelation buried for decades. It was a terrible betrayal of a brave young Australian digger who had done all he could for his country and fellow POWs.

2

ANZACS IN NAZI UNIFORMS

*'My friend and I vowed we would never speak about it and I
never have – not even to my family or my wife of forty years.'*

Four years into the war, Germany had detailed plans to form
a special combat unit inside the elite Waffen SS, a frontline
force of hardline Nazi fanatics operating separately from the
German army. The new unit was to be made up of British and
dominion servicemen who were sympathetic to the Nazi cause
and willing to fight against the 'true enemy' – the supposed
Jewish conspiracy of communists in the Soviet Union.

It was the brainchild of English Nazi John Amery, the 31-year-
old son of aristocrat Leo Amery who had gone to Harrow
School with Winston Churchill and was a minister in Churchill's
wartime government. In the early 1930s Leo Amery, a rabid
anti-communist, built extensive business connections with
German metal-manufacturing firms and met Hitler on at least
one occasion.

John Amery was the black sheep of the high-society family; expelled from Harrow School, a spendthrift and bankrupt layabout, he became a fascist and strong supporter of Hitler. He raged against Jews, upsetting his family who had Jewish heritage. When he married a former prostitute it was the final straw for his family and they cut off his money. He left for France where he joined fascist groups in Paris. When war broke out, Amery moved to Berlin to broadcast Nazi propaganda on radio to the United Kingdom, along with 'Lord Haw-Haw' William Joyce.[1]

But Amery wanted to do even more for the Nazi cause. By 1943 the German army had formed dozens of special SS military units made up of non-German Nazi sympathisers, as well as conscripts from German-occupied lands. Up to a million volunteers and conscripts made up the special Waffen SS non-German divisions from Scandinavia, Poland, France and the Balkans with names such as Viking, Nordland, Baltic Legion and Charlemagne. Nearly all fought on the Eastern Front against Russian troops. The worst of them joined the ruthless SS Death's Head Unit – extermination forces massacring resistance fighters and Jews.

Amery envisaged a mighty British Legion made up of British and dominion troops held in prisoner-of-war camps who could be persuaded to defect and volunteer to fight for their former enemy. German leaders thought it had a good chance of success. After all, more than 2000 Indian troops captured in North Africa held in POW camps had already agreed to volunteer for the Free India Legion, nicknamed the Tiger Legion, with promises that they would lead a liberation force against British-ruled India.

Amery believed he would have little trouble finding enough volunteers to pull on Nazi uniforms among the tens of thousands of British and dominion POWs, particularly among the lower ranks. Conditions in the POW camps, even for officers, were not nearly as pleasant as depicted in movies like *The Great Escape* or *The Wooden Horse*. Privates, corporals and sergeants were kept separate from officers and were held in significantly worse conditions. POW camps for the ordinary British and dominion troops were dreadfully overcrowded, bitterly cold in winter and uncomfortably hot in summer. Most prisoners weren't properly clothed and went hungry most of the time. They were forced to work in horrendous conditions. Medical help was minimal, and bashings and humiliations were common, administered by both guards and racketeering standover thugs among the prisoners. The camps were a continual struggle for survival.

The Germans distributed pamphlets throughout the camps that argued that the true war was against the Bolshevik barbarians and the 'dragon of Asiatic and Jewish bestiality'. The pamphlets said hundreds of British and dominion soldiers, including senior officers, had already joined the British Legion. They said the crews of RAF planes had defected and landed their planes in Germany to join the Nazi force.[2] It was all a lie, but the prisoners didn't care. The pamphlets were welcomed and seized upon by the prisoners. They made excellent toilet paper.

Amery persuaded the German authorities to offer more incentives. The prisoners were told new 'holiday camps' had been set up near Berlin to welcome converts with good food, new clothes, access to women and freedom to wander outside the camp. This worked for some. A handful of British lower ranks agreed to join up. Most volunteers had already held fascist beliefs and pro-German attitudes before the war. When they left the camps, many told their fellow prisoners they were joining up only to spy on the Germans and hopefully escape to neutral territory, while sabotaging the Germans behind the lines. None of them were exactly exemplary soldiers.

Accepting the Nazi's offer was no simple lark just to get away from the POW camp. Pulling on the uniform of the enemy and agreeing to fight for them is – any way you read it – the act of a traitor. The Germans weren't threatening to shoot POWs if they didn't comply. These men stepped forward and volunteered. If caught, they risked being executed by firing squad.

One of the first to join was a corporal from the New Zealand Expeditionary Force. Roy Nicholas Courlander, thirty-six, was born in London but grew up in the New Hebrides where his Jewish stepfather owned a copra plantation. At the outbreak of war, Courlander sailed to Auckland where he joined the New Zealand army. He served in New Zealand's 18th Battalion in North Africa and Greece, where he was captured in 1941. For two years Courlander was in a POW camp in Austria. He took to posing as a White Russian émigré in the hope of earning some extra food and favours from his German captors. He believed Germany would win the war and spouted his belief that Russian communists were the real enemy. He sucked up to the camp commandant and was made camp interpreter, a position that immediately made him suspect among his fellow prisoners. He was ostracised and shunned.[3]

When the Germans asked Courlander whether he would make some propaganda broadcasts against the Soviets, he readily agreed. He was taken to Berlin and housed in the new 'holiday' camp – a boarding house in the outer suburb of Genshagen. He was given civilian clothes and a pass that allowed him to travel daily to the broadcast building in Berlin. Courlander thought he'd landed in clover. He made friends with several British soldiers who'd also accepted the holiday camp offer. Some had been members of the British Union of Fascists before the war. These men were to form the nucleus of what Amery hoped would grow into the British Free Corps division of the Waffen SS.

Around 200 British prisoners were persuaded to give the holiday camp a try. Most took up the offer because they thought they might have a chance to escape. Besides, anything was better than the dreadful conditions inside the POW camps. When escape proved difficult, most asked to be returned to their POW camps. Courlander was one of the small number who wanted to stay on. He told German authorities he would join the British Free Corps if he were made an officer. But the Germans were coming to the conclusion that they would have trouble attracting enough turncoat recruits to form anything more than a platoon – thirty to forty men.

Amery and a small group of German commanders persisted, thinking the propaganda value of forming a British Free Corps wearing Waffen SS uniforms far outweighed the small size of the unit. The German commander of the recruitment operation, SS Hauptsturmführer (equivalent of captain) Hans Werner Roepke, agreed with a committed core of six pro-Nazi defectors, including Courlander, who argued they'd attract more recruits if they didn't have to swear an oath to Adolf Hitler, nor have their blood group tattooed under their arms like regular SS members. They would receive the same pay as German soldiers and would wear the field grey Waffen SS uniform, not the black of the Death's Head SS. An optimistic army bureaucrat ordered 800 uniforms for the unit – possibly so the commander could bluff his superiors and Hitler into believing that the operation was a great success.[4] The British Free Corps uniforms were German-army grey with a shield bearing the Union Jack on the left sleeve, silver SS lightning flashes on one black collar and a patch of three silver lions on the other black collar. The English words 'British Free Corps' were embroidered in silver Gothic lettering on a black sleeveband.

The British Free Corps officially came into being on 1 January 1944. The eight members, still waiting for uniforms, were moved to a former monastery at Hildesheim, south of Hanover, that had been used to train other foreign units of the SS. Courlander was given the SS rank of Unterscharführer, the equivalent of sergeant, and appointed chief recruiter. Prison guards distributed thousands of pamphlets in the POW camps calling for recruits for the British Free Corps. The pamphlets read:

Fellow countrymen!

We of the British Free Corps are fighting for YOU!

We are fighting with the best of Europe's youth to preserve our European civilisation and our common cultural heritage from the menace of Jewish Communism.

MAKE NO MISTAKE ABOUT IT! Europe includes England. Should Soviet Russia ever overcome Germany and the other European countries fighting with her, nothing on this earth would save the Continent from Communism, and our own country would inevitably sooner or later succumb.

We are British. We love England and all it stands for. Most of us have fought on the battlefields of France, of Libia [sic] Greece or Italy, and many of our best comrades are lying there – sacrificed in this war of Jewish revenge. We felt then that we were being lied to and betrayed. Now we know it for certain. This conflict between England and Germany is racial SUICIDE. We must UNITE and take up arms against the common enemy. We ask you to join with us in our struggle. We ask you to come into our ranks and fight shoulder to shoulder with us for Europe and for England.

Published by the British Free Corps.[5]

Once again the pamphlets were welcomed and quickly pocketed by POWs as excellent toilet paper. Some prisoners, however, read the pamphlet and saw a chance to get out of the atrocious conditions in the camp. A handful actually agreed with the racist nonsense. Courlander spent several weeks going from camp to camp interviewing those who came forward. By April he told his superiors he had 300 likely recruits – certainly an exaggeration, but then the whole operation was based on lies.

One of the first to put his hand up was Australian Corporal Lionel Herbert Battison Wood. He was a 31-year-old former bus driver from Melbourne who was captured at El Alamein. After two long years in squalid and overcrowded POW camps, Wood liked the notion of getting out from the barbed wire fence to a 'holiday' camp. He agreed to join, and then certainly enjoyed himself at the so-called holiday camp. In an act that should have earned him severe retribution at the end of the war, Wood participated in a ceremony at which he swore before an SS captain that he was neither a Jew nor a criminal and that he would fight the Russians. He pulled on German army fatigues, but without the smart Waffen SS uniform with all the Teutonic embroidery. That wouldn't be ready for a few more weeks. Wood was paid the German army rate of one Reichs mark a day, and was able to wander around the town, stopping at pubs for a beer and chatting up local women.

Most of Wood's time was spent idly cleaning barracks and doing a bit of physical training, but in this early stage of forming the corps, Wood and the other recruits had no access to weapons. After three weeks, Wood's conscience got to him and he demanded to be returned to the POW camp. He was sent to a punishment camp.

The next digger to step forward was Private Robert 'Charlie' Chipchase, an English-born 25-year-old former labourer from Perth. Chipchase had a history of nicking off for a few days at a time, and his record was riddled with instances of his pay being docked for going AWOL. He was captured at El Alamein in 1942 and found conditions in the POW camp hard. Like Wood, Chipchase decided to accept the Nazis' offer.

When the war was over, Chipchase told British intelligence investigators that he only went with the Nazi recruiters so that he could explore opportunities to escape. He said he spent two months in the British Free Corps camp but refused to sign the formal enlistment papers. The angry Germans stripped him of his German uniform and bundled him off to a punishment camp. Inside this camp he ran into his old mate Lionel Wood. The two agreed they would never reveal the shameful thing they had done.

Chipchase was never charged with treason, or any other crime, for defecting to the Nazis. His official military record had segments expunged, and it is still restricted. The National Archives of Australia maintain that the restricted material falls under Section 33(1)g of the Archives Act, as the 'information relates to the personal affairs of the individual and is the type of information that continues to be sensitive'.[6]

In a decision that seems aimed at covering up Chipchase's involvement in the British Free Corps, the National Archives stated: 'The information is of a kind that most members of the community would not want disclosed about themselves and which, if publicly disclosed, in this case could reasonably be expected to distress or embarrass the individual and/or members of their family.'

It wasn't until 1994, when Chipchase was tracked down at age seventy-eight for a feature on the British Free Corps in *The Weekend Australian*, that he finally broke his silence. Wood had died ten years earlier, so there was no point in keeping the secret any longer.

'My friend and I vowed we would never speak about it and I never have – not even to my family or my wife of forty years,' Chipchase told reporter Red Harrison.[7]

'I have never enjoyed talking about the war because there was nothing enjoyable about it. I never told my family because I had no reason to tell them.'

Chipchase admitted he agreed to join the traitors' unit, but insisted that at the last moment he'd refused to sign the enlistment papers.

'There were clear-cut motives to start with. The ultimate aim, we were told, was to work behind the lines and do underground work for the Allied forces. I never had any intention of working for the Germans.'

Two other Australians who joined up with the SS weren't so squeamish about getting their hands dirty in collaborating with the enemy.

Corporal Albert James Stokes, a 27-year-old former labourer from Fremantle, had spent almost two years in POW camps after being captured at El Alamein. Stokes didn't know Chipchase before the war, but their records show they joined up in Perth on the same day, 4 March 1941, and then both fought in Palestine, Egypt, Libya and Syria before their platoons were overrun by Rommel's Afrika Korps. They were both captured on the same day – 17 July 1942.

Stokes was recruited by Courlander and arrived in the corps barracks near Berlin in early April 1944. The barracks was in a great state of excitement, as the unit was about to have its inauguration parade on April 20 – Hitler's birthday. The brand-new British Free Corps SS uniforms were ready and Stokes didn't hesitate. He signed papers declaring his loyalty to the British Free Corps, and he was given the rank and pay of a private in the Waffen SS. Stokes was to later tell British interrogators that he had no plan to fight for the Germans, but would use the freedom of the uniform to escape and sabotage the German war effort.

'For the first fortnight I didn't do anything but walk around in uniform enjoying myself,' Stokes told his interrogators.[8] 'I always saluted German officers in the camp and in the streets with the Nazi salute. We also gave the Nazi salute when we entered and left the camp dining room.'

Members of the British Free Corps were advised by the German officers in charge to sign up under a pseudonym. Perhaps the Germans knew their war was doomed, and they were trying to help their recruits avoid a firing squad. There were about thirty recruits at this time, mostly British soldiers who had been members of the British Fascists before the war, but also some Canadians, South Africans and the handful of Australians. Not all changed their names. Some genuinely believed in the Nazi cause and wanted to fight the Russians. Courlander signed up under his own name. Stokes enlisted in the SS as comic book hero Flash Gordon. Chipchase chose the unimaginative nom de guerre of Bill Jones. Wood called himself Aussie Williams.

At this point a fourth Australian joined up. Ronald David Barker, from Goulburn, New South Wales, was a merchant seaman captured in 1941 after the German pocket battleship *Admiral Scheer* sank his ship, MV *British Advocate*, in the Indian Ocean. Adrian Weale, a British army intelligence officer and historian who uncovered the records of the British Free Corps for his 1994 book *Renegades: Hitler's Englishmen*, paints Barker as a crude and brutish character who joined the Nazis because they promised booze, smokes and women. British investigators later described Barker as 'a man of very inferior intelligence'.[9] Barker was, however, the only Australian member of the SS to evade capture at the end of the war.

The swearing-in parade of the British Free Corps on Hitler's birthday provided great propaganda material for the Nazi war machine. Photos were taken of the turncoats posing and smiling in their brand-new SS uniforms. Posters went up around the Reich showing a band of Teutonic-looking British Free Corps personnel, with the call 'Britains Awake!' (sic) and the Union Jack flying alongside the Nazi red and black swastika flag in a marching parade, declaring 'Our flag is going forward too'.[10] The British Free Corps had barely enough men to form a platoon; nevertheless the new SS recruits were taken away to be moulded into a fighting unit. For the next five months, until October 1944, the misfits practised using German machine guns and flamethrowers. They learned about mine-laying and took turns on city guard duty alongside German troops.

However, no German military commander trusted these converts enough to put them in the frontline against the Russians. After all, if these soldiers turned traitor against their birth country, why wouldn't they turn traitor against their adopted country? The British Free Corps was shunted to barracks in Dresden, a military backwater that was a major railway junction filled with refugees fleeing the Russian advance. They were there on 13 February 1945 when 1000 Allied warplanes began the three-day bombing raid on Dresden that set off a ferocious firestorm that killed at least 25,000 people.

Stokes was with a German girlfriend on the night the bombs started to rain down on the historic city. They huddled together in the cellar of her building, the ground shaking from the impact of the thousands of bombs. For three days the bombs continued pulverising the city. When the bombs finally stopped, ninety per cent of the city was destroyed. Stokes emerged and rejoined the corps. Together with German troops, they went into the streets to dig for survivors and bodies. They used flamethrowers to burn the piles of corpses stacked on every street corner. Stokes later told British interrogators that he saw German civilians throwing pictures of Hitler into the flames.[11] It was probably an embellishment to impress his questioners, as nobody else reported seeing that happen.

The horror of Dresden marked the end of the British Free Corps. It was clear to all but the most committed fascist among them that Germany could not win the war. Some members deserted and disappeared into the chaos of war. The remainder were ordered back to Berlin to join the 3rd SS Panzer Division assigned to halt the steadily advancing Russians. The battle-hardened panzer officers didn't want anything to do with these traitors. They ordered them to dig trenches and direct traffic for the hordes of refugees fleeing from the east.

The remaining members of the unit were startled when a tall, blond man in a black SS Panzer uniform with fresh British Free Corps insignia on his sleeve marched into their barracks room and, in a posh English accent, announced he was Hauptsturmführer (Captain) Douglas Webster St Aubyn Berneville-Claye, and had come to lead them into battle. He told them he had been a captain in the Coldstream Guards and was captured while on a mission behind the lines for the Special Air Service. He 'accidentally' let drop he was distinctly upper crust – a Cambridge graduate from a distinguished old aristocratic family. In his toffee upper-class accent he modestly proclaimed he didn't use his title of earl, and urged the men not to call him 'My lord'.

The man was a total charlatan. Born Doug Clay, he came from a working-class family in Leeds. He was a bigamist and a thief. He joined up as a private and was caught stealing from mess mates several times. Despite this, once he 'reluctantly revealed' he was an aristocrat and had gone to the best English schools, the British army made him a captain. He was captured in Egypt and then duped the Germans with the phony story of his aristocratic background. He was keen to get out of the POW camp, as his fellow officers suspected he was a fraud and an informer. Senior German officers welcomed this communist-hating English aristocrat coming to their side in the Reich's darkest hours, and gave him the uniform and rank to lead the British Free Corps.[12]

Berneville-Claye told the twenty or so remaining members of the British Free Corps that Churchill was about to declare war on the Soviets and join the Germans in fighting the true enemy – the communists. He said that once this happened, and Britain joined Germany in a new war against the Soviets, the British Free Corps would be praised for leading the charge against the Red Army.[13] Berneville-Claye told the men they would now all mount up in two armoured vehicles and he would lead them in an heroic attack against the Russians, who were now just kilometres outside Berlin. The bedraggled turncoats looked at each other. One liar quickly recognises another, and the men told the conman to get stuffed. Faced with this refusal to fight, Berneville-Claye grabbed one of the men as a driver, climbed into an armoured vehicle and drove off. Outside the barracks, instead of turning right to take on the advancing Russians, he turned left and joined the flood of refugees heading west. He threw away his smart black SS tank uniform, pulled on a British uniform he'd taken from a prisoner and surrendered to British paratroopers 200 kilometres outside of Berlin.[14]

For some reason, Berneville-Claye was never questioned about his time in the SS. He spoke good German, so he was restored to his British army rank of captain and put in charge of guarding German POWs at a camp in Yorkshire. He resumed his bigamist and thieving ways and was court-martialled three times. He was eventually cashiered out of the army for forging cheques, bigamy, stealing and fraud.[15] With yet another wife in tow, he migrated to Australia, where he changed his life story yet again – working as a radio announcer, deportment school manager and schoolteacher at St Gregory's College in Campbelltown, west of Sydney. In 1964 he told the *Canberra*

Times he had been one of the top five British agents of World War II, fighting with the French resistance and disguising himself as an SS tank officer.[16] In 1967 he was fined fifty dollars for wearing war medals he wasn't entitled to and falsely claiming to be a retired major.[17] He died in 1975, and was honoured by St Gregory's with a debating trophy in his name. In 2008 his past was exposed and the school removed his name from the trophy.[18]

Once Berneville-Claye skedaddled from Berlin, the remainder of the Corps was left to drive trucks and direct traffic around Berlin. After two weeks of that pointless task, and with the Russians forcing their way into the city, the men decided to follow their short-lived leader and run. Despite all Barker's claims of wanting to fight communists, the man from Goulburn slipped out of the barracks, ditched his uniform and headed north towards the German ports, hoping to jump on a freighter. He was never seen again. Stokes decided to join the mass of people fleeing the Russians. Thousands of German soldiers were throwing down their guns and heading west, intent on surrendering to the British or Americans rather than the Russians. Stokes shrugged out of his SS uniform and pulled on prison clothing. There were thousands of Allied POWs roaming around the countryside, as their guards had run away. Stokes headed west until he ran into a British patrol and told them he was an escaped prisoner of war.

British intelligence MI5 was aware of the British Free Corps, and after the war started picking up those known to be involved. Courlander was known because of his propaganda broadcasts, and when he was captured in Brussels he quickly informed on the others. A total of thirty-nine British and dominion soldiers were listed as members of the British Free Corps. Most were captured during May and June 1945. Many claimed to have changed sides in order to spy on the other traitors or to sabotage the German propaganda effort. Courlander was sentenced to fifteen years' jail. He served seven years behind bars, then passed many years earning free beers in Auckland in exchange for his tales of being the only Kiwi to serve in the Nazi SS. He moved to Australia, where he died in Sydney in 1979, aged sixty-five.

Three days after the official German surrender, on 8 May 1945, Stokes was flown to the Australian army transit camp in Eastbourne, England, where he was given some money and sent on leave. Stokes told no one what he had been doing for the past year. 'I was too scared stiff to mention it.'[19] But when MI5 eventually confronted Stokes with Courlander's statement, he confessed. 'I want to get it off my chest. I did not volunteer but was tricked into it by Courlander . . . I was a fool.' He insisted he 'did his damnedest' to try and escape.

Stokes was charged, not with treason but the far lesser charge of voluntarily aiding the enemy. His charge sheet, dated 27 July 1945 and signed by Lieutenant-General Edward Smart, stated 'in Germany between March 1st 1944 and April 30th 1945 having been made a prisoner of war he voluntarily aided the enemy by joining and working for . . . the British Free Corps and by joining the armed forces of the enemy.'[20] The military court dismissed his claim of wanting to escape, saying he was able to wander around Germany more or less free for fourteen months without making any attempt to escape or sabotage the enemy.

Chipchase and Wood were the only prosecution witnesses at the court martial. They were not proceeded against as they had only been with the corps for a few months before demanding to return to a POW camp. On 18 August 1945, Stokes was found guilty and sentenced to one year's imprisonment. He was sent back to Australia in the brig of the troopship *Aquitania*, and formally discharged from the army on 3 December 1945. After his release from jail, Stokes worked around Australia until he was able to get a service pension. He died in 1989.

The upper crust Brit who started the British Free Corps, John Amery, pleaded guilty to treason and was sentenced to death. His trial lasted just eight minutes. He was hanged on 19 December 1945 and buried in an unmarked grave in Wandsworth prison.

3

THINKING THE UNTHINKABLE

'The less that was put on paper on this subject the better ...'

Incredibly, Douglas Berneville-Claye's claim, in the last weeks of the war, that Britain was about to switch sides and join Germany in attacking the Soviet Union, wasn't totally insane.

It was the most tightly held secret in the last months of the war that Churchill had quietly ordered his military chiefs to draw up plans to recruit defeated German troops and together start a new war against the Soviet Union.

Churchill's aim was to drive the Red Army out of eastern Europe. If necessary he would have British and German troops fight side by side all the way to Moscow to beat Stalin into submission and have him bow to the will of the West.

The mere thought of Britain rearming defeated German troops, making them allies, and then marching side by side eastwards toward the Red Army, was truly shocking.

World War II had left more than 27 million Russians dead – thirteen per cent of the entire Soviet population. The Soviet military lost 5.7 million people – thirty-one per cent of its forces. Yet Churchill wanted to kill more of them. Rather than seeing the enormous sacrifice the Russians had made in defeating Germany, Churchill saw only an advantage. The Russians were exhausted and Churchill knew they were vulnerable to a surprise attack, having suffered massive losses during four long years of continually fighting the Nazis.

World War I left 16.5 million dead, but as soon as the war ended Churchill pushed the Allies to mount a multinational invasion of Russia to crush the Red communist Bolsheviks who were still fighting the aristocrat White Russian forces. His rabid hatred of the Bolsheviks shocked even the most ardent conservatives. He described communists as 'swarms of typhus bearing vermin', 'ferocious baboons' and 'enemies of the human race that had to be put down at any cost'.[1]

In 1919 Churchill was still Minister for War and, against the wishes of the majority of the British cabinet, clandestinely sent two British makeshift brigades – including 150 Australian volunteers – to Archangel and Murmansk to fight the Red Army. Many troops mutinied rather than be ordered to fight yet another war; Churchill had to offer extra pay to get enough volunteers. The Australians who volunteered were mostly troops who'd arrived after the fighting in France was over and didn't want to make the long voyage back home without a scrap.[2] Churchill persuaded the United States, Czechoslovakia, France, Greece, Estonia, Japan, Italy and China to join the invasion of Russia with a combined force of 166,000 troops. Two years later the folly was over. The Bolsheviks had won and foreign troops withdrew, leaving 2000 White Russian allies dead as well as 4112 Czechs, 167 Americans and 526 British troops, including ten Australians. Churchill failed, but his virulent hatred of communist Russia did not dim.

Secret British military files buried in the UK National Archives reveal that just one month after D-Day, British military leaders were already thinking about the carve-up of post-war Europe. On 27 July 1943 the chief of the Imperial General Staff, Field Marshal Sir Alan Brooke, met the British Secretary of State for War, Sir James Grigg, to discuss whether, once Germany was defeated, they should try and persuade the beaten enemy to become a new ally to meet the threat from communist Russia, a conflict they saw was inevitable once the war was over.[3]

Military men saw a post-war threat from the Soviets coming much more quickly than the Foreign Office. The British Foreign Office calculated that the exhausted Soviet Union couldn't be a military threat to Britain or the West for at least a decade. The Soviet Union had borne the brunt of the war, and without Soviet forces tying up the bulk of the German army on the Eastern Front, the Western Allies would not have been able to success-fully invade France. On D-Day, Germany had 155 divisions on the Eastern Front and just 66 divisions in the west to face the Allied invasion of France.

The key, as before the war, was Poland. In October 1944, the Polish prime minister in exile, Stanislaw Mikolajczyk, warned Churchill that once the Red Army had pushed back the Germans, Stalin would continue to occupy Poland and turn it into a vassal communist state. The evidence for this seemed clear when the Red Army halted its advance to watch and wait while the Germans crushed the Warsaw Uprising – an attempt by Polish resistance to liberate Warsaw from German occupation – then continued to advance towards Berlin across war-torn Poland. Churchill had little choice at the time but to rebuff Mikolajczyk.

On 4 February 1945, Stalin, Churchill and an ailing President Roosevelt met amid the ruins of the war-damaged Crimean resort town of Yalta to sort out the future of the world once Germany was defeated. It was obvious the end of the European war wasn't far off. Soviet troops were closing in on German territory. American troops had beaten back a German counterattack at the Battle of the Bulge and, together with the British, were advancing towards the Rhine. Churchill was determined to restore the British Empire after the war, regaining colonial administration in nations such as India, despite its moves for independence. Roosevelt had no sympathy for Churchill's ambitions of empire, and wouldn't listen to his warning that Stalin intended to occupy eastern Europe. Roosevelt needed Stalin to declare war on Japan to hasten the end of the Pacific War. When Roosevelt said he planned to remove nearly all American troops from Europe within two years of Germany's surrender, Churchill was horrified. He saw Britain and France being left alone to face the looming threat from the Soviet Union. Stalin was overjoyed at Roosevelt's declaration. It meant his plan for a string of vassal states across eastern Europe, to act as a buffer against another attack from the West, would have no meaningful opposition.

That changed on 12 April 1945 when Roosevelt said to an artist painting his portrait to hurry up, as he had only fifteen minutes left. Roosevelt then stiffened, clutched his head and collapsed out of his wheelchair. He was dead. Vice President Harry Truman was an unknown Democrat Party hack who had had little to do while Roosevelt was in office. He had been chosen for the deputy's position because he came from Missouri and the ticket needed a Midwesterner. But President Truman was to prove a far tougher opponent for Stalin, and a far greater ally for Churchill, in the post-war world. Stalin knew he'd lost what he called an 'honest broker' in Roosevelt, and decided to speed up the Red Army's advance, ordering the attack on Berlin to start four days after Roosevelt's death on 16 April so Russians would beat any Western troops to the German capital. The Red Army had already conquered Vienna after fierce fighting, and Stalin intended to install a puppet government in Austria.

Churchill was desperate, and possibly paranoid. He could see Stalin swallowing up half of Europe. Where would the communist advance end? Throughout the war the most effective resistance guerilla forces in France, Italy, Greece and across eastern Europe had been mostly communist. Could Stalin call on these seasoned and fierce fighters to lead a communist takeover in the post-war governments of France and Italy? Royal Air Force Bomber Command chief, Sir Arthur 'Bomber' Harris, warned Churchill that the Soviets could continue advancing all the way to the French coast and conquer all of Europe.[4]

In mid-April Churchill approached the Chiefs of Staff Committee and ordered them to prepare a top-secret plan for the use of military force to 'bring Stalin to heel'.[5] The high-powered committee, made up of the most senior military chiefs, lay outside the normal chain of command. It was answerable only to the prime minister. Field Marshal Sir Alan Brooke was chairman. First Sea Lord, Admiral Sir Andrew Cunningham, and Chief of Air Staff, Air Marshal Sir Charles Portal, made up the rest of the committee, with General Sir Hastings 'Pug' Ismay acting as secretary. Ismay was an influential figure, as he was also Churchill's personal chief of staff and his close confidant on military and strategic matters.

The chiefs' initial brief from Churchill was to assess Britain's 'potential ability to exert pressure on Russia by the threat or use of force'.[6] They were tasked with calculating the chances of the success of a surprise strike on the Soviet Union led by British and US forces within two months of the surrender of Nazi Germany. The aim of the attack was to force upon Stalin 'the will' of the Western Allies by first recovering Polish territory, then penetrating the territory of the Soviet Union itself. Once the Red Army was defeated, the Western Allies would determine the fate of post-war Europe.

It was an astonishing plan, one of utmost treachery against a long-standing ally in the fight against Nazi Germany; treachery against a people who had suffered far more destruction and death than Britain, and far, far more than the US. Research for the plan was handed piecemeal to the Joint Planning Staff, a tight group of senior officers operating in maximum secrecy who worked on contingency plans for all sorts of scenarios, some of them highly improbable. They were already working on plans for possible fanatical Nazi holdouts in Bavaria, operations in Burma and Borneo, and other campaigns. All those secret preparations were put aside to draw up fresh military plans to start World War III.

Throughout April 1945 the Red Army fought one of the fiercest and most deadly battles of the war as they advanced street by street into Berlin. On 18 April, German forces in the Ruhr surrendered to British and American forces. On 28 April, Italian dictator Mussolini was captured by partisans and hanged. Concentration camps at Buchenwald, Belsen and

Dachau were liberated. On 30 April, Hitler committed suicide in his bunker. On 2 May, German troops in Italy surrendered. On 7 May, General Alfred Jodl, chief of Operations Staff in the German High Command, signed the unconditional surrender of German forces at General Eisenhower's headquarters in Riems. On 8 May, Germany formally surrendered to the Allies in the presence of Soviet and Western military chiefs. It was V-E Day – Victory in Europe. In the Pacific, the war against Japan continued.

Regardless of victory in Europe, in London the Joint Planning Staff continued to work right through April and May preparing a battle plan for World War III. They even set a date for launching the new war – 1 July 1945.

In a report[7] prepared for the Chiefs of Staff Committee on 22 May, the planners outlined basic assumptions needed for the treacherous surprise attack on the Soviet Union to work:

(a) The undertaking has the full support of public opinion in both the British Empire and the United States and consequently, the morale of British and American troops continues high.
(b) Great Britain and the United States have full assistance from the Polish armed forces.

The report then dropped a sensational assumption, one that was truly unthinkable but one which the planners stressed was included in the instructions given when they had been ordered to draw up the plan. Apart from Polish fighters joining the Allies in this new war against the Soviet Union, the planners

said they could 'count upon the use of German manpower and
what remains of German industrial capacity'.[8]

In other words, Churchill's plan to start a war with the
Soviet Union immediately after the defeat of Nazi Germany was
to rearm German troops and then have British and American
troops fight alongside their former enemy against their former
ally. Intelligence reports in the last months of the war found many
German POWs were keen on continuing to fight. Some had
asked if they could enlist to fight Japan. They feared communist
Soviet occupation of half of Germany and were aware of the
terrible revenge that had been taken by Red Army troops on
German civilians and military prisoners. Two million German
troops surrendered to the British in 1945, and around a quarter
of a million were anticipated to be used as labour to rebuild a
shattered Britain. Many German soldiers were being used by
American forces to help maintain order in US-occupied areas,
and there was already widespread fraternisation.

The report did not delve into the question of what to do
with Nazi fanatics, members of units that committed atrocities
or suspected Nazi war criminals. Would Nazis be excluded from
any new German allied force? Who would lead the German
force? Revelations of the horrors of concentration camps had
already emerged, which made it hard to persuade the British
and American public that Germans should now be accepted as
military allies.

Those closest to Churchill had their doubts about what he
was doing. Fifteen years after the war, Ismay published in his
memoirs: 'Should they [Britain and the US] have forgotten all
that they had said about their determination to destroy Nazism,
taken the Germans into their fold, and proceed with their help

to crush their recent allies? One is forced to the conclusion that such a reversal of policy, which dictators have taken in their stride, was absolutely impossible for the leaders of democratic countries even to contemplate.'[9]

Ismay wrote that the British people had for years been told the Russians were a brave and faithful ally who had done the lion's share of the fighting and endured untold suffering. Any attempt to now paint them as an evil that must be obliterated would have a 'catastrophic' effect on the unity of the people.[10] The British people were also exhausted from six years of war and were not likely to look kindly on starting a new war.

It is not known whether Ismay told Churchill of his doubts and concerns, but the planners' report left little doubt that starting a war with Russia would end badly. The report said that the object would be to 'impose upon Russia the will of the United States and British Empire'. It continued:

> Even though 'the will' of those two countries may be defined
> as no more than a square deal for Poland, that does not neces-
> sarily limit the military commitment. A quick success might
> induce the Russians to submit to our will at least for the time
> being; but it might not. That is for the Russians to decide. If
> they want total war, they are in a position to have it.[11]

The planners seemed to recognise the extraordinary treachery of the plan. They called it Operation Unthinkable. The thirty-seven page file was classified top-secret and titled 'Russia threat to Western civilization'. The report went on to assess the chances of success.

The only way in which we can achieve our object with certainty and lasting results is by victory in a total war. The result of a total war with Russia is not possible to forecast, but the one thing certain is that to win it would take us a very long time.[12]

The report then outlined various scenarios and battle plans. It predicted that if the Russians withdrew eastwards, as they did with the German invasion, the Western Allies would face the same difficulties of supply that the Germans had, and would be unable to produce a 'decisive result'. Like it had been for Hitler and Napoleon, the Russian winter would be a formidable obstacle. An attack on Russia would require the full resources of the United States as well as the 're-equipment and re-organisation of German manpower' and all the Western European allies. The Red Army was battle-hardened and would be a formidable opponent. The planners predicted it would become a world war. Russia would form an alliance with Japan, prolonging the Pacific War. Russia would probably seize Turkey and block naval access to Greece. Russia would also seize the oil fields of Persia (now called Iran) and Iraq.

Western air and naval superiority would count for little, as Russian industry and military strongholds were widely dispersed and not easy to destroy. The West could mount at most forty-seven divisions in an attack, while the Red Army had 170 divisions – around seven million troops. These odds meant launching an offensive would be 'a hazardous undertaking'.[13] It concluded that even if the Western Allies were to win a quick war in Europe and get the concessions they wanted from Russia, the military power of Russia would not be broken and they could counterattack at any time.

The planners estimated the new German allies could supply ten divisions, but they could not be 'reformed' or re-equipped for the early stages of an attack starting on 1 July. They might be ready to join the fighting by autumn.

All these preparations meant that the Russians probably would not be taken by surprise by an attack launched on 1 July. Russia could be expected to enlist communist former resistance fighters and freed Russian POWs held in the West to sabotage Western Allied lines of communication in France, Belgium, Holland and Germany.

On 8 June, Ismay wrote a top-secret note to Churchill saying: 'Prime Minister: In the attached report on Operation UNTHINKABLE the chiefs of staff set out the bare facts, which they can elaborate in discussion with you, if you desire. They felt the less was put on paper on this subject the better'.[14]

The chiefs of staff made it clear to Churchill that his pondering on a war with Russia was pure folly. 'Our view is that once hostilities began it would be beyond our power to win a quick but limited success and we should be committed to a protracted war against heavy odds. These odds, moreover, would become fanciful if the Americans grew weary and indifferent and began to be drawn away by the magnet of the Pacific War.'[15]

On 10 June Churchill sent a reply to the chiefs of staff through General Ismay, acknowledging that Russian forces outnumbered the West by two to one. A surprise attack on Russia might not be feasible, but Churchill now feared what might happen if the United States withdrew its forces from Europe altogether. He pointed out this withdrawal would allow Russia to advance all the way to the North Sea and the Atlantic.

'Pray have a study made of how then we could defend our island, assuming that France and the Low Countries were powerless to resist the Russian advance to the sea.'[16]

Churchill wanted to know how much of the navy, army and air force should be kept ready to protect Britain, and where they should be based. He suggested the RAF should occupy captured airfields in Denmark to keep open the sea passage to the Baltic, and the army maintain control of bridges in France and the Low Countries.

'By retaining the codeword Unthinkable the [Chiefs of] Staffs will realise that this remains a precautionary study of what, I hope, is still a purely hypothetical contingency.'[17]

The date of 1 July, set for a surprise attack on Russia, passed without incident. On 11 July the chiefs replied to Churchill. They said that Russia did not have enough ships to be able to invade Britain, and wouldn't have them for many years. No Russian warships or warplanes were available to threaten the Royal Navy. However, the chiefs said that if Russia did plan to invade Britain they would make full use of new weapons such as rockets and pilotless aircraft. Britain could expect a 'far heavier scale of attack than the Germans were able to develop'.[18]

There were, of course, some in the Allied military who were enthusiastic to be first in to liberate Berlin and confront the Red Army much deeper inside east German territory. US General Patton bragged that his 3rd Army could thrash the Red Army on its own, and the Allies should strike against the communists before they could recover from fighting the Germans. Amid a flurry of propaganda photos, American units first met up with the Red Army on 25 April at Torgau on the Elbe River, just north of Leipzig. This was just 100 kilometres from Berlin, but Stalin had made it clear his forces must be first to enter Berlin. Churchill was keen on throwing out the earlier agreement with Stalin that British and US troops would halt along a line that would leave eastern Germany, Poland, Czechoslovakia, the Baltic provinces, a large part of Austria, Yugoslavia, Hungary, Romania and Bulgaria under Soviet control. On 4 May Churchill wrote a top-secret memo to his foreign minister, Anthony Eden, stating that this matter must be settled before the US withdrew their forces from Europe. Churchill wrote that failure to act now would mean 'there are no prospects of a satisfactory solution and very little of preventing a Third World War.'[19]

Amid fears that the Red Army would land forces in Denmark, British forces raced east to seize the German port city of Lubeck. They arrived with just hours to spare to stop the further advance of Russian forces. Fighting effectively ended on all fronts on 7 May.

A flashpoint was developing further to the south. In Austria, Soviet forces had advanced deep into the country, seizing control of Vienna. Churchill feared that on the other side of the Alps the communist Yugoslav partisan forces under Tito would try to take the north-east corner of Italy – a long-contested stretch of mountainous country called Venezia Giulia, around Trieste, that was the gate to the Balkans. Churchill wanted the British 8th Army that was advancing north through Italy to occupy Trieste, then push troops up the Danube River valley towards Vienna. Tito also wanted to occupy Trieste, as it would be an important port for Yugoslavia, and his troops advanced into the city. Despite Tito being a wartime ally, Churchill was prepared to go to the brink to ensure that Trieste remained in Western hands. He urged Truman, only recently installed as US President, to join Britain in fighting Tito for control of Trieste and the region. Truman wasn't keen on starting a new fight in Europe while the US was still battling Japan. The British reached Trieste and faced off against Tito's partisans, who had Soviet backing. Truman said the US would only become involved if Tito attacked British forces in the region. Truman knew the American public had no desire for further fighting in Europe.

A week after the war against Germany was over, in London Churchill privately met the British commander, Field Marshal Montgomery. Montgomery later wrote he was ordered not to destroy weapons of the two million Germans who had surrendered to the British. 'All must be kept, we might have to fight the Russians with German help,' Churchill told him. Montgomery added: 'This was Himmler's view.'[20]

Churchill ordered that all of Britain's war equipment be preserved, to halt the reduction of Bomber Command and slow the demobilisation of the army. Churchill was readying for a defence of the British Isles if the Soviets did as he feared and kept advancing right across Germany all the way to the coast. But all that was about to change.

On 16 July in New Mexico, the scientists of the Manhattan Project exploded the world's first atomic bomb. Two days later Truman told Churchill of the successful test. Churchill was jubilant. The Soviet threat had evaporated. Stalin wouldn't dare launch a land attack on the West now that they had the atom bomb and could obliterate Moscow at any time. Churchill was anxiously awaiting the result of the British election held on 5 July and, at Churchill's request, Truman did not inform Stalin about the atom bomb until 24 July. Even though the bomb changed everything in the strategic balance, Stalin did not seem surprised. Soviet spies had kept Stalin informed on the progress of the top-secret bomb. On 26 July, the result of the British election came in. In a shock result, Churchill, the British Bulldog, stalwart bastion of Britain during the long war, had been voted out.

Churchill's Labour Party successors – Prime Minister Clement Attlee and Foreign Minister Ernest Bevin – largely agreed with Churchill's ambition to restore the British Empire and had no qualms about atom bombs being part of the arsenal to hold back the Soviet Union's territorial advances. Two weeks after Labour took office, the US dropped atom bombs on Hiroshima and Nagasaki. Japan surrendered on 2 September.

•

In many places in South East Asia, such as Vietnam, there were no Americans, Britons or Australians to accept the Japanese troops' surrender. Japanese troops simply hung around their barracks waiting for the victors to arrive. Vietnamese nationalists – the largely communist Viet Minh – had for years fought a guerilla war against the Japanese invaders, with some assistance from a handful of US special forces. With the war over, the Viet Minh, led by Ho Chi Minh, sought to take control of their country from the invaders. The situation was chaotic in Saigon (now Ho Chi Minh City) and Hanoi as partisans stormed government buildings, fighting French colonialists, crime gangs and religious fanatics for control of key positions. However, at the Potsdam Conference in July, the US and Britain had promised France it could restore its pre-war colonial rule over Vietnam. To help with disarming Japanese troops, the Allies decided to divide Vietnam at the 16th Parallel, cutting the country in half. Britain had responsibility for disarming the south while Chinese Nationalist forces of strident anti-communist Chiang Kai-shek would be responsible for the north.

The British officer in charge of the south was Major General Douglas Gracey, an old-school imperialist who arrived on 13 September with 2000 seasoned Indian troops. Gracey immediately armed 5000 French soldiers who had been released from POW camps, and allowed them to attack Viet Minh held buildings.

As violence escalated, Gracey took the extraordinary step of rearming surrendered Japanese marines and asking them to help crush the Viet Minh. The sight of the defeated Japanese, who had committed so many atrocities on their people, being rearmed by the British further infuriated the Vietnamese. It was a terrible act of treachery against the Vietnamese.[21] The Viet Minh hit back, attacking a European residential enclave in Saigon, killing 150 French civilians. Fighting intensified, with Japanese troops fighting side by side with British, Indian and Gurkha troops against the Vietnamese. Gracey called in reinforcements. US ships and planes brought in thousands of French troops. By December the Viet Minh had lost more than 3000 fighters and been forced out of Saigon. Gracey handed South Vietnam back to its old French colonial masters.

In rearming Japanese troops, Gracey had exceeded his orders, but he didn't face justice. On the contrary, the following year Gracey was promoted, awarded a knighthood and given command of British forces in India. His actions in Vietnam helped lay the foundation for a bitter thirty-year war that was to drag in France, the United States and Australia before peace could come to the country. Gracey continued to be fêted for the rest of his life, granted higher rewards until he died in 1964 at the same time that the US was becoming more deeply embroiled in the Vietnam War.

Despite the victory over Germany and Japan, there was only a short celebration by Western political and military leaders. Anti-communist hawks in Washington and London immediately started planning for World War III against the Soviet Union. They envisaged atom bombs raining down on Soviet cities, unaware that the US had only one bomb left in its arsenal. Washington didn't know about Churchill's Operation Unthinkable, but by November 1945 the US Joint Chiefs of Staff were drawing up detailed maps of Soviet military offensive capability. US military chiefs concluded that the Red Army could easily overpower Western Europe, with more than sixty infantry divisions, 25,000 tanks and 60,000 heavy artillery guns.[22] On 2 March 1946, the US Joint War Plans Committee produced its own version of Operation Unthinkable. Called Operation Pincher, it saw the biggest threat of Soviet expansion heading south towards the oil- and gas-rich Caucasus and Middle East. The American planners warned that 'another war will be the equivalent of an Armageddon and that must count on the use of atomic weapons . . . This point is essential basis for US planning'.[23]

In December 1947 the plan was updated. It concluded that America must revise its strategy and strike first with atomic bombs, biological weapons and chemical weapons as a means of defence once it was clear that the enemy was mounting an offensive campaign. US military chiefs believed the Soviets would have atom bombs of their own within a few years, and that they already had biological and chemical weapons. By this stage America had nine atomic bombs. The hawks argued that if the US was going to embark on a 'preventative war' and strike first, now was the time.[24] Truman didn't buy it. He noted in his memoirs that it was foolish to theorise that 'war can be stopped by war . . . you don't "prevent" anything by war except peace'.[25]

Washington didn't expect the Soviets to have their own atom bomb until 1952, so when the Soviets exploded their first bomb in 1949 the whole plan of first attack had to be rewritten. By this time, the US had 400 atomic bombs available to launch against the Soviet Union. The Cold War risked becoming a very hot war, one that would see both countries probably wipe out each other – and the rest of the world along with them. The tactical situation was labelled MAD – Mutually Assured Destruction – and there never was a truer acronym.

The top-secret Operation Unthinkable might have remained buried forever in the locked vaults of Whitehall but for the actions of the man who ordered it. In 1954 Churchill was back as prime minister. He was giving a low-key stump speech in his local constituency when he made a bizarre statement to the crowd: that in the last year of the war he ordered Field Marshal Montgomery to preserve captured German weapons and be ready to hand them to 'German soldiers whom we should have to work with if the Soviet advance continued'.[26] Reporters who had been nodding away during the stock speech suddenly perked up. They had a sensational story, and it flashed around the world. Montgomery said he did not recall ever getting a formal order along those lines, but he later wrote that Churchill had given him a verbal order. Churchill received a storm of criticism for planning to start World War III with Nazi stormtroopers joining British troops in attacking a wartime ally. It was a bitter issue, and many dignitaries refused to sign a book marking Churchill's 80th birthday.

So why, at the height of the Cold War, did Churchill reveal how close he had come to doing the unthinkable? It may have been a serious leak of a terrible secret or, as Churchill himself admitted privately, he'd made a 'goose' of himself.[27] Seven years after the world war was over, Churchill was back as prime minister and was again planning for an unthinkable war with the Soviet Union. This time he was doing it with the willing cooperation of Australia's prime minister, Robert Menzies. From 1952 to 1963, Britain exploded a dozen atom bombs in the Australian outback, and hundreds of other atomic explosions. The aim was to find out how quickly troops could be sent into the radioactive blast zone after an atom bomb explosion. The atom bomb was to be used as a battlefield weapon rather than held as a doomsday threat to deter war.[28] Once again, the unthinkable had become thinkable.

4

NAZIS RUN THE RATLINES

*'One hundred dead are a catastrophe, one
million dead are nothing but a statistic.'*

Josef Mengele, Klaus Barbie, Adolf Eichmann, Walter Rauff, Franz Stangl, Alois Brunner ... some of the most notorious Nazi war criminals to survive World War II were helped to flee justice thanks to the blind eye or unabashed assistance of the Catholic Church, the CIA, MI6 and the International Red Cross.

World War II was over, but the Catholic Church and Western intelligence agencies were intent on fighting a new war – a global fight against godless communism. Justice for the millions of victims of the Holocaust was discarded because key members of the Nazi Party – many of whom had behaved monstrously – were deemed to be useful as allies in the new Cold War against the Soviet Union.

The Allies also discarded the solemn vow they had made to pursue war criminals to the bitter end once Nazi Germany was

defeated. The leaders of the three major Allied powers – UK
Prime Minister Winston Churchill, US President Franklin D
Roosevelt and Soviet Union President Josef Stalin – all signed
a pact drawn up in Moscow on 30 October 1943 to bring the
perpetrators of wartime atrocities to justice:

> The United Kingdom, the United States and the Soviet Union
> have received from many quarters evidence of atrocities,
> massacres and cold-blooded mass executions which are being
> perpetrated by Hitlerite forces in many of the countries they
> have overrun and from which they are now being steadily
> expelled . . . most assuredly the three Allied powers will
> pursue them to the uttermost ends of the earth and will deliver
> them to their accusors in order that justice may be done.[1]

The first to strike a deal with the Nazis was the Catholic Church.
In fact, Hitler could not have gained power without the assistance of the Catholic Church and its political arm in Germany,
the Catholic Centre Party. In 1932 just one in three Germans
voted for the Nazi Party, but in the splintered and chaotic
Weimar Republic, the Nazis emerged as the largest single party
in the Reichstag (parliament). Hitler lacked a majority to form
government, and his SA Brownshirt thugs were running rampant,
bashing and intimidating anyone who opposed them.

Conservative political leaders and wealthy industrialists
wanted stability. They persuaded President Hindenburg to turn
a blind eye to the Brownshirts and convinced the president they
could control Hitler. Hindenburg relented and appointed Hitler
chancellor in January 1933. But the Nazis only increased their
terrorism, arresting, bashing and murdering leftist opponents,

particularly communists and socialists who stood up to them in the Reichstag. After the suspicious Reichstag fire a month later, on 27 February, Chancellor Hitler demanded absolute control. It was the Catholic Centre Party that provided the crucial votes to pass the Enabling Act that handed dictatorial powers to Hitler.

In return, the Führer promised the Party that the Catholic Church could keep its prime clerical powers in Germany, such as schools, community groups and seminaries. The Catholic Church hierarchy didn't want to lose access to the enormous amount of money it sourced in Germany through tithing.

The deal was formalised four months later in the *Reichskonkordat*, a formal agreement between the Nazi government and the Vatican. Cardinal Eugenio Pacelli, Vatican Secretary of State, worked for years to secure this agreement with Hitler.

Six years later Pacelli became Pope Pius XII. He was later dubbed 'Hitler's Pope', not necessarily because he actively supported Hitler or shared Nazi anti-Semitic values, but because Pacelli's determination to save the church from losing power to the Nazis meant turning a blind eye to Nazi atrocities. 'Pacelli behaved like a fellow traveller to the Nazi cause – one who ostensibly remained aloof from Hitler's ideology while accepting his beneficence,' wrote John Cornwell in a new 2008 preface to his controversial 1999 book *Hitler's Pope*.[2]

There were individual Catholic priests and bishops in Germany and Italy who spoke out against the brutality of the Nazi and Fascist regimes. Some priests even risked their lives to protect people from the Nazis. The Vatican Nuncio in Berlin protected 28,000 Jews from the Nazis by insisting that the church could not allow German Catholics to divorce their Jewish spouses.[3]

But throughout the terror of the Nazi regime, most historians agree that the policy of the senior hierarchy of the Vatican was to ensure the Catholic Church emerged as unscathed as possible from the horrors going on around them. Throughout the war, Pacelli, as Pope Pius XII, failed to use his extensive power with Catholics to speak out publicly against the persecution of the Jews and the horrors of Nazi extermination camps as the truth of the extent of the Holocaust emerged.

Cornwell noted that Pope Pius XII did urge bishops in occupied lands – including Holland, Belgium and Luxembourg – to speak out against Nazi attacks on Catholics, but he himself remained silent on the fate of the Jews.

'That failure to utter a candid word about the Final Solution in progress proclaimed to the world that the Vicar of Christ was not moved to pity and anger. From this point of view he was the ideal Pope for Hitler's unspeakable plan. He was Hitler's pawn. He was Hitler's Pope,' Cornwell wrote.[4]

That became clear in September 1943 when German troops occupied Rome. Mussolini had fallen. The Allies were advancing north after landing in southern Italy. Pope Pius XII was trapped inside the Vatican. German Field Marshal Albert Kesselring declared martial law in Rome. The German ambassador to the Holy See, Baron Ernst von Weizsäcker, urged the Pope to maintain his impartiality. In return, German forces would respect the territory of the Vatican. (The baron's son Richard was a captain in the German army who was involved in plots to assassinate Hitler. Richard later became a popular president of the Federal Republic of Germany.)

At first the Germans demanded the Jews of Rome hand over fifty kilograms of gold to avoid deportation. The people of Rome – Jews and Christians – came together and donated the gold. The Pope offered an interest-free loan for Jews to buy the gold, but the Jews found the fifty kilograms themselves and it was sent to Berlin.[5] However, the gold didn't save their lives. Holocaust organiser SS Obersturmbannführer (Lieutenant Colonel) Adolf Eichmann ordered all Italian Jews be rounded up and transported to concentration camps in Germany where they would be used as forced labour until they dropped dead or were executed. SS Death's Head troops began dragging Jews from their homes in Rome on a rainy October night in 1943.

Pope Pius XII was told immediately the troops started their raids. The church spy network had always been extremely efficient. Priests reported that Jewish men, women and children were being forced into army trucks. Some trucks drove right past the boundary of St Peter's Square, and terrified Jews called out to the Pope for help.[6] Von Weizsäcker privately wrote that he and many people, including the German consul in Rome, Albrecht von Kessel, were urging the Pope to make an official protest at the forced removal of Jews.[7] German diplomatic officials feared the SS action could spark an uprising in Rome. The Pope remained silent. Instead, he got Bishop Alois Hudal, rector of the German Catholic Church in Rome, to lodge a protest letter to von Weizsäcker and the German military. Hudal requested the action against the Jews be suspended 'otherwise I fear the Pope will take a position in public as being against the action'.[8]

Von Weizsäcker wrote to the German Foreign Ministry that the Vatican was 'especially upset considering the action took place, in a manner of speaking, under the Pope's own windows'. He warned that the Pope was being put in a position where he may have to openly condemn the action. He suggested that to avoid a schism between the Catholic Church and the German government the Jews be 'employed in labour service in Italy'.[9]

The German officials may have been trying to do all they could to save the Jews from the Nazis, but the Jews were forced into railway cattle boxcars and taken by train north to Germany. Catholic clergy along the route reported back to the Pope that many of the thousands being transported were dying of thirst and cold, and urged the Pope to protest. Still the Pope remained silent. Pius XII seemed to be more concerned about the possibility of a communist-backed uprising in Rome than about the fate of the thousands of Jews. The Pope told the United States representative to the Vatican, Harold Tittmann, that while the Germans had at least respected the Vatican's territory and property in Rome, he feared communist resistance fighters would invade Vatican grounds.[10]

More than 2000 Jews transported from Rome were murdered at Auschwitz and Birkenau extermination camps. Some Italian Jews survived, hidden and protected on Catholic Church property thanks to brave actions taken by individual priests and Italian Catholics. The roundups were cut back after von Weizsäcker's warning, undoubtedly saving many lives. In truth, the Pope's concern about the risk of upsetting Hitler if he publicly denounced Nazi atrocities was misplaced. Frankly, Hitler didn't care what the Pope might say or do. In July 1943 as German troops prepared to move into Italy, Hitler ranted in his headquarters: 'I'd go straight into the Vatican. Do you think the Vatican impresses me? I couldn't care less . . . we'll clear out that gang of swine . . . then we'll apologise for it afterwards.'[11]

SS General Karl Wolff told the 1946 Nuremberg War Trials that Hitler gave him secret orders in 1943 to occupy the Vatican, seize all its treasures and imprison the Pope and the curia.[12] Wolff claimed he deliberately delayed the action until it was too late, and warned Hitler that such an act would cause a major uprising against German forces across Italy and provoke a negative reaction from German Catholics, including troops fighting on the front. Wolff claimed Hitler reluctantly acquiesced and the plan was dropped. Some historians challenge Wolff's credibility, suggesting he was trying to save his own neck at the trials. Other Nazis corroborated Wolff's story. John Cornwell maintained in *Hitler's Pope* that the episode demonstrated that even Hitler recognised the Pope was the strongest social and political force in Italy in 1943, and that the influence of Pius XII and the power of the Catholic Church spread far across Europe. It was power that Pius XII failed to use to save lives.[13]

The Allies liberated Rome on 4 June 1944 and the Pope opened the doors to the Vatican, offering food and a home to thousands of refugees. Pius XII was hailed as the saviour of Rome. The eternal city had survived the war intact. The Pope insisted that the Allies enter Rome immediately after the Germans left so that communists couldn't take over the city. He had also sent a formal request to the Allies that 'no Allied coloured troops would be among the small number that might be garrisoned at Rome after the occupation.'[14]

The Catholic Church wasn't so particular about the sort of people it wanted in Rome when it came to Nazis fleeing justice from the Allies. As the Allies moved steadily into German territory, Rome became the key gateway for escaping Nazis. Like rats leaving a sinking ship, as early as 1943 key Nazi leaders were looking for boltholes outside Germany. Russia was turning the tide on the Eastern Front and America was throwing its vast resources into the Western Front. It was obvious to all but the most fanatical Nazi that Germany could not win the war. With defeat would come the inevitable retribution for the atrocities they had committed.

As early as 1942, the Pope's Secretary of State, Cardinal Luigi Maglione, set up an agreement with Argentina to accept European Catholics fleeing the war as immigrants.[15] Within three years this well-meaning arrangement become the ratline – the main underground escape route for Nazis fleeing justice. Neutral Spain and Portugal were the first jumping-off points for ships and flights to South America. In 1943, the first to make use of this Vatican escape route were leaders of the French Catholic far right monarchist group Action Française, who had fallen foul of the Vichy French. By early 1945 hundreds of Nazis, SS and other war criminals had made their way to Spain and Portugal, aiming to get to Argentina.

Once Germany surrendered, the flow of fleeing Nazis became a raging torrent. Cities lay in ruins, refugees clogged the roads and millions of defeated German troops were shoved into camps by war-weary Allied troops. The Allied search for war criminals began immediately. They knew who they were looking for, and most Nazis in senior positions were quickly rounded up.

The Nazis knew what awaited them. When the Allies had signed their pact in Moscow in 1943, Stalin originally proposed executing 50,000 to 100,000 of the most senior German staff officers. President Roosevelt, perhaps jokingly, said 49,000 should be sufficient. Churchill, who saw Stalin as a tyrant, condemned the notion as a cold-blooded execution of soldiers who had been fighting for their country. It was Roosevelt's successor, Harry

Truman, who pushed for a public war crimes trial where prisoners would be allowed German defence lawyers.

At the Nuremberg Trials, twelve of the leading Nazis were condemned to death by hanging, including the absent Bormann. Hermann Göring escaped the noose by biting into a cyanide pill the night before his execution. Those hanged on 16 October 1946 were Governor of Poland Hans Frank, Interior Minister Wilhelm Frick, General Alfred Jodl, Gestapo chief Ernst Kaltenbrunner, Field Marshal Wilhelm Keitel, Foreign Minister Joachim von Ribbentrop, Eastern Territories Minister Alfred Rosenberg, slave camp boss Fritz Sauckel, Governor of Netherlands Arthur Seyss-Inquart and propagandist Julius Streicher.

Five others were sentenced to lengthy jail terms. Another 1600 Germans were tried in military courts of the western Allies. Dozens of concentration camp guards and SS officials were executed, particularly those held for crimes committed at the extermination camps. Many more were imprisoned. Some were acquitted.

Soviet forces had captured 3 million Germans and other nationals found in German uniforms. For years after the war, these prisoners were kept in terrible conditions in POW camps, forced to work, repairing the damage done by Germany during the war. Official Soviet figures said 381,067 German POWs died in captivity.[16] Some German estimates put that figure at more than 1 million dead. Those suspected of being Nazi war criminals were often executed on the spot by Russians, or they disappeared into Gulags in the vast wastes of Siberia. The last German POW didn't return home from Russia until 1956.

•

But many of the worst war criminals got away. Top of the most wanted list was Martin Bormann, Hitler's right-hand man. He fled Hitler's Berlin bunker in the final days of the war and vanished into the teeming mix of millions of refugees and dazed German troops trying to find what remained of their homes. Bormann was later tried *in absentia*, along with 200 of the most senior Nazis including SS and military officers, Reich officials, jurists and industrialists. (In 1972, remains found in Berlin were deemed to be those of Bormann, killed trying to flee the city in the final days of the war.)

The International Military Tribunal trials at Nuremberg from 1945 to 1946 were the most extraordinary achievement in bringing war criminals to justice in history. Some of the worst Nazi war criminals, however, managed to escape both the Soviets and Western Allies by scurrying down the ratline. Auschwitz extermination camp SS doctor Josef Mengele conducted sadistic medical experiments on children, women and men. He liked to focus on twins, torturing one to see what effect it had on the other, before killing them both to dissect their bodies. He would feign kindness to children, giving them sweets, before conducting deadly experiments on them, earning him the moniker 'The Angel of Death' among the prisoners. A more vile and evil man is hard to imagine.

Mengele knew he would be executed by the Soviets, and with Russian troops just days away from capturing Auschwitz, he fled westwards. He was captured by American troops in June 1945 and gave his name as Mengele but claimed to be a simple Wehrmacht army private. Although Mengele's name was on the list of wanted SS war criminals, he didn't have the telltale SS tattoo of his blood type in his armpit. When he'd joined the SS,

Mengele had successfully argued that as a doctor he didn't need it. The secrets of Mengele's Auschwitz horror lay in documents hidden in the Soviet occupation zone.[17] The man in front of the Americans presented as rather bland and a bit simple. Evil doesn't come spitting fire with horns and a tail. Like hundreds of thousands of prisoners in the chaos after the war, Mengele was released by Americans from his prisoner-of-war camp and allowed to find his way home.

Instead of going home, where he feared Nazi hunters would be waiting for him, Mengele went to ground. His family insisted to American war crimes investigators who came calling that Josef Mengele was dead. Meanwhile, they secretly supplied him with money. A German doctor got him a false identity card in the name of Fritz Hollmann, and for the next three years Mengele worked quietly as a farmhand in Bavaria. Friends and fellow Nazis supported him and kept his identity secret. He even managed to return to the Soviet-occupied zone to recover hidden research notes he'd made during his Auschwitz experiments. Mengele never regarded what he'd done as wrong. To him, it was just science.

In December 1946, the trial of twenty-three Nazi doctors began in US military tribunals in Nuremberg and the full horrors of the medical experiments in the concentration camps were revealed to a shocked world. Seven doctors were given the death penalty and nine got lengthy jail terms. The rest were acquitted. Some of those acquittals were extraordinary. Dr Adolf Pokorny left the 'Doctors' Trial' tribunal a free man, even though he'd said in a letter to Himmler that 'the enemy must not only be conquered but exterminated'.[18] Pokorny worked on finding the best method to sterilise millions of people in Nazi-occupied eastern Europe. His method was tested in experiments in concentration camps.

Mengele had conducted the same experiments, or worse, and knew he would be hunted down as a mass murderer. But the American hunt for Nazi war criminals was largely in disarray at the time with breakdowns in intelligence and ineffective officials. Mengele wasn't even on their radar.[19]

In 1949 Mengele decided to run the ratline to Argentina. Like many Nazi war criminals before him, he travelled from Innsbruck through the Brenner Pass and into German-speaking South Tyrol in northern Italy, where Nazi sympathisers put him up in their homes and inns. Innkeeper Jakob Strickner, who was mayor of the border village of Gries am Brenner from 1945 to 1969, later boasted to guests that he had helped Mengele escape. It wasn't until 1985, when Nazi hunter Simon Wiesenthal exposed Strickner's Nazi past, that German newspapers reported the local mayor's key role in the ratline.[20] Four years after the end of the war, the ratline was a smooth-running machine. The Nazi network gave Mengele a false ID as a local Tyrolean. Through the Swiss embassy he was issued with false International Red Cross identity papers that functioned as a Red Cross 'passport'.

Within weeks, Mengele landed in Argentina and was welcomed by a network of old Nazis in a right-wing nation ruled by a dictator and a people who largely embraced German immigrants – turning a blind eye to their Nazi past. The Germans were good for business, and Nazi cash flowed in. Mengele got odd jobs but also practised medicine without being registered, often performing illegal abortions. Within a few months he was on his way to becoming a successful businessman selling farm machinery. He made frequent trips to the corrupt and impoverished nation of Paraguay, a sanctuary for some of the worst Nazi war criminals and run with an iron fist by President Alfredo Stroessner. The military strongman was an ardent anti-communist and was backed by the United States for most of his time in power, no matter how many opponents he tortured and murdered. Mengele was in like-minded company. No one was looking for him in South America. The 1946 Nuremberg Trials had been advised that Mengele was probably dead, and with the trials over, few in authority in the US, UK or West Germany were keen on continuing the hunt for war criminals.

Mengele felt safe in Argentina, and by 1956 he was so confident he was untouchable that he ordered a copy of his own birth certificate from the West German embassy. He used it to obtain a West German passport in his own name. No official checked whether the Josef Mengele standing at the counter in the embassy could be the same notorious medical butcher known as the Angel of Death. The lack of scrutiny may have been due to the fact the West German ambassador in Argentina, Werner Junkers, had been an active member of the Nazi Party and senior aide to Hitler's foreign minister Joachim von Ribbentrop. Junkers later told author Gerald Posner it was the job of the consular section to issue passports, not check on their war history. 'I didn't know who Mengele was,' Junkers insisted.[21]

Mengele brazenly travelled around South America on his German passport, making no attempt to conceal his true identity. He even flew to Germany under his own name and met members of his family in his picturesque hometown of Günzburg in Bavaria. In Argentina he lived openly under his real name. He became part-owner of a pharmaceuticals company. All was going swimmingly until he was questioned by Argentinian police over an abortion racket for underage girls. He slipped into Paraguay where, with the help of the Nazi network, he was granted citizenship.

By 1960, Nazi hunters from Israel were on his trail, but Mengele managed to stay just out of reach thanks to sympathetic officials and old Nazis who hid him on remote farms. Pesky newspaper reporters managed to snap a photo of him in Paraguay, so Mengele was smuggled by fellow fugitive Nazis over the border into Brazil. He lived a comfortable family life managing remote farms owned by fellow Nazis. Israeli Mossad agents came close to mounting a mission to snatch Mengele in Brazil, but thanks again to the Nazi network he eluded capture. By 1977 Mengele was in poor health and his son Rolf visited him at a villa near Sao Paolo. Rolf later told author Gerald Posner that he found his father was still an unrepentant Nazi who claimed he had never personally harmed anyone and had only done his duty.[22] In 1979, Mengele was staying with friends at a Brazilian coastal resort when he had a heart attack while swimming and drowned. He was buried in a grave bearing the false name Wolfgang Gerhard.

Mengele's pursuers weren't aware of the death of their quarry, and searches continued for many years. In 1982 Simon Wiesenthal offered a $100,000 reward for Mengele's capture. In 1985 a trial was held in Mengele's absence in Jerusalem, where more than a hundred victims of his experiments told of his horrific deeds. The trial sparked a worldwide manhunt and, after months of searching, investigators followed the trail to the grave of Wolfgang Gerhard. The body was dug up, and forensic tests determined that the remains were highly likely to be those of Mengele. In 1992, DNA testing of the remains confirmed that the Angel of Death was indeed dead. Ten years later, a diary kept by Mengele in Brazil attracted huge bids at an international auction. It was bought for a quarter of a million dollars by a Jewish collector of war artifacts.[23]

During Mengele's business trips around South America he frequently met up with other Nazi veterans living comfortable lives. In Chile, Mengele met Walter Rauff, the SS colonel who developed the mobile gas vans that killed 97,000 Jews, Russian POWs and partisans. As Gestapo chief in northern Italy, Rauff executed thousands of Jews and partisans. At the end of the war Rauff was about to be lynched by an angry Italian mob when American troops stepped in and arrested Rauff, putting him in a POW camp. Rauff escaped and hid in Catholic convents under the protection of Bishop Alois Hudal before he was hired to work for Syrian intelligence.

Later, between 1958 and 1962, Rauff worked for West German intelligence agency BND in Chile. According to German files, the BND wanted him to travel to Cuba on business and spy on Fidel Castro. Rauff used his cover to return twice to Germany for training in 1960 and 1962, but was eventually sacked by the BND – not for his Nazi past, but because of his 'drunkenness' and being 'untrustworthy'.[24] The German justice department didn't know the German secret service already had Rauff in their hands, and in 1961 requested Rauff's extradition. The request was blocked by a Chilean court on the grounds that the 100,000 murders he allegedly committed had passed Chile's statute of limitations.[25] Chile's US-backed dictator, Pinochet, refused extradition requests from Germany and Israel, and Rauff was protected by Chile for the rest of his life. Rauff died from lung cancer in 1984 aged seventy-seven, a totally unrepentant Nazi. Dozens of old Nazis gathered at his funeral in Santiago saluting 'Heil Hitler, Heil Rauff'.[26]

•

The process of ditching a Nazi identity and slipping into a new name with a clean past had been laid out for fleeing SS war criminals as early as 1944. The Central Office for Germans in Italy (ZDI in German) acted as an unofficial consulate for Germans in Rome. When the Americans occupied Rome in June 1944, the Office of Strategic Services (OSS – the wartime US intelligence agency that was the forerunner of the CIA) helped finance the ZDI to act as a central registry of Germans in Italy. The ZDI worked closely with German priests in the Vatican, including Bishop Hudal, who made no secret of his anti-Semitic and pro-Nazi views. Most of the Germans the office assisted with aid and ID papers were genuine refugees, but among them were some of the worst war criminals.

Franz Stangl was commandant of the Treblinka extermination camp, the most efficient death factory of the Third Reich, where 900,000 Jews were murdered in gas chambers. He liked to wear a white uniform and carry a whip. He viewed the people he killed simply as cargo to be destroyed. He competed with other extermination camp commanders to see how many prisoners they could kill. Once it became clear Germany would lose the war, SS guards bulldozed Treblinka in a pathetic attempt to wipe it from history. Stangl was captured by Americans and, despite not hiding his name, remained untouched in a camp for German POW soldiers for more than two years. At the end of 1947, administration of the camp was transferred to Austria.

Stangl was moved to an open camp near Linz, and in the spring of 1948 he simply walked out. He kept walking and hitchhiking all the way to Rome. Once there, Stangl asked for Bishop Alois Hudal. All the ratline runners knew to ask for the Austrian bishop. Stangl later told journalist Gitta Sereny: 'The bishop came into the room where I was waiting and he held out both his hands and said, "You must be Franz Stangl. I was expecting you".'[27] Hudal billeted Stangl in church quarters, and two weeks later presented him with his brand-new International Red Cross passport. It was made out to Paul F Stangl. When the Nazi mass murderer pointed out the slight error, saying his correct name was Franz D Paul Stangl, Hubal patted his shoulder and said, 'Let sleeping dogs lie – never mind.' Stangl told Sereny that Hubal supplied money and arranged a visa to Syria for him and a job in a textile factory in Damascus. Once there, he met several other SS senior officers and Nazi officials living in Syria and Egypt. Stangl's family joined him, and three years later they migrated to Brazil.[28]

In 1961, Austrian authorities finally issued a warrant for Stangl's arrest. Six years later, Nazi hunter Simon Wiesenthal tracked Stangl down in Brazil where he was brazenly working under his own name at the Volkswagen factory. He was arrested by Brazilian police and extradited to West Germany. In 1970 Stangl finally faced justice. He was tried for the deaths of 900,000 people and convicted to life in jail. A year later Stangl died of heart failure in Düsseldorf prison.

Adolf Eichmann, one of the architects of the Final Solution (the Nazis' euphemism for the annihilation of Jewish people), was the next big-name Nazi to come down the ratline. He knew what was to come if Germany lost the war. When asked by one of his officers what would happen if the world asked about the millions of dead, Eichmann replied: 'One hundred dead are a catastrophe, one million dead are nothing but a statistic.'[29]

Like Stangl, SS Obersturmbannführer (lieutenant colonel) Eichmann was captured by Americans after the war and kept prisoner in a special POW camp for SS officers. He had false identity papers saying he was Otto Eckmann, but fearing his true identity was about to be exposed, he escaped from a work detail and went to ground inside Germany living as a forester under a different false name. The Nuremberg trials of 1946 exposed the efficient, evil work Eichmann did as chief bureaucrat of the mass extermination of Jews. He knew he had to get out. By 1948 the ratline was well established and Eichmann made his way to South Tyrol. Nazi sympathisers gave him a false Italian ID card as Ricardo Klement. With the support of Bishop Hudal's organisation, the Red Cross issued him with a passport and he sailed to Argentina. Nazi hunter Simon Wiesenthal and agents from the Israeli secret service Mossad tracked down Eichmann in Argentina in 1960. They kidnapped him and smuggled him to Israel where he faced trial. Eichmann was sentenced to death and executed in 1961.

In 2006, buried among 27,000 newly declassified CIA files in Washington, were documents that revealed US intelligence services had known for years exactly where Eichmann was, and the false name he was living under. A secret CIA memo dated 19 March 1958 from the station chief in Munich to headquarters noted that German intelligence had just passed on a list of high-ranking former Nazis, including Eichmann, and their locations.[30] What is shocking is that the documents reveal that the CIA failed to act on the information about Eichmann because they decided it did not serve their interests in the Cold War struggle. Canadian–American historian Timothy Naftali from the University of Virginia found documents that revealed the US feared that bringing Eichmann into the light would attract global attention to the fact that the Americans and West Germans had recruited former Nazis in the fight against communism.[31] The CIA clearly didn't see its job as tracking down Nazi war criminals. After all, ex-Nazis were rabid anti-communists and useful in the CIA's new Cold War. Some had been placed in senior positions. Eichmann's own wartime deputy, Dr Hans Maria Globke, an unremarkable civil servant who drafted the Nuremberg Race Laws (described by Eichmann as 'basic for the Final Solution of the Jewish people'), had risen to the top of the government of the new Federal Republic of Germany.[32]

After the war, while Eichmann hid in South America, Globke claimed he'd been just a minor public servant doing his job. He avoided prosecution by blaming his vile paperwork on those more odious than him, or the dead. By 1948 Eichmann's face-less functionary was running the back rooms of the new West German government as state secretary for Chancellor Konrad Adenauer. With a shortage of competent officials who survived the war, Globke managed to find jobs for his former colleagues in the Nazi administration in the back rooms of seven key ministers.[33] If Globke were exposed as a former senior Nazi official, it would severely damage the new West German government, which was essential as a bulwark against the Soviet's new Eastern Bloc of communist-run nations. When the CIA learned *Life* magazine was about to publish Eichmann's memoirs, it persuaded the publisher to delete any mention of Globke.[34]

The files also revealed the extraordinary depths to which the CIA had sunk in covering up the Nazi past of the Germans it hired after the war to spy on the Soviet Union. One of those most concerned about the truth coming out was Otto Albrecht von Bolschwing, who had been an SS Hauptsturmführer (captain) in the SD, the notorious SS intelligence agency. At one time he was adjutant to Eichmann and helped organise mass exterminations in Romania.[35] Towards the end of the war, von Bolschwing had a key role in confiscating the assets of Dutch Jews for the Reich. Despite his past, von Bolschwing was recruited by the US Counter Intelligence Corps (CIC, a forerunner of the CIA) almost immediately after the Allies took control of the Netherlands. The Americans sent von Bolschwing to Salzburg, where he worked his way up the ranks of the American secret service. In 1949 von Bolschwing obtained a senior position in the Gehlen Organisation, an unofficial clandestine German intelligence operation set up by the US occupation forces. The Gehlen Organisation mainly consisted of hundreds of former Nazis led by Major General Reinhard Gehlen, former head of German military intelligence on the Eastern Front.[36] The CIA papers reveal that von Bolschwing pleaded with his CIA case officer to ensure Eichmann was silenced. The CIA did their best to keep Bolschwing's past secret, and in 1954 he became Gehlen's representative in the US. He became a US citizen in 1959 with a job as a defence contractor. In 1981 he was finally charged by the Justice Department for concealing his Nazi past, but died before legal action could commence.

•

Klaus Barbie earned his moniker 'The Butcher of Lyon' for the torture and murder of thousands of French men, women and children during the war when he was Gestapo chief in the French province. In April 1947, despite being known for his savagery and sadism, Barbie was hired by the American army's CIC and became a paid employee of US intelligence.[37]

At the time, Barbie was on the run from British, American and, most of all, French war crime investigators to face justice for his war crimes. But the CIC wanted Barbie's skill and local knowledge to garner information on communist agents and influence in Europe. Barbie had a track record – he'd hunted down French communist resistance fighters around Lyon and personally tortured them. He was a sadist who liked to skin his victims alive, bit by bit, while interrogating them. He beat children to a pulp in front of their parents. He was responsible for massacring up to 4000 Jews, resistance fighters and innocent villagers.[38] US intelligence knew full well what this monster had done, but chose to ignore it and instead had him spy on their wartime Allies – the French and British – as they believed they were riddled with communist spies and Red sympathisers.

The French had sentenced Barbie to death *in absentia*, and somehow learned he was working with the CIC. The US intelligence agency lied and told French investigators they didn't know who Barbie was. In 1951 they secretly shuffled Barbie and his family to Bolivia via the ratline network with the assistance of the Croatian Roman Catholic leader in Rome, Father Krunoslav Draganovic. A declassified CIA document revealed that 'because of French and German efforts to apprehend subject, the 66th Detachment resettled him in South America.

Subject was documented in the name of Klaus Altmann and routed through Austria and Italy to Bolivia.'[39]

Barbie adopted the identity Klaus Altmann and prospered in South America, surrounded by fellow Nazis and Bolivian generals. As a businessman, he travelled to the US and Europe under his new identity without drawing attention. In 1965 Barbie worked as a spy for West Germany's BND intelligence agency in South America under the code name 'Adler' (eagle). BND files describe Altmann/Barbie as 'intelligent, receptive and adaptable, discreet and reliable'. A year later the BND dropped him, fearing the Soviets might be able to blackmail him because of his Nazi past.[40]

In 1972 Barbie drew attention to himself when he gave the Nazi salute and yelled 'Heil Hitler' at the West German ambassador to Bolivia. It led French Nazi hunters Serge and Beate Klarsfeld to pick up his trail, and they exposed Altmann as the wanted Barbie. The old Nazi was protected, however, by the extreme right-wing Bolivian military government. It wasn't until 1983 that Barbie was finally extradited to face justice in France. In 1987, after a sensational trial in Lyon, Barbie was sentenced to life in jail. He died in jail four years later, aged seventy-seven.[41]

•

Another wanted Nazi war criminal to evade justice after the war was Adolf Eichmann's assistant Alois Brunner, the hands-on organiser of the deportations of Jews to extermination camps. Responsible for the death of hundreds of thousands of Jews, he also personally shot dead many Jews. At war's end Brunner worked for several years alongside many other Nazis at the Gehlen spy organisation, funded and supported by the US to hunt communist agents in occupied West Germany. Brunner felt safe, as he was confused with another SS officer named Anton Brunner who had been executed for war crimes. He didn't leave Germany until 1954 when he shimmied down the ratline with documents he said were issued by US authorities to Syria. Under the name Georg Fischer he is said to have advised the Syrian regime on torture techniques, living a protected life and surviving several assassination attempts by Israeli agents. In 2001, *Spiegel* magazine reported that BND files indicated Brunner may have worked for BND in the 1960s, but much of the evidence had been destroyed. He was an unrepentant Nazi, telling German magazine *Bunte* in 1985 that his only regret was that he didn't kill more Jews.[42] In 2014 the Simon Wiesenthal Center said it had confirmed that Brunner died in 2010, living to the ripe age of ninety-eight.[43]

These were just some of the worst Nazi mass murderers, sadists and mad scientists who escaped justice at the end of the war with the secret assistance of Allied intelligence agencies and the Catholic Church, all done with the new fight against communism in mind. The Federation of American Scientists examined CIA files released under the 2006 US War Crimes Disclosure Act and found more than 100 high-ranking Nazi war criminals had been employed by US intelligence agencies through Germany's Gehlen organisation.

One of these was SS Oberführer (a senior Nazi rank equivalent to between colonel and brigadier) Willi Krichbaum, who rounded up hundreds of thousands of Hungarian Jews, 300,000 of whom died in concentration camps. Krichbaum never faced trial and later worked for BND. Another was SS Oberführer Dr Franz Six, who commanded a Death's Head SS unit that exterminated the Jews of Smolensk. Six was sentenced to twenty years jail at the Nuremberg Trials, but served only four years before being released. If Germany invaded Britain, Six was to have been in charge of exterminating British Jews and rounding up any opposition. Six later became publicity manager at Porsche. Several other SS officers who had served at Auschwitz, Treblinka, Buchenwald, Dachau and other concentration camps were also employed by Gehlen.

The CIA was set up by an act of Congress in May 1949, taking over the role of military intelligence agencies in Europe. The new US overseas spy agency had the widest possible powers, untraceable funds and virtually no oversight in Washington. Congressman Richard M Nixon voted for the act and when he became president remarked simply, 'If it's secret, it's legal'.[44] A tiny sub-clause of the act allowed the CIA to settle up to 100 individuals a year in the US, no questions asked. In his groundbreaking history of the CIA, Tim Weiner said one of the first people the CIA brought into the US was Ukrainian Mykola Lebed, a fascist and sadistic collaborator with the Nazis who slaughtered many Jews. The CIA's task was simple – fight communism however and wherever it could, regardless of who was doing the fighting.

Who was committing the real treachery and treason – those ex-Nazis who joined their former enemy to spy on their other former enemy, or the Allies who secretly protected them from prosecution and allowed them to live long, undisturbed lives, betraying the millions of people who fought and died to bring down these evil men? As life-long Nazi hunter Simon Wiesenthal said, 'Justice for crimes against humanity must have no limitations.'[45]

5

AUSTRALIA WELCOMES NAZIS

*'His file was marked "should be allowed
to escape", and he did.'*

Buried in US National Archives in Maryland just outside
Washington are secret CIA files that reveal the US intelligence
service sought to dump its unwanted Nazis in Australia. The files
concentrate on a network of former Nazi officers who worked
for US intelligence in south-western Germany between 1949 and
1955. Given the code name 'Kibitz', the 125-strong unit of ex-SS
and Nazi officers were protected from war crime investigations
by the CIA and its intelligence forerunners in the US army while
they were spying on communists and suspected Soviet agents
in Europe. The former Nazi officers were trained in the use of
radio sets, provided with money and weapons hidden in secret
dumps, and were paid to act as undercover US agents if the
Soviet Union ever invaded West Germany.

Unfortunately for the CIA, the Nazis proved to be awful spies. They frequently fabricated or exaggerated information they passed on to their American paymasters. Most seemed intent on keeping the dollars rolling in and exploiting their blackmarket rackets in the chaos of post-war Germany rather than tackling the evil of communism. West German authorities were also concerned that the protected ex-Nazis were encouraging the formation of neo-Nazi political groups in the new German democracy.

By 1952 the CIA decided to dump the most useless of their former SS agents, particularly those who were unrepentant Nazis. A secret CIA file numbered 'EGFA 313', declassified under the Nazi War Crimes Disclosure Act in 2005, reveals that the CIA arranged to disperse their Nazi agents among their Allies. One agent, code-named Kibitz 171 – a former SS officer who had been given the alias Hans Schaeffer – was meant to be 'disposed of' by migrating to Australia. The file shows the CIA got the Australian consul general in Frankfurt to meet Kibitz 171 on 13 October 1952. The deal put forward by the CIA was that if Australia agreed to take the former Nazi, Australia would cover the cost of the journey while the CIA would give him enough money to start a new life.[1]

Historian Timothy Naftali, who examined the declassified CIA documents, found that Australia *didn't* accept Kibitz 171, whom he managed to identify as Horst Otto Ims, and he had ended up migrating to Canada.

But Australia wasn't always so reticent in accepting Nazi migrants.

Australia was determined to build up its population after the war, fearing a future Asian invasion from the north. An agreement was signed with the International Refugee Association (IRO) to sort out suitable refugees. The IRO was charged with excluding Nazis and Nazi collaborators – a tough task, given the millions of refugees seeking new homes in Australia, the US, Canada, South Africa and South America.

The Labor government set a target of 70,000 immigrants a year – so long as they were all white. The White Australia policy had been running since the nation was formed in 1901, with the Immigration Restriction Act. British immigrants were favoured over all other Europeans. This was reinforced after World War I and intensified immediately after World War II. Despite the bitterness of the war, Germans were acceptable as migrants to Australia because, and only because, they were white.

The first shipload of 4000 displaced persons from war-torn Europe left Germany bound for Australia on 30 October 1947. These migrants were carefully selected from the Baltic states of northern Europe and Germany. The faces that would beam from photographs filling the Australian press on their arrival were all young, good-looking, mostly blonde and with 'Aryan features', later wrote the Labor government's Immigration Minister Arthur Calwell.[2] Calwell was such a staunch advocate of the White Australia policy that he readily deported wartime refugees from Malaya, Indonesia and China, even those who had married Australian citizens. When asked in parliament about the deportation of a Chinese man called Wong, Calwell notoriously remarked, 'Two Wongs don't make a White'.[3] Despite the horrors of the Holocaust being fresh in the world's mind, immigration officials were ordered to keep the number of Jews in each group of migrants to less than fifteen per cent. Approvals never got even close to that figure.[4]

Under the program with the IRO, Australia took more than 170,000 migrants from Europe between 1947 and 1951. Perhaps it isn't surprising that a few Nazis, and others wanted for war crimes, would adopt false identities and slip through the vetting process to land in Australia. The IRO screening process was full of holes. Those who feared being knocked back for their wartime activities found it quite easy to get false identity papers. Often they didn't need to. Many IRO clerks were former collaborators themselves who coached Nazi applicants in how to beat the screening process. Some were simply corrupt and filled out papers for applicants and got them rubber-stamped approvals in exchange for cash or favours.[5] Australian officials, mostly military men, then examined the IRO-approved applicants. The officials were overworked and most spoke only English. They were under pressure to approve healthy, strong applicants and get them onto ships as quickly as possible. Their examinations were perfunctory at best. In 1951, the military men were replaced with ASIO agents. ASIO was on the lookout for migrants with experience in intelligence who could work for the agency in the new Cold War against communism. The war crimes of ex-German SS or wartime Nazi collaborators could be overlooked if they would be useful in this struggle against communism in Australia.

The war criminals heading for Australia were predominantly from central and eastern Europe, particularly Slovakia, Hungary, Romania and the former Yugoslav states of Serbia and Croatia.

In 1948, alarm bells started ringing inside Australia's Jewish community that former SS members and concentration camp collaborators were among the new migrants arriving in Australia. Some had scars that suggested the removal of SS tattoos.

Complaints were made to the authorities, but Calwell immediately dismissed them as a 'farrago of nonsense'.[6]

The Australian government wasn't alone in dismissing concerns about war criminals being let loose in the post-war community. In 1948 the British government sent a top-secret message to seven Commonwealth governments, including Australia, stating that 'punishment of war criminals is more a matter of discouraging future generations than of meting out retribution to every guilty individual. Moreover in view of future political developments in Germany envisaged by recent tripartite talks, we are convinced that it is now necessary to dispose of the past as soon as possible'.[7] The Commonwealth countries all agreed, or at least didn't oppose the move.

But stories of SS war criminals infiltrating Australia reached the press, and articles started appearing in Melbourne's *Truth*[8] and Sydney's *Daily Telegraph* about Heinrich Bontschek, a former Jewish 'capo' inmate of Auschwitz who allegedly collaborated with SS guards, and eleven former members of the SS who had been approved as migrants. *Truth* demanded an independent tribunal to investigate. It was becoming a big story. Calwell banned members of the press from boarding ships carrying displaced persons arriving as migrants, and from entering the settlement camps. *Truth* hit back with seven statutory declarations from former Jewish inmates saying that they had witnessed Bontschek punish prisoners with great cruelty and that he was wanted for war crimes by Dutch authorities. After a cursory inquiry, the government closed the case. Similarly, claims against the eleven men who were alleged to be members of SS extermination squads were investigated lightly, then dismissed. Government officials noted that the accused men were not causing any trouble in Australia and they were all good anti-communists. They claimed the accusations came from communist sympathisers and Jewish activists.

At the end of 1949 there was a change in government. Robert Menzies was back as prime minister and new immigration minister Harold Holt mounted a campaign to recruit even more migrants from the ruins of Germany. Holt appeared to be more receptive to complaints about war criminals being admitted to Australia, but he also said that once the Germans were accepted as migrants, all past bitterness should be set aside. According to Jewish historian Leslie Caplan, Holt regarded Nazi atrocities as a matter for 'historic record rather than government action'.[9] Caplan said Holt became increasingly annoyed at strident demands from the Jewish community to investigate and charge war criminals who'd reached Australia, and eventually threatened to freeze Zionist funds bound for Israel unless the demands stopped.

It wasn't only the Jewish community that was rebuffed in their calls for justice. In 1950 the Yugoslav government formally requested the extradition of Branislav Ivanovic, an alleged collaborator during the Nazi occupation of Serbia. In a letter marked confidential to the Foreign Affairs Department, Holt's Department wrote that the Ivanovic family had settled in Australia and handing them over to the Yugoslavs would harm the immigration program. The Foreign Affairs Department told the Yugoslav government, 'it has not been possible to identify this person in Australia.'[10] It was a lie that wasn't exposed until the files were opened thirty years later.

Yugoslavia tried again. They asked for Milorad Lukic and Mihailo Rajkovic to be tried as war criminals. They were charged with denouncing resistance fighters to the Gestapo. Lukic had allegedly boasted in Perth pubs that he had killed many of Tito's fighters by telling the Gestapo where to find them.[11] Both men were involved in anti-communist activities inside the Slavic community. ASIO stepped in. It whispered to Foreign Affairs that the men were valuable in the fight against communism and were working with ASIO. The extradition request was denied.

The Yugoslavs made one more try. They wanted Bogojub Rancic-Veljkovic for allegedly stealing government money. Request denied. Czechoslovakia tried to extradite two of its wanted men. Request denied. In 1951, after several press stories of Nazis hiding in Australia, Holt declared only three former Nazis had ever made it into Australia, and two of them had already been deported. The other was deemed too ill to travel.

In 1961 the Soviet Union asked Australia to hand over Ervin Richard Adolf Viks to face trial for war crimes. Viks was alleged to have been deputy head of an extermination division at a concentration camp in Estonia and personally participated in the execution of 12,000 prisoners in a ditch near the town of Tartu. As Gestapo chief in Estonia, Viks allegedly supervised the mass murder of 2000 people and sent 6000 to concentration camps.[12] Unlike previous cases, the evidence against Viks would have been substantial. Gestapo chiefs liked paperwork, and were proud of the long lists of people they had executed.

Attorney-General Garfield Barwick, a highly regarded man of law, found refuge in the small print of legal statutes. Barwick told parliament there was no extradition treaty between Australia and the Soviet Union, so Viks would stay in a country that enabled 'men to turn their backs on past bitternesses and make a new life for themselves and for their families in a happier community

. . . the time has come to close the chapter' on prosecuting Nazi war criminals in Australia.[13] The Liberal Government of Robert Menzies had just declared an amnesty for Nazi mass murderers, torturers and other war criminals living in Australia.

In 1962 the Soviet Union tried Viks and camp guard Karl Linnas, who was living in the US, *in absentia*. Former camp guards testified that Viks had personally ordered the execution of thousands of inmates, many of whom were elderly, women, children and babies. Viks was sentenced to death on the evidence, and the Soviets once again asked Australia for his extradition.[14] They got no reply. Viks died a free man in 1983. Linnas wasn't so lucky. In 1982 he faced court in New York using evidence from the Soviet trial. He was found guilty and deported to the Soviet Union in 1987. A few months later Linnas cheated the hangman, dying of natural causes.

However, like a painful splinter embedded deep in the body, the truth has a way of working its way into the open. In 1979, ABC journalist Mark Aarons picked up a tip that the CIA's discarded former Nazi spies and war criminals had been inserted among German migrants entering Australia in the late 1940s and 1950s. Aarons began digging and quickly realised he was going to need hard evidence if he was ever to be able to broadcast a story that successive governments had been denying for decades. Aarons was extremely motivated to write the exposé. He came from a left-wing socialist/communist family that had been under close observation by ASIO and other government spy agencies since the 1930s. ASIO has 209 volumes of files on four generations of Aarons, amounting to 32,000 pages – the largest in its history.[15] Aarons was a Jew, and determined that justice should come to those who had committed the horrors of the Holocaust.

Aarons spent years researching the wartime activities of Lyenko Urbanchich, who migrated from Slovenia to Australia in 1950. By the 1970s Urbanchich had emerged as a powerful backroom figure in the extreme right wing of the governing Liberal Party. Brooding, humourless and aloof, and with a fiery temper, he ran Slovenian nationalist paramilitary training squads at his rural property and was leader of a hard right Liberal Party faction dubbed 'the Uglies'. Even conservative rivals in the party described him as a Nazi. In 1979 the New South Wales Labor government described him in parliament as 'an alleged war criminal'.[16]

Aarons trawled through files in Slovenia and interviewed dozens of witnesses. In a groundbreaking ABC radio broadcast on 27 August 1979, Aarons accused Urbanchich of being an organiser for the wartime Slovenian militia called Domobranci, or White Guard, that operated under orders from the SS. The White Guard was ordered to guard railways and bridges, freeing up German soldiers to fight the Allies.

Nazi hunter Simon Wiesenthal said Urbanchich had been declared a war criminal by Yugoslav investigators. Wiesenthal produced pro-Nazi anti-Semitic propaganda papers written by Urbanchich. Aarons discovered the twenty-year-old Urbanchich had given rousing pro-Nazi speeches, acted as propaganda officer for the puppet government and had been described as a 'little Goebbels'.[17] In one article, Urbanchich wrote: 'Jewry, in its mean greediness for profit, pushed millions into the war . . . we went to war for Jewish interests for the benefit of international communism'.[18] Urbanchich was on a US list of Nazi collaborators and would have faced war crimes trials in Tito's Yugoslavia. But, in a processing camp, his war record was 'bleached' by British officials from the black category – which meant he must face trial for his crimes – to the less serious category of grey. White meant you were cleared for migration. Grey meant he wouldn't be handed over to Tito's communist Yugoslav government to face justice. Urbanchich was an avowed anti-communist and the Western Allies did not send anti-communists back to communist governments. They just might be useful in the coming Cold War. Urbanchich was allowed through western lines and was accepted for migration to Australia.

Aarons's ABC report was raised by Labor in both the federal and state parliaments. Labor Whip Les Johnson accused Urbanchich of being 'a friend and a tool of Adolf Hitler'.[19] The Liberal Party still would not expel Urbanchich. The wartime Nazi propagandist insisted that Nazi censors had inserted the anti-Semitic words into his article. He said he'd never given the Hitler salute. That seemed to satisfy the Liberal Party state executive. It ruled that Urbanchich was young when he wrote the articles, and that the war was a turbulent time. However, after the ABC exposé, Urbanchich was poison in Liberal Party circles, and his influence waned. Urbanchich died in 2006, but that wasn't the end of his story. Several of his young disciples in the 'Uglies' of the 1970s later grew into the top ranks of the hard right in the Liberal Party.

•

Thirty years after the war was over, the newly formed Federal Republic of Germany was passing laws to allow people to keep hunting war criminals and to bring them to justice. But in

Britain, Canada, the US and Australia the government attitude was to turn a blind eye to war criminals. It wasn't until Jewish activists and journalists exposed Nazis hiding in the midst of society that governments felt pressured to act.

In 1978 the US enacted legislation facilitating the deportation of war criminals and set up the Office of Special Investigations (OSI) to expose them and deport them. In its first ten years, the American OSI investigation led to more than twenty men losing their US citizenship, another twelve being deported, and 50,000 names being added to a watchlist. Over the border in Canada, in 1985, after significant pressure and claims that 1000 war criminals were living in the country, the government finally set up an inquiry. Two years later, Canadian investigators had a list of 650 persons of interest and fifteen cases likely to pursue in court. Pleas for extradition from West Germany and Israel began to be accepted by US and Canadian authorities.

In 1986, Yugoslavia successfully had Andrija Artukovic extradited from the US. Artukovic, the 'Butcher of the Balkans', was charged with taking part in the murder of 700,000 Serbs, 40,000 Gypsies and 25,000 Jews when he was Interior and Justice Minister in the Nazi's puppet government in Croatia. He was found guilty of mass murder but died in custody in 1988 before his death sentence could be carried out.

Also in 1986, John Demjanjuk was extradited from the US to Israel. A Ukrainian fighting in the Soviet Red Army, Demjanjuk was captured by the Germans and allegedly volunteered to serve as a guard in the Treblinka extermination camp. His cruelty led him to be dubbed 'Ivan the Terrible' by inmates. However, witnesses at the trial were unable to confirm that Ivan the Terrible was the same man who stood in the dock before them.

When it was established that Demjanjuk was not at Treblinka but was actually a guard at Sobibor concentration camp, he walked free. In 1993 he returned to the US. West German lawyers took up the case and in 2001 he was charged again, this time for crimes he allegedly committed while a guard at the Sobibor and Majdanek camps in Poland. After ten years of legal battles, he was finally convicted in a Munich court of 27,900 counts of accessory to murder – one charge for each person who died at Sobibor while he was a guard. He was sentenced to five years jail. He appealed, but died in a German nursing home in 2012 before his appeal was heard. This meant, under German law, that he died a free man with no conviction recorded against him.

These highly publicised trials led to a fresh focus on the Nazi pasts of prominent people. Kurt Waldheim was a distin- guished and respected Austrian diplomat who was elected to the important international post of United Nations Secretary- General from 1972 to 1982. It wasn't until 1986 when he ran for president of Austria that details emerged of his wartime activities. Waldheim had always claimed that his wartime service effectively ended in 1941 when he was wounded on the Russian front. Not so, investigative journalists found in the dusty military files. Waldheim was only out of action for three months, then he was a lieutenant in a Wehrmacht intelligence unit that committed war crimes in the Balkans. He wasn't accused of pulling the trigger himself, but his unit was accused of mercilessly executing partisans, POWs and Jews. Uncovered files revealed that Waldheim had joined the Nazi Party at age nineteen, as well as the bully-boy SA Brownshirts. 'The disclosures sparked a nationalist backlash in Austria that aided Waldheim's election as president,' the *New York Times* said in his 2007 obituary. 'Many

Austrians apparently viewed Waldheim's life as a parable of their own. They identified with his attempts to deny complicity with the Nazis and to view himself as a citizen of a nation occupied by German invaders and forced into their military service.'[20] Was it Austrian guilt or pride that kept Waldheim as president from 1986 to 1992? Throughout his term as president, Waldheim was officially deemed persona non grata by the United States and he could not enter the country.

While governments in the rest of the world were turning on Nazis during the 1980s, and bringing some to justice, Australia was slow to join the movement. It took more prodding from the media and activists before the grudging gears started turning Down Under. In 1986, Mark Aarons hit the airwaves again with fresh revelations of Nazis hidden in our midst.[21] This time Aarons was with American lawyer John Loftus, who had uncovered CIA protection of former Nazis in the US. The hard-hitting program accused Western politicians and intelligence services of conspiring to protect hundreds of Nazis and war criminals and using them as agents in the Cold War. The program targeted Liberal Party member Srecko Rover, accusing him of being a leader in the Ustashi, an ultra-nationalist Catholic Croatian fascist organisation. The program claimed Rover was a Nazi collaborator and had participated in the Ustashi slaughter of half a million Jews, Gypsies, Serbs and communist Croats. The program said that after the war, Western intelligence agents helped Rover and others revive Ustashi terrorist networks. Rover was twice arrested for war crimes, but each time was released – first by US intelligence, then by British intelligence. Rover arrived in Australia in 1950 and the program alleged he was protected by ASIO.

The Ustashi terror campaign against Tito's regime in Yugoslavia collapsed in 1948. Loftus traced up to a hundred Ustashi members who had been settled in Argentina, Australia, Canada, the United States and West Germany. Curiously, the file of Ustashi leader Ante Pavelic, held by US intelligence, was marked 'Hands Off'.[22]

After the war, despite protests from the Vatican, Bishop Gregory Rozman, Catholic Bishop of Ljubljana and Nazi collaborator, was arrested by British military authorities. The program reported that his file was marked 'should be allowed to escape', and he did. He then became a key figure in the 'ratlines' before he settled in Ohio, making frequent trips to Argentina.

Rozman died in 1959. In 2013 his body was reburied in Ljubljana Cathedral.

Another East European named in the ABC program was Dr Laszlo Megay, a Liberal Party member who was active on the party's Migrant Advisory Council. During the war, Megay was mayor of the Hungarian town of Ungvar. The program alleged that Megay had supervised the confinement of 14,000 Jews in a ghetto under appalling conditions, and that he was personally responsible for many acts of brutality. He arrived in Australia in 1950 and quickly rose through right-wing political ranks to become Australian representative on the Anti-Bolshevik Bloc of Nations, a front for British intelligence to coordinate ex-Nazi terrorist organisations around the world.[23] Megay was still on the way up the conservative political hierarchy when he died in 1959.

Aarons reported, 'of the three Western nations in which allegations have been made of post-war infiltration of Nazis, only Australia has taken no systematic action to investigate them.'[24]

Just after the uncompromising radio report aired, the ABC television flagship current affairs program *Four Corners* followed
up asking, 'Has Australia been used as a dumping ground for
Nazi war criminals?' Loftus told the program: 'Australia was
the dumping ground for fugitive Nazis.'[25] Now there was no
hiding for the politicians. Right-wing commentators tried to
rubbish the astounding amount of documentation presented
in the programs, arguing it was impossible thirty years after
the war to understand what people had to do to survive Nazi
oppression.

But the pressure on governments was growing. The Federal
Labor government of Bob Hawke was persuaded to act, saying
it had ordered the Immigration Department to investigate. But it
stipulated that the inquiry was to be done in a sensitive manner,
taking care not to harm innocent people. In other words, it
would be done discreetly, behind closed doors.

In the New South Wales Parliament, Labor minister Frank
Walker (no relation to the author) named six men in the
Liberal Party as war criminals and Nazi collaborators, including
Urbanchich, Rover and Megay. Not one to pull his punches,
Walker said 'the federal Liberal Party government of the 1950s
was an accessory to a monstrous conspiracy against the people
of the western democracies'.[26] He accused the Menzies government of being part of a conspiracy that allowed thousands of
war criminals to escape punishment and allowed many to settle
in Australia.

He said war criminals from extremist groups such as the
Croatian Ustashi, Slovenian White Guard and Hungarian Arrow
Cross were allowed to continue their political activities in
Australia. Walker also said the United States and Canada had

initiated investigations, but that in Australia little had been done to bring war criminals to justice. Walker said it was likely 1000 Nazi war criminals had entered Australia, and he demanded the federal government mount a full and open investigation. 'We as a nation cannot take the view that we will diligently bring to justice future or present criminals if we now grant amnesty to perpetrators who have successfully hidden their terrible crimes for the past forty years,' Walker thundered.[27]

The debate in the NSW parliament, along with increased demands for action from the Jewish community, placed even more pressure on the Hawke Labor government in Canberra, and it beefed up the discreet internal inquiry it had already ordered.

In June 1986 the Hawke government appointed a retired deputy secretary in the Attorney-General's Department, Andrew Menzies QC, to head the inquiry. The government insisted that Menzies's inquiry be held behind closed doors.

Six months later, Menzies produced his report. It cleared Australian officials of wrongdoing. Instead, Menzies said immigration checking procedures were faulty. No doubt many survivors of the governments of the late 1940s and 1950s breathed a sigh of relief.

Was the report a whitewash? Was it a deliberate cover-up? Was Menzies stymied by ASIO and Immigration officials who kept crucial files from him? A confidential part of his report did look at Western intelligence post-war involvement with war criminals, but the summary released to the public was heavily censored.[28]

But Menzies did provide the government with a secret list of seventy people he believed should be investigated as possible war criminals. Most were from eastern Europe, and Menzies recommended Australia agree to requests from foreign nations to extradite individuals back to the countries where their alleged war crimes were committed. Cabinet papers released in 2014 reveal Labor's attorney-general at the time, Lionel Bowen, was reluctant to allow extradition of war criminals to East Bloc countries because of their 'suspect legal system'. But extraditing to West Germany or Israel, nations with which Australia has an extradition treaty, would be acceptable. However, Bowen wanted to have 'absolute discretion' to refuse requests for the extradition of Australian citizens.[29]

The pressure was on the government to act, and in 1987 the Hawke government set up a Special Investigations Unit (SIU) to investigate and prosecute any individuals in Australia believed to have committed crimes against humanity during World War II. Former public prosecutor and senior lawyer on the National Crime Authority, Robert Greenwood QC, was appointed director of the SIU. He had an enormous task. It is far easier to identify an individual as a war criminal than to produce enough evidence forty years later that would stand up in court. It wouldn't be enough for the accused to have just been part of a unit that had committed atrocities. To satisfy the law under the *War Crimes Amendment Act 1988*, a person charged with war crimes would have all the legal defences of any other Australian citizen facing serious criminal charges. Obviously, proving identity would be difficult after forty years. The source of the necessary paperwork was often in East Bloc nations, making access a problem. However, the new law did stipulate that the excuse 'I was just following orders' would not be a valid defence.

Menzies insisted that most of the seventy suspected war criminals on his list had lived 'apparently blameless lives in Australia for many years'. But there were some who may have been guilty of serious war crimes. These included the 'murder of many persons, in some cases hundreds of persons in circumstances of the utmost cruelty and depravity'. Menzies recommended that only those suspected of 'really serious' atrocities be investigated for possible prosecution.[30]

Greenwood got off to a roaring start. He'd gathered a skilled team of fifty investigators and they quickly delved into files held by both the Immigration Department and ASIO. Experienced Nazi war criminal researchers, such as Professor Konrad Kwiet, dug into dusty wartime files in Europe. The Germans were fanatical about keeping efficient files, and they had meticulously documented all their executions and mass murders. SIU investigators scoured eastern Europe to find witnesses to the atrocities committed. It wasn't easy, but they interviewed ex-guards and former soldiers as well as survivors of massacres to try and prove that the suspects they had on their files could be identified as the perpetrators of specific war crimes.

Greenwood tramped through the corridors of power in Germany, Israel, the East Bloc, Canada, the US and the Soviet Union to secure support for the Australian investigation. It was difficult to convince the Soviets that Australia was at last serious about bringing Nazi war criminals to justice. It took a lot of talking – and drinking. Greenwood told Aarons about one vodka-filled night in Rovno, Ukraine, with local and Soviet officials, that went till three in the morning. On the steps of his hotel, a very drunken KGB colonel finally swore he would do everything he could to help and gave Greenwood a massive bear hug. The Australian lawyer heard his ribs crack and ended up in hospital being treated with electric shocks.[31]

One theme that came through time and again was that many of the suspected war criminals had been used as anti-communist spies by Allied intelligence organisations after the war. They were then protected by these organisations as they were settled in communities in the US, Canada, Australia, Germany and Britain. It was to prove a major barrier to bringing charges against them. Twelve months before Greenwood died in 2001, he said in an interview with Mark Aarons that the files they'd found on suspected war criminals held by ASIO didn't look like they were suspects being monitored as possible enemies of the state. They 'had much more the smell of personnel files about them', Greenwood said.[32] While Greenwood's unit didn't get full access to ASIO files, he suspected ASIO had recruited several of these war criminal suspects as agents. Their mission was to report on communist influences in the ethnic communities in Australia that they mixed in. Greenwood told Aarons he realised he would be wasting energy and bashing his head against a wall to continue pursuing this line of investigation. 'So somewhat reluctantly I abandoned my campaign in respect of ASIO,' he told Aarons.[33]

ASIO was still keeping its role secret thirty years later when it had to release old files under the Archives Act. The ASIO file on one suspect who arrived in Australia in 1951 – Nikolai Alferchik – was so heavily censored that 123 pages out of 190 were not released, as they were still classified.[34] The files released to the public were made up of newspaper clippings, translations of Russian war crimes allegations and heavily censored ASIO observations of Alferchik's life.

The Americans weren't so bashful. Alferchik's extensive file held by US intelligence, and released under US Freedom of Information, reveals that during the war Alferchik was part of Nazi intelligence in Poland. The US files reveal that, as Germans advanced eastward, Alferchik was part of an *Einsatzguppe* (extermination squad) that took part in mass murders in Minsk and Smolensk. After the war he was hired by US intelligence to stay in Austria and spy on Russian émigrés. When the Soviets issued an arrest warrant on him for war crimes, Alferchik was supplied by US authorities with a new identity as Nikolai Pavlov, and he was cleared to migrate to Australia in 1951. Upon arriving in Australia, Alferchik, aka Pavlov, settled in Melbourne and worked for the Victorian Electricity Commission. The US files show that by 1954 ASIO knew all about his wartime activities and his work with the SS. Although hard evidence is missing from National Archive files, heavily censored letters from ASIO chief Brigadier Charles Spry to his staff indicate that he had a strong interest in Alferchik's reports on the activities of Polish communists in Australia. Greenwood found enough evidence in wartime files and statements from witnesses to conclude that Alferchik had been a key participant in massacres of thousands of Jews and political prisoners. However, by the time it came to charge Alferchik he'd had a stroke, and many of the witnesses needed for a case against him in court were dead or too old and ill to travel to Australia. The case against Alferchik never proceeded.

This became a recurring and frustrating situation for Greenwood's investigation. Argods Fricsons was a Latvian lawyer who joined the Latvian political police once the Germans invaded and worked with the Gestapo. In that role he is alleged to have been involved in mass murders of Jews and partisans. His file held in the National Archives of Australia[35] is extremely heavily censored, even more so than that of Alferchik. But, again, it reveals Spry's strong interest in this former Nazi spook, and suggests he probably became an informant for ASIO in the Latvian community soon after migrating to Australia. Greenwood couldn't get enough hard evidence to charge him.

Petro Hrushchewskij had been Nazi police chief in the Ukrainian city of Rovno and was said to be involved in the murder or deportation of 100,000 Jews, partisans and Cossacks. In Melbourne he became a priest and in 1956 was walking along the street in his smock when a passer-by, former Cossack captain H Bosyj, was shocked to recognise the man who had executed his former colleagues. Bosyj reported him to police, but nothing was done for decades. When the SIU sought to bring Hrushchewskij to justice he was old and ill, deemed unfit to stand trial. He died in 1992.[36] Several other strong cases gathered by the SIU against Nazi war criminals in Australia failed to make it to court for the same reasons.

But the Nazi hunters of the SIU did find strong enough evidence on four suspects to bring the cases to court. The first was Ivan Polyukhovych, who witnesses said played a major role in the massacre of 850 people in Ukraine. Greenwood's capacity for vodka consumption played a key role in the case. The KGB colonel who had broken Greenwood's ribs in a bear hug fulfilled his promise to help and agreed to dig up a ditch near a country lane where SIU investigators were told the massacre took place. They found the remains of dozens of bodies. The SIU charged Polyukhovych, and he faced an Adelaide court in 1990. However, the judge disallowed crucial photographic evidence as proof of identity. A second blow came when the judge ruled that the memory of eyewitnesses – who said they saw Polyukhovych shoot boys as they fled the massacre – couldn't be relied on sixty years later. Other historical circumstantial facts were ruled inadmissible under South Australian rules of evidence. In the end it was inevitable that the jury took one hour to acquit Polyukhovych.

The second case involved another Adelaide resident, Mikolay Berezovsky, for his alleged involvement in the murder of 102 Jews in the Ukraine village of Hnivan. Due to a prosecution blunder in the committal stage, the defence successfully argued that Berezovsky had an alibi, as he wasn't in the village at the time. The case never went to trial. A third SIU case was brought against yet another Adelaide resident, Heinrich Wagner, charged with being involved in the massacre of 104 Jews in the Ukraine village of Izraylovska. The massacre included babies and young children. Witnesses from around the world testified that Wagner was in the police unit involved in the killings. In the middle of committal hearings, Wagner had a heart attack. Independent medical evidence said the pressure of a trial could kill him. The trial was no-billed. It was over before it began. Wagner lived a fairly active life for another seven years, a free man. It was the last war criminal case the SIU presented. None had been successful.

It was a huge blow to Greenwood and the SIU. The cost of the investigation and the lack of convictions in court were felt in Canberra. With Lionel Bowen gone as attorney-general, the SIU lost its biggest ally in Canberra. After the Polyukhovych failure the Labor government decided funding for the unit would end on 30 June 1992. Greenwood quit in disgust. His deputy, Graham Blewitt, took over, and he came under immediate pressure to wind up operations.

Determined investigations on war criminals in the US and Canada came to embarrass Australia, in particular the extraordinary case of Konrads Kalejs. He arrived in Australia in 1950 telling immigration authorities he'd been a simple farm labourer. He later admitted to being a lieutenant in the Latvian army until the German invasion in 1941. It was the first in a string of lies Kalejs was to tell over the coming decades. He neglected to inform Australian immigration authorities that he had deserted Soviet-led forces to become a Nazi collaborator, working for the Latvian security police. In Australia, Kalejs was appointed to the critical post of documentation and processing clerk at the Bonegilla migrant camp. He handled sensitive information about new arrivals from war-torn Europe. He moved to Melbourne and became a citizen in 1957. Two years later he moved to the US, and over the next thirty-five years accrued a fortune through property development.

In 1985 Kalejs was arrested as a suspected Nazi war criminal. US prosecutors said he had been a company commander in the notorious Arajs Kommando, a Latvian unit that massacred entire villages of Jews, killing up to 5000 men, women and children per day. Kalejs was accused of committing fraud on his visa application to the US, as he hadn't mentioned his Nazi connections. In 1988 Kalejs was ordered to be deported back to Australia. Kalejs made it to Canada, where he was arrested in 1997 and deported to Australia. He went underground with the right-wing Latvian community in Melbourne, but he was shadowed by hostile publicity. In 1999 Kalejs slipped out of Australia to England where he was discovered in a luxurious nursing home run by the Latvian Welfare Fund. In 2000 he travelled back to Australia. Latvia demanded his extradition to face trial for war crimes. In May 2001 a Melbourne court ordered Kalejs' extradition to Latvia. He appealed, but the case was delayed by his illness and dementia. Kalejs died in Melbourne in 2001, still a free man. Nazi hunter Mark Aarons said at the time there were around a dozen Nazi war criminals still living quietly in Australia's suburbs. 'The probability is that the last Nazi will die peacefully in his bed somewhere in Australia in the next few years.'[37]

In 2010, a 600-page report on the international hunt for Nazi war criminals, commissioned by the US Justice Department four years earlier, finally became public. It had harsh words for Australia. It described the Australian government's attitude to pursuing war criminals living in the Australia as 'ambivalent', and quoted the Simon Wiesenthal Center that Australia's poor record in pursuing Nazis was explained by 'a lack of the requisite political will'.[38]

•

In 2014, respected historian Professor David Horner published the official history of ASIO in a volume covering the years 1949 to 1963. It was the first time an outsider, albeit one who had to submit to security clearances and extensive vetting of his writing, provided the first official acknowledgement of the agency's complicity and protection of Nazi war criminals in Australia. It disclosed that as early as 1952 that ASIO chief Brigadier Spry ordered that 'low level' Nazis could be approved for entry to Australia.[39] When a certain Australian citizen applied to sponsor his German father-in-law, his wife and daughter, it was pointed out the German had been a member of the Nazi Party since the early days of 1933 and that this would disqualify him. Spry decided to approve the application to allow the family to come together.

Such compassion was not shown for anyone who showed the slightest communist connection. As late as 2016, hundreds of elderly migrants who had come to Australia after the war continued to be denied citizenship. They were never given a reason for being denied naturalisation, but newly declassified ASIO files show that they had been recorded as national security risks because of their suspected association with communist groups, trade unions or leftish community groups. The files showed thousands of these migrants were earmarked for potential internment and other restrictions because of their political beliefs. Right up until the 1970s, hundreds of these left-linked migrants were kept under surveillance. ASIO sought information on their backgrounds from right-wing governments such as Greece. Nothing like this happened to migrants with Nazi associations.[40]

Horner reveals that as early as 1950 ASIO was agreeing to British requests to accept twenty to thirty people a year who had been of use to MI5, such as Soviet defectors, East Bloc refugees and former Western agents. Horner found evidence in ASIO files that ASIO protected alleged Nazis who were actively anti-communist. Horner cites the case of Laszlo Megay, who ASIO approved for citizenship despite knowing he was leading pro-Nazi Hungarian émigré groups in Sydney. ASIO knew he had collaborated with the Nazis as mayor of Ungvar during the Nazi occupation of Hungary. ASIO's report on Megay discounted accusations that he had committed war crimes, as these accusations had been made by members of Sydney's Hungarian Jewish community. This ignores the obvious fact that if anyone were to know about Megay's war crimes it would be the Jews who came from his region.

'ASIO seemed willing to overlook possible right-wing war criminals as long as they were not communists,' wrote Horner in the official history.[41] Megay became an influential figure, meeting government ministers to press for aid to Hungarian refugees fleeing communist rule. But when questions were put in parliament about Megay's Nazi past, ASIO simply lied. It said allegations were coming from a nation under communist rule and were therefore unreliable.

Horner also revealed that ASIO hired alleged Latvian war criminal Argods Fricsons in 1954 to spy on Australia's Latvian community. ASIO had been told that Fricsons was part of the Gestapo. His ASIO file, secret until Horner's official history, states that Fricsons had 'assisted us in the past and our current assessment is that he is a very strong anti-communist . . . he is not considered a security risk'.[42] The mass murderer worked for ASIO for six years until 1960. He died a free man in 1990.

Horner confirms that Nikolai Alferchik, aka Pavlov, was also hired by ASIO in Australia, ignoring his wartime massacres with the Gestapo in Byelorussia (now Belarus). 'In its determination to defeat the communist threat ASIO was willing to overlook the fact that some of its sources might have been war criminals. ASIO's reluctance to pursue possible war criminals would continue for years,' Horner wrote.[43] 'There is sufficient evidence that in some cases ASIO turned a blind eye to war criminals once they reached Australia as long as they were very strongly anti-communist.'[44]

The actions of these Allied governments was a gross betrayal of the men and women of all Allied forces who sacrificed so much to fight the evil of Nazism. Sixty million people died in World War II. Six million Jews were brutally murdered by the Nazi regime. Forty thousand Australians and 11,700 New Zealanders died fighting Germany and Japan, terrible enemies who committed the worst atrocities imaginable.

Yet Allied post-war governments allowed enemy war criminals to escape justice and even encouraged them to live out their lives among us in our peaceful suburbs as neighbours – all in the name of combating communism. The evil did not end with the Allied victory, it just changed out of a uniform into a suit.

6

TRADING WITH THE ENEMY

'IBM designed and supplied indispensable technological equipment that allowed the Nazis to achieve what had never been done before – the automation of human destruction.'

It was an extraordinary moment. The conservative arch-enemy of communism in Australia, Robert Menzies, desperately clinging to the coat-tails of Australia's most hard-line communist to get through an angry crowd screaming 'Pig Iron Bob!' at him.

It was an extraordinary moment for another reason. For the first time in Australian history, wharf workers refused to load a ship they feared would carry material that would be turned around and fired back at Australians as shells and bullets in a looming war.

It was November 1938. For the past seven years Japan had battled its way down through Manchuria and China, brutally suppressing any resistance to its invasion. In 1937 an estimated 300,000 disarmed Chinese soldiers and hundreds of thousands of civilians were massacred by Japanese troops in Nanking (today called Nanjing). In the two years since the invasion of China, Japan had killed more than a million Chinese troops. It was obvious to everyone at the time that Japan was intent on conquering all of South East Asia. Would they stop when the vast north of Australia was wide open? It seemed inevitable that Australians would soon be fighting for their survival against the powerful Japanese military.

Japan was desperate for iron for its war machine and Australia's largest mining company, BHP, had been selling ore to Japan for several years. In 1938, Japan made a deal with an English front company to mine iron ore from Yampi Sound off the coast of north-west Australia. BHP protested that this new mining deal threatened its own lucrative sales of iron ore to Japan. The United Australia Party government of Joseph Lyons (a right-of-centre party that was the forerunner of the Liberal Party) ordered a ban on the sale of all iron ore to Japan after public revulsion at reports of atrocities Japan's forces were committing in China. But the government threw a lifeline to BHP. While the company couldn't export iron ore to Japan, it was allowed to export to Japan 300,000 tons of pig iron – transportable ingots of smelted iron ore. This deal was even more profitable for BHP than iron ore because Japan could convert it more quickly into war machines. BHP convinced the government that the extra profit it made from the sale would enable the company to build war machines for Australia.

In 1937 Australia's union movement imposed a boycott on all Japanese goods. In 1938 wharf workers in Port Kembla, a small coastal mining town 100 kilometres south of Sydney, learned that a British tramp steamer called SS Dalfram was due in November to load pig iron for Japan. The workers had read pamphlets, circulated by unions, of a supposed Japanese plan to conquer Asia and the South Pacific. Called the *Tanaka Memorandum* it was reputed to have been written in 1927 by Japan's Prime Minister Tanaka Giichi as a memorandum to the emperor. It was published in China and in communist newspapers in the early 1930s, asserting that if Japan conquered China 'the rest of the Asiatic countries and the South Sea countries will fear us and surrender to us.'[1] Today some scholars doubt its authenticity, but in the 1930s and early war years it was taken as gospel.[2] On 15 November 1938, Port Kembla's wharf labourers voted to refuse to load BHP's pig iron on to the *Dalfram*. They said they could not load a ship with iron bound for Japan that would come back to Australia as bullets and bombs.

The action by the 200 wharfies rapidly became a national test of strength. At the time, Menzies was both attorney-general and minister for industry. It was his job to get the ore delivered to Japan. Menzies ordered the wharf workers to carry out government policy and load the ship. Although the wharf workers' action was not officially a strike, on 28 November Menzies announced he was enforcing tough anti-strike laws that would require all wharf workers to apply for a licence to work. Those who didn't have one couldn't enter the wharves. Unions dubbed it the 'Dog Collar Act'.[3] It was a harsh measure. Workers and their families were still suffering the effects of the Great Depression and most lived in poverty. It would deny them access to work unless they buckled to the government and loaded the ship. But the workers stuck to their principles. Only one wharf labourer applied for the licence and then publicly burned it in front of a cheering crowd.

On 17 December, BHP announced that, because of the workers' refusal to load the ship, 3500 Port Kembla steel workers would be retrenched. Another 500 would join them right after Christmas. That hit the struggling mining town hard. Many members of the public supported the wharfies' refusal to load the ship. Indian crew on the *Dalfram* refused to move the ship to another dock where non-union labour could load it. Chinese grocers in Sydney, grateful that the workers were helping their former homeland, drove down from Sydney with food and money for the workers, who hadn't received pay for weeks. Wharf workers in Sydney and other ports also refused to load pig iron bound for Japan. It was blowing up into a major test for the government, and many prominent Australians supported the workers.

Australia's much-respected retired governor general and former High Court Chief Justice, Sir Isaac Isaacs, wrote at the time:

It is wholly contrary to British Democracy to coerce a private citizen to do something not requested of him by law, simply because it is the policy of the Government, however unconscientious that may be, that is a dictator's rule. The Government had used the economic pressure of possible starvation to force the men to act against their conscience. I believe that Port Kembla, with its studied but peaceful and altogether disinterested attitude to the men concerned, will find a place in our history beside the 'Eureka Stockade' as a noble stand against executive dictatorship.[4]

After a deadlock lasting nine weeks, Menzies felt he had to step in personally. He drove to Port Kembla to warn the workers that unless they loaded the pig iron they would have to get licences to work on the waterfronts. He was met outside Port Kembla's Town Hall by a large and hostile demonstration of a thousand men and women. They carried placards reading 'No pig iron for Jap bullets' and angrily yelled out a new nickname that would stick like mud to Menzies for the rest of his life – 'Pig Iron Bob'. Police asked union leaders, including communist union official Ted Roach, to usher Menzies through the angry crowd into the Town Hall where he would meet a delegation from the workers. Roach later remarked, 'The irony of this, Menzies number one Red baiter, had to be protected by a communist'.[5]

Inside the room, Menzies told the workers that the job of government was to carry out the will of the people, and the government would not be dictated to by a minority. But Menzies gave a concession. He said if the *Dalfram* was loaded this time, the government would review the issue of the export of pig iron to Japan. The workers hung on for another two weeks, but the pressure of starving families and the fear of losing their right to work altogether meant that they couldn't hold on forever. After ten weeks and two days they finally loaded the pig iron under protest, and the *Dalfram* sailed to Japan with its load.

In 1942, with Japan at war with Australia, Menzies defended his reputation as 'Pig Iron Bob' in one of his weekly radio chats. He was in the political doldrums and felt the need to clear his name. Menzies had taken over as prime minister in April 1939 after Lyons died, and then declared Australia at war with Germany five months later. But in August 1941, Menzies was faced with a cabinet revolt over the amount of time he'd spent in Britain while Australia faced invasion from Japan, and he resigned. Labor's John Curtin became prime minister and

Menzies had to cool his heels in Opposition. In Menzies's weekly radio talk he defended his pre-war pig iron stance, arguing that in 1939 the US exported twenty times as much scrap iron to Japan as Australia did over two years. Menzies asked why no one protested about the export of Australian wool to Japan before the war. 'Many thousand of bales of Australian wool have probably gone into Japanese uniforms, and a soldier cannot fight without a uniform,' Menzies said.[6]

Unfortunately, despite the example of the principled stand of the working-class wharf labourers, who endured hunger and poverty to act according to their conscience and block the supply of material for an aggressive nation's war machine, other industrialists chose to follow profits instead.

Many industrialists had no qualms about selling equipment that aided the enemy's war efforts, or in providing machines that assisted in the genocide of millions of people. The two years between the war starting in Europe in September 1939 and the United States joining the war in December 1941 provided an opportunity for American corporations to increase the sale of material to Nazi Germany. There were restrictions on what American firms could trade, but many found a way around any obstacles. Some American billionaire industrialists had strong links with the Nazi regime and were strongly anti-Semitic. Their motives for trading with Hitler and his cronies went further than just profits.

•

In 1930 the world's central banks, principally those of the US, Britain, France, Italy and Germany, set up the Bank for International Settlements (BIS), based in Basel, Switzerland.

The BIS was designed to be a global clearing house for discreet payments for cross-border deals that weren't meant for public eyes. It was the brainchild of Hjalmar Schacht, president of Germany's Reichsbank and later Nazi Minister for Economics. Schacht grew up in New York and had powerful Wall Street connections. In reality, BIS was a front for Nazi leaders and billionaire financiers to shift funds once war made regular transfers difficult. Based in neutral territory, BIS was immune from any investigation, seizure or censure, whether or not its owners were at war with each other. By the time war broke out, BIS was under Hitler's control. It was his link to international finance. Directors included the head of IG Farben (a German chemical corporation) Hermann Schmitz; German banker Baron Kurt von Schröder, who financed the Gestapo; Nazi Minister for Economic Affairs Dr Walther Funk; and Reichsbank vice-president Emil Puhl.

In March 1938 the Nazis marched into Austria and immediately looted much of the gold and valuables from the Jews of Vienna. The booty was stored in vaults of banks controlled by BIS. In 1939, within days of Germany entering Czechoslovakia, the BIS helped shift fifty metric tons of gold reserves held in Czech accounts in the Bank of England to the Reichsbank.[7] Alarm bells should have rung at the Bank of England at the theft of Czechoslovakia's gold reserves, but the Czech bank's governor, Montagu Norman, was an admirer of the Nazis and a close friend of Hitler's Economics Minister Schacht. Norman simply gave the theft the all-clear. The gold didn't physically travel to Germany; that's where the BIS came in. At the Basel headquarters of the BIS, the value of the gold was laundered and quietly slipped to the Reichsbank.[8] Similar transfers of gold and cash through the BIS to the Reichsbank came as Germany invaded other European nations.

The BIS's wartime president, Thomas McKittrick, a Harvard-educated American, allegedly assisted not only the Reich in looting Europe's gold reserves but also arranged deals with Nazi industrialists to guarantee their profits after the Allied victory. Despite being an American and a supposed enemy, McKittrick mixed with Nazi bankers in neutral Switzerland. After the war, McKittrick described the BIS to *Newsweek* as 'a sort of club'.[9] The Basel-based BIS was a money-bound sanctuary for cigar-smoking bankers carrying on business as usual in neutral Switzerland while men and women were dying in their millions. Gold teeth ripped from corpses in the concentration camps, and stolen property and loot from millions of Jews, was funnelled, in one form or another, to Nazi coffers through banks in Switzerland. In all, the Nazis stole around $800 million in gold ($10.7 billion in today's money) from the nations of Europe.[10] In 1944, some in Washington wanted to try McKittrick as a traitor and close down the BIS. It never happened. In fact, after the war McKittrick got a cushy job as vice-president of Chase National Bank (renamed Chase Manhattan Bank in 1955 and Chase Bank in 2000) and was fêted by Wall Street until he died in 1970.

It shouldn't be surprising that McKittrick got a job with Chase. Owned by the Rockefellers, Chase National Bank was the richest and most powerful financial institution in the United States at the time. It was extremely close to top Nazi leaders, and had two prominent Nazis as directors of its German subsidiary. Chase kept its Paris branch open throughout the war and, with the knowledge of head office in New York, did deals with

German financiers. Chase acknowledged it assisted Hitler's Third Reich by converting German marks into US dollars between 1936 and 1941.[11]

Allied banks were also involved in stealing assets from Jews who were being exterminated in the Holocaust. After the war, Britain's Barclays Bank had to pay $3.6 million to Jews whose assets were seized from French branches of the bank during the war. Chase National Bank also admitted that it had seized around 100 accounts held by Jews in its Paris branch after the German invasion.[12]

•

In the late 1930s, Brown Brothers Harriman (BBH) was said to be the world's largest private investment bank. One of the directors of this American bank was Senator Prescott Bush, founder of the Bush political dynasty that included his son George H W Bush, who would become president of the United States in 1989, and his grandson President George W Bush.

While there is no suggestion that Prescott Bush had Nazi sympathies, documents at the US National Archives reveal that BBH acted as the US base for German industrialist Fritz Thyssen, who was an early financial backer of Adolf Hitler. In 1928 Thyssen bought a building to serve as Nazi headquarters in Munich. BBH set up another bank in New York, Union Banking Corporation (UBC), and Prescott Bush was made a director of that bank to represent Thyssen's interests in the US. In the lead-up to the war, Thyssen had the largest steel and coal company in Germany, and grew rich from Hitler's rearmament drive. During the 1930s, UBC bought and shipped millions of dollars in gold, fuel, steel and coal to Germany, assisting the Nazi build-up to war. Prescott Bush continued to work for the bank after America entered the war.[13]

Trading with Germany after Europe went to war wasn't illegal for Americans – until the US itself joined the war at the end of 1941. After the US joined the war, suspicions grew that the gold held for Thyssen by BBH and UBC was a secret nest egg for Thyssen and other Nazi leaders. In October 1942 a string of assets controlled by BBH, including Prescott Bush's UBC, were seized under America's Trading with the Enemy Act.

The assets were returned to the banks after the war and no action was taken against Prescott Bush or other prominent directors of BBH.[14] After the war, Prescott Bush was reported to have sold his share in UBC – a bank that had made vast profits trading with the enemy – for $US1.5 million. It was a huge amount at the time, about $US120 million in today's money.

•

Today, IBM (International Business Machines) is a massive New York based multinational technology corporation with operations around the world. It has annual revenue of $US81 billion and 380,000 employees. Finance magazines *Barron's* and *Fortune* dub IBM the world's most respected and admired company. However, the huge corporation has a dark, secret past it doesn't tell you about in its glossy brochures listing Nobel prize winners and technological breakthroughs.

What they don't tell you is that in the 1930s IBM was instrumental in providing groundbreaking technology that assisted the Nazi regime in identifying and tracking down Jews for its methodical program of genocide. One of the machines is displayed in a place of prominence at the United States Holocaust Memorial

Museum in Washington DC. The IBM badge can be clearly seen. It was a technical marvel of its time, the forerunner of today's computers. The complex-looking machine was a punch card and card-sorting system initially built to assist the collation of vast amounts of information gathered in a census.

In the 1930s, IBM was one of the largest firms in the world, a true multinational conglomerate, with its headquarters in New York. Oddly, IBM has Germanic origins. Herman Hollerith was the son of German immigrants. Working in the US Census Bureau, he was still in his twenties when he devised a machine using punch cards to tabulate the 1890 census. A smart businessman, he didn't sell the machines or the punch cards but only leased them to whoever needed work done. It was a formula that kept the money rolling in. His machines were used in censuses around the world, as well as for major operations such as railways and shipping. Hollerith set up a subsidiary in Germany called Deutsche Hollerith Maschinen Gesellschaft – Dehomag for short – and assigned it all of his patents. In 1911 Hollerith sold his firm to financier Charles Flint, who put tough and ambitious salesman Thomas Watson in charge. The name was changed to International Business Machines, IBM for short, and the company grew and grew. In 1924 IBM owned eighty-four per cent of Dehomag, and the firm's New York headquarters kept a close eye on all that its German subsidiary did throughout the war.

American investigative author Edwin Black was deeply shocked when he saw the IBM–Dehomag machine in Washington's Holocaust Museum. The museum said on the display that IBM was responsible for organising the German census of 1933, which for the first time identified all Jews in the German population.

Black was mystified how an iconic American corporation could be involved in the Holocaust, the most evil act of the twentieth century. He then spent decades digging up the links between IBM America and the Nazi genocide of millions of Jews and other inmates of the concentration camps. He said IBM tried to block his access to the firm's records at every turn. But from archives around the world, and some files from IBM, he managed to assemble 20,000 documents that revealed IBM's horrific role in the war, and in 2001 Black published his groundbreaking findings in *IBM and the Holocaust*. It was shocking. Black wrote that IBM headquarters in New York knew all about its German subsidiary designing and supplying indispensable technological equipment that allowed the Nazis to achieve what had never been done before – 'the automation of human destruction'.[15] Buried deep in the files of the IBM company and German archives, Black alleged he discovered IBM boss Thomas Watson was an enthusiastic supporter of the Nazis from the very early years of the rise of Hitler.

'IBM NY always understood from the outset in 1933 that it was courting and doing business with the upper echelon of the Nazi Party,' Black wrote.[16] Watson was obsequious in pandering to the Nazi hierarchy, writing a grovelling letter in 1937 to Nazi Economics Minister Hjalmer Schacht declaring that the world must extend 'a sympathetic understanding to the German people and their aims under the leadership of Adolf Hitler'.[17] To show his gratitude to Watson and the support of IBM, Hitler personally bestowed on Watson a special swastika-bedecked medal to honour his unique service to the Reich – the Order of the German Eagle with Star. Black writes that in June 1940 Watson was forced to return the medal after public outrage that such a prominent American business leader would be in possession of a Nazi medal while Nazi troops occupied Paris.

Black found documents showing that Watson encouraged the IBM German subsidiary to build and supply 2000 of the card punch machines to Nazi Germany and thousands more in nations that the Nazis conquered. From the moment Hitler came to power in 1933, IBM used its monopoly on punch card technology to 'organise, systemise and accelerate Hitler's anti-Jewish program, step by step facilitating the tightening noose'.[18] After years of investigating IBM's connections to the Nazis and the Third Reich, Black is in no doubt that 'Thomas Watson and his corporate behemoth were guilty of genocide.'[19] Black concludes that for Watson and IBM, trading with the monster of Nazi Germany wasn't about anti-Semitism or National Socialism. 'It was always about the money.'[20]

Machines belonging to IBM's subsidiary Dehomag were set up in every concentration camp. IBM's custom-made punch cards from the camps sorted inmates by religion, nationality, sexual orientation, family history and political leaning. Each camp had its own number on the cards. Auschwitz was 001, Buchenwald 002, Dachau 003, and so on. It then showed each prisoner's classification. An 8 designated a Jew, homosexuals were 3, 'anti-socials' (which meant political prisoners) were 9, Gypsies were 12. The manner of death in the camps was recorded by its own number – 4 was execution, 5 was suicide, 6 was the gas chamber, 3 was death by natural causes such as starvation or disease. Black said documents released by the German archives show that staff from IBM's German subsidiary had to create codes to differentiate between a Jew who had been worked to death and one who had been gassed. The machines methodically recorded the fate of every prisoner. Every two weeks, staff from IBM's German subsidiary visited the camps to service the machines, deliver new blank cards, print and collate the punched cards, and reconfigure the machines if any change in information was requested by the SS or Gestapo.[21]

Black found documents showing that IBM's German subsidiary built a reinforced-concrete bombproof blockhouse to protect its twelve valuable machines at Dachau. 'IBM equipment was among the Reich's most important weapons, not only for its war against the Jews, but in its general military campaigns and control of railway traffic,' wrote Black. 'Watson personally approved expenditures to add bomb shelters to Dehomag install-ations because the cost was borne by the company. Such costs cut into IBM's profit margin. Watson's approval was required because he received a one per cent commission on all Nazi business profits.'[22]

As the Third Reich expanded across Europe, IBM's subsidi-aries in the Netherlands, Poland, France and other conquered nations supplied machines to aid the Nazi genocide of Jews, Gypsies, homosexuals and other peoples. Since the machines were leased, not sold, the Nazi regime had to keep on paying for them throughout the Holocaust years. The profits were enormous. Invoices for every machine and punch card went from the Third Reich subsidiaries to the IBM office in Geneva, and then on to headquarters in New York. In May 1941 the Geneva office reported to Watson in New York that Dehomag was cutting the price of its rented machines for the Nazis by ten per cent. 'This would mean a reduction of approximately 1,500,000 Reichsmarks in the gross annual production of the company.'[23]

As Nazi Germany advanced across Europe in 1939, 1940 and 1941, pressure mounted on the United States to stop sitting on the sidelines and join Britain, the Commonwealth and the Soviet Union in fighting the Nazi evil. Nazi atrocities received coverage in the American press, but that didn't stop IBM from keeping its business going with the Nazis. IBM's communications with its subsidiaries in Nazi-controlled Europe became difficult, but Black found documents indicating that the US State Department had been extremely helpful behind the scenes. In January 1941, Watson wrote to the assistant chief of the US State Department's European Affairs division thanking him for passing on letters to an IBM salesman in Berlin. US embassies in Nazi-occupied lands were also helpful in passing on messages to IBM salesmen busy setting up subsidiaries to do business with the new Nazi occupiers.[24]

In September 1941, war with Germany seemed inevitable for the Americans. President Franklin D Roosevelt banned trade with the Nazi regime unless the government issued a special permit for each transaction. IBM had to tell its subsidiaries that from now on they would have to operate on their own. Watson did not order IBM's German subsidiary to stop supplying machines to the Nazis. On the contrary. Watson expected them to keep making money for the IBM empire even though, after December 1941 when war was declared, they were the enemy.

In war, Watson saw yet another business opportunity. Through a new US subsidiary, Munitions Manufacturing Corporation, Watson quickly converted a large slice of IBM's US production capacity to making weapons – 20-millimetre anti-aircraft cannon, Browning automatic rifles, bomb sights, M1 carbine rifles – all stamped with the IBM logo.

The punch card machine also proved profitable on home ground. If a US official wanted to know where a particular soldier or sailor was, an IBM machine could pinpoint his location anywhere in the world. The day after the attack on Pearl Harbor, IBM machines were used to locate every person of Japanese origin in the United States for internment. IBM punch cards identified every American by race. The company also developed code-breaking machines. 'It was an irony of the war that IBM equipment was used to encode and decode for both sides of the conflict,' Black wrote.[25] War was good for IBM. Ninety days after Pearl Harbor, an excited Watson told the press that IBM had secured $150 million in defence contracts.[26] IBM's total wartime sales and rentals grew from $46 million in 1940 to $140 million a year by 1945.[27] Watson cloaked himself in the US flag and embarked on an expensive public relations campaign to put himself and IBM at the forefront of patriotism and the US war effort. He proclaimed IBM only made one per cent profit from the sale of military equipment it made for the US government. Democrats asked Watson to run for Governor of New York. He declined.[28]

In 1943, however, the Economic Warfare Section of the US Justice Department, the unit responsible for investigating cases of trading with the enemy, looked into IBM's deals with Nazi Germany. It didn't like what it saw. The unit's chief investigator, Howard J Carter, wrote a memo to his superiors warning that corporations like IBM had become larger and more powerful than nations. Carter was denied access to crucial files by IBM that could have proved how closely it was linked to the Nazi regime. In reality, there was nothing Carter could do to challenge

IBM. The company was simply too big and too essential to the US war machine.

As Allied troops rolled back the German army in 1944 and 1945, IBM officials followed right behind them, anxious to secure the equipment and records of its pre-war subsidiaries. Every file and banknote recovered was sent to IBM's Geneva office. Dehomag emerged from the ruins of Germany relatively unscathed. 'Its machines were salvaged, profits preserved and corporate value protected,' wrote Black.[29] With the war over, IBM was able to recapture its highly profitable German subsidiary and assimilate all the profits Dehomag had made trading with the Nazi regime.

Former IBM employee James T Senn was a US army corporal but considered himself part of the 'IBM Army', a network of former IBM employees in the military services who had all been promised their jobs back when the war was over. On 26 April 1945, Senn wrote to Watson that he had just visited the Dehomag firm in Sindelfingen, 644 kilometres south-west of Berlin. Senn said he and his captain – another member of the IBM Army – were the first Americans to set foot in the plant since the war and that they had been greeted by Dehomag employees. 'The entire factory is intact, spared for some unknown reason by our airmen . . . every tool, every machine is well preserved and ready to start work at a moment's notice . . . a card stock of over a million cards is ready for shipment,' an excited Senn wrote to his old boss. Senn concluded by saying that Dehomag managers Herr Haug and Herr Wiesinger 'would like to be remembered to you'.[30]

Edwin Black reports that IBM files from 1945 contain many such letters. One IBM Army officer, Lieutenant Colonel

Lawrence Flick, proudly told Watson how he tried to assist Dehomag managers who had been detained or arrested by the Allies and get them back to work for IBM. Watson was furious. He didn't want the German managers restored to their positions; he had other plans, and told the top army brass to tell Flick to stop interfering. The Pentagon acted swiftly, promptly retiring Flick and sending him back to the US.

IBM immediately took back control of the rest of its European subsidiaries and demanded the profits they had made during the war. In this demand IBM had the assistance of the US government, who was keen on IBM getting back its machines because they were needed to run the military occupation of post-war Germany. When it came time to put German industrialists and Nazi leaders on trial, it was IBM machines that stored and collated the evidence and translations. While many German war profiteer corporations, such as the mammoth IG Farben, were stripped for war reparations, Dehomag was untouched. By 1949 the German subsidiary was 100 per cent owned by IBM New York and the name was changed to IBM Germany. Dehomag was gone. Nobody questioned the role of the IBM machine and its Dehomag subsidiary in the Nazi death camps or the Nazi war machine. In the ruins of post-war Europe, IBM was back in business big time. Allied military administrations turned to IBM to compile statistics on post-war Germany. Wartime Dehomag managers were employed in IBM Germany to do the job. They never faced justice for their involvement in the automation and information collating that enabled the Nazis to carry out mass genocide.

Thomas Watson retired an extremely wealthy man in 1956, aged eighty-two. He was a respected businessman and generous philanthropist who helped set up Binghamton University and served as trustee of Columbia University. He died five weeks after retiring. His eldest son, Thomas Watson Junior, took over his position as chief executive officer of IBM. He died in 1981. Another son, Arthur, was president of IBM World Trade Corporation. He died in 1974.

On the publication of Edwin Black's book in 2001 about IBM and its link to the Holocaust, IBM released a statement acknowledging that IBM equipment supplied by Dehomag had been used by the Nazi government. But IBM insisted that during the war Dehomag and hundreds of other foreign-owned companies came under the control of Nazi authorities. The IBM statement[31] said most records concerning Dehomag were lost or destroyed during the war, but documents that did exist had been placed on the public record to assist research and historical scholarship. 'IBM and its employees around the world find the atrocities committed by the Nazi regime abhorrent and categorically condemn any actions which aided their unspeakable acts,' it said. In a 2002 statement,[32] IBM denied assertions by Black that the company was withholding documents and material from the wartime era.

•

While IBM and its boss Thomas Watson passed through the war unchallenged, untroubled and unscathed as far as the public was concerned, and of course a darn sight wealthier, in the course of 1942 several American industrial giants were exposed for trading pacts with the enemy. The results of an investigation by US Treasury and Justice Department officials were presented to a special Senate committee investigating war production. It was chaired by Senator Harry S Truman, who was to become US vice president on 20 January 1945 and president on the death of Franklin D Roosevelt on 12 April 1945.

The first giant to be exposed was the biggest giant all. On 27 March 1942, the *Chicago Tribune* carried a long story blaring the headline, 'Truman accuses Standard Oil of rubber "treason"'. It reported that Senator Truman had accused Standard Oil of New Jersey of 'treasonable' relations with Germany before and after the United States entered the war. It was a bombshell. Standard Oil of New Jersey was the largest petroleum corporation in the world, controlling eighty-four per cent of the US petroleum market. It was owned by the Rockefellers, but the second-largest stockholder was the enormous German conglomerate IG Farben, which had financed the rise of Hitler and was integral to the Nazi war machine.

Truman and the members of the Senate committee had heard evidence that Standard Oil had handed IG Farben crucial secrets for creating synthetic rubber – a product desperately needed by the German military – while withholding the same technical information from the US and UK military. The secret formula produced a better product than natural rubber, especially for inner tubes and tyres.

In 1938, shortly before the outbreak of war, the German Luftwaffe urgently needed 500 tons of tetraethyl lead, an additive used in aviation gasoline. IG Farben got it from Standard's subsidiary in Britain, Ethyl. In 1939, just months before Germany invaded Poland to trigger the war, IG Farben bought another $15 million worth of the aviation fuel additive from Ethyl. This was despite an internal memo in the US War Department warning: 'Germany is secretly arming and ethyl lead would doubtless be a valuable aid to military aeroplanes'.[33] 'The result was that Hitler's air force was rendered capable of bombing London, the city that had provided the supplies,' wrote British–Australian journalist and author Charles Higham in his revealing 1983 book *Trading With the Enemy*.[34]

In the 1930s, Standard Oil chairman Walter Teagle and president William Farish made frequent trips to Nazi Germany and struck close relationships with senior IG Farben bosses as well as influential leaders of the Nazi Party. Teagle, a bear of a man, loved shooting and often went hunting with IG Farben boss Hermann Schmitz and Reichsmarschall Hermann Göring. (Reichsmarschall was Nazi Germany's highest military rank.) IG Farben made Teagle director of IG Farben's US subsidiary, American IG. The firm was a front for the Nazi regime and hired New York gun public relations agent Ivy Lee to improve the image of Nazi Germany in the US. Lee was paid the enormous sum of $25,000 a year, several million dollars in today's money, to smooth over the more evil aspects of Hitler's regime and spread anti-Jewish propaganda inside the US.[35]

However, the evidence against Standard Oil and the treachery of the firm's bosses was mounting. Documents revealed that Standard Oil and IG Farben had made a pact to maintain their secret arrangement to keep synthetic rubber for the exclusive use of IG Farben throughout the war, 'whether or not the United States came in'.[36] This secret deal left a major shortage of synthetic rubber in the Allied nations, so that the price – and Standard Oil profits – went up and up.

In 1940 and 1941 it also meant German ships would not have to run the gauntlet of the British naval blockade to bring in rubber. Instead, IG Farben could make synthetic rubber in

Germany for its war machines, much of it with slave labour from the Auschwitz concentration camp. Also, in 1939, when the British Royal Navy started blockading Germany, the Nazi regime desperately needed fuel and oil. In stepped Standard Oil. The company changed flags on Standard Oil tankers to that of neutral Panama, put on Nazi crews, and carried oil from South America and Africa to the neutral Canary Islands. There the oil was transferred to German tankers for shipment to Hamburg. German submarines were refuelled directly from tankers in the Canary Islands. As Higham noted ironically: 'Standard tankers supplied the self-same submarines which later sank American ships . . . by a humorous twist of fate, one of the ships the U-boats sank was the *SS Walter Teagle*'.[37] After the US entered the war at the end of 1941, Higham says that in 1942 Standard Oil continued to get oil to Nazi Germany via trucks through neutral Switzerland.

In March 1942, US Assistant Attorney-General Thurman Arnold declared Farish and other senior officials of Standard Oil and related companies had pleaded 'no contest' in a New Jersey criminal court to conspiring with the Nazi government.

Before the trial proceeded, government lawyers and Arnold held a closed meeting with Farish. Standard Oil's president was presented with the evidence of the firm's treachery in trading with the enemy. Farish, normally reserved and scholarly, reacted furiously. He challenged the government to do anything against Standard Oil, a company that was fuelling a high percentage of the US Army, Navy and Air Force. He said without Standard Oil the Allies would lose the war. Unfortunately, Farish was right. The government caved in and the charges were dropped in exchange for Standard Oil releasing its German patents to

America and paying a fine of just $50,000 – only a few million dollars in today's money. Farish, a multimillionaire, paid a fine of $1000 – just two days' salary. It was an incredibly lenient penalty, one that allowed Standard Oil to make even more money producing synthetic rubber for the Allied war machine.

But there were more determined men in the US Senate who were intent on making the bosses of Standard Oil face questioning in public. Document after document was presented by the Senate Committee. With Pearl Harbor fresh in the public mind, the Senate Committee asked the Standard Oil bosses why, in early 1941, Standard Oil had advised its Japanese customers to ask IG Farben to provide the synthetic rubber formula. They asked why Standard Oil put profits before its own country when making statements like: 'We fear US government in the near future may have grounds for action unfavourable to American–Japanese trade, we consider timely for us to organise with Japanese partners whose influence would be valuable later toward our reestablishment after interruptions in our trade.' The oil mandarins had been exposed. But there was to be no justice. The Senate committee concluded in its report that there had been no 'unpatriotic motive'.[38] The senators, who had their own close links to big business, declared it was only 'big business playing the game by the rules' with a heavy price 'to be borne by the entire nation'.[39] The war, as far as the giant oil corporation and its cronies in government and congress were concerned, was merely an annoying temporary suspension of making profits from trade, regardless of whom it was with.

Standard Oil and its bosses didn't suffer from this exposure of treachery. Standard Oil New Jersey is today's ExxonMobil.

Standard Oil California is today's Chevron. Standard Oil Indiana became Amoco.

Walter Teagle resigned as president of Standard Oil New Jersey shortly after the shocking revelations of treachery before the US Senate. In 1944 he established the Teagle Foundation 'to advance the well-being and general good of mankind throughout the world'. He died in 1962, aged eighty-three, revered and honoured as a great American businessman.

•

Standard Oil wasn't alone in making secret deals with firms inside Nazi Germany. There were profits to be made in restricting US and Allied production of crucial wartime material so that prices would skyrocket, while at the same time German firms expanded production for the Nazi war machine. War was coming and war was good for business. Below are just some examples of businesses that profited from human misery.

Before hostilities broke out and the killing started, American light metals giant Alcoa struck an agreement with IG Farben to suppress the production of magnesium in the US while Germany developed the greatest magnesium industry in the world. Alcoa had a worldwide monopoly on aluminium and dominated other minerals needed for electricity production. Before the US and Nazi Germany went to war, Alcoa sent so much aluminium product to Germany that the Nazi economy made sixty per cent more aluminium products than America. It left a massive shortage for America, but Alcoa was rolling in profits.[40]

As war approached, Sosthenes Behn, boss of the giant tele-communications firm American International Telephone and Telegraph (ITT) Corporation, made good friends in the Nazi hierarchy. He frequently visited Göring and Hitler to ensure ITT could continue to do business with Nazi Germany. He had already aided General Franco to win the Spanish Civil War, and ITT ran telephones across Europe.[41] After war broke out, ITT manufactured telephone equipment in its Spanish factory and sold it to Germany. At the conclusion of the war, Behn was awarded the Medal of Merit, America's highest award for a civilian. ITT also received millions of dollars in compensation for war damage to ITT's plants in Germany.[42]

In 1938, General Electric made a secret pact with Friedrich Krupp of the Ruhr industrial powerhouse to divide the world production of tungsten carbide between them. Krupp would have a world monopoly while GE would have the sole right in the US and Canada to produce tungsten carbide, which is vital in the process of hardening machine tools such as drillbits. In 1940 the US government indicted GE and Krupp for conspiring to maintain a monopoly on 'carboloy' – a trade name for tungsten carbide. The government alleged that, after the 1938 agreement between GE and Krupp, the price of carboloy in the US soared from $48 a pound to $453 a pound. Internal GE files showed tungsten carbide could be produced for just $8 a pound. GE was clearly exploiting the US war effort for its own gain.

The case was suspended when the US joined the war in 1941, and the public heard virtually nothing about the conspiracy. When the case resumed in 1947, only one reporter from the American electrical union newspaper *UE News* sat in court to cover the trial. Evidence presented at the trial showed that GE obeyed Krupp's dictates (which came in letters signed 'Heil Hitler') not to sell tungsten carbide to Russia or China.[43] This denied the vital material to Allied nations already fighting the

Axis powers of Germany and Japan. GE was found guilty of breaching anti-trust laws, but the judge rejected prosecution appeals for six-month jail sentences for GE managers. Instead, Judge Knox made it clear that he didn't want to hit GE executives too hard, saying the crimes were up to nine years old. He fined GE just $56,000, declaring that not imposing a penalty would be misinterpreted by many people.[44] The prosecutor protested that such a miniscule fine would be regarded by corporations as simply the cost of doing business and wasn't a penalty at all. It could even be claimed as a loss on taxes.

•

War machines run on steel ball bearings. Without them, gun turrets can't turn, tanks can't move, ships don't sail and planes don't fly. During World War II eighty per cent of steel ball bearings were made by the Swedish company SKF. Luckily for the war machines of both Axis and Allied nations, Sweden was neutral. Sweden was happy to sell to both sides. In reality, SKF was an arm of the Swedish government and its overseas representatives were often ambassadors or consuls. Its biggest customer was Germany, and SKF was closely tied to the Nazi hierarchy. SKF chairman Sven Wingquist was a dashing playboy industrialist who liked to mix with Göring and the pro-Nazi Duke (the abdicated King Edward VIII) and Duchess of Windsor (Wallis Simpson). SKF decided that if ball bearings ran low at SKF's German plant in Schweinfurt they would be supplemented by ball bearings from SKF plants in Philadelphia and Sweden.[45]

One of the directors of American SKF was Hugo von Rosen, second cousin by marriage to Hermann Göring. Von Rosen was under orders from Stockholm to supply Nazi-affiliated firms in South America with ball bearings from Philadelphia, regardless of the need for the critical product in the US. SKF Philadelphia frequently failed to meet orders for the extremely vital Pratt-Whitney fighter plane engines.[46] During the war, von Rosen also sent US industrial secrets to Sweden, slipping them into the diplomatic bags of the Swedish embassy in Washington to prevent them from being intercepted by British or American secret services. Diplomatic bags of neutral countries are barred from examination in times of war. Von Rosen set up a subsidiary that shipped 600,000 American-made SKF ball bearings a year to South America in ships registered in neutral Panama, an idea he probably got from Standard Oil. The ball bearings then sailed from Rio for Sweden on Panama-registered merchant ships, sailing through the Royal Navy blockade of Europe untouched. From Gothenburg in Sweden the ball bearings had only a short journey to German factories. Higham found documents showing that the British government ordered special Navicerts (documents exempting them from seizure or search) for the Panama ships. Obviously, the British too needed SKF ball bearings from Sweden, as Britain's plant had been destroyed by the Luftwaffe.

But the 'hands-off SKF' message didn't reach General Henry 'Hap' Arnold, US Army Air Force chief, who ordered massive bombing raids on SKF's Schweinfurt factory on 14 October 1943. Arnold was staggered when the bombing raids were met with such fierce resistance that the US lost sixty planes in the attack. He figured that the Germans had to have been expecting them. 'I don't see how they could have prepared the defence they did unless they had been warned in advance,' a furious Arnold told the London *News Chronicle* five days later.[47] What Arnold didn't know was that a week before the raid, SKF Philadelphia director

William Batt and several senior US Defence officials flew from London to Stockholm to meet Wingquist and other SKF officials to secure further supplies of ball bearings for American manufacturers. Did they know about the upcoming raid on Schweinfurt? Did they tip off SKF Sweden, who then told the Germans? It is impossible to know, but the US High Command in London was frustrated that the Swedes were tripling their supply of ball bearings to Germany. US General Carl Spaatz thumped the table at the US Ambassador to Britain, John Winant, shouting: 'Our whole bomber offensive is being nullified!'[48]

The US Ambassador to Sweden, Herschel Johnson, protested to Sweden's Foreign Minister, Christian Günther, but was coldly told SKF was fulfilling contracts signed before the war – contracts approved by the US government.[49] The Swedish government feared Germany might simply invade Sweden and seize the ball bearing plant if they refused to supply them. Britain rejected US calls for SKF products to be put on a blacklist, which would end the Navicert clearance for shipping, as Britain also needed SKF ball bearings. So the US tried to simply buy off SKF. US officials flew to Stockholm and struck a deal – for $8 million SKF would reduce its supply of ball bearings to Germany. However, the secret deal also said that after the war SKF would keep all its German properties, and all SKF links to Nazis would be forgiven and never investigated or exposed.[50]

Back in the US some disillusioned American SKF managers leaked to the press that SKF had strong links to the Nazis and had secretly sent ball bearings to the enemy. Unions started calling for strikes against their Nazi collaborator bosses. However, as soon as the secret deal with SKF was signed in Stockholm, the US Treasury issued a statement declaring SKF was totally absolved of all 'alleged collusion' with the enemy.[51]

Throughout 1944 and 1945, SKF Sweden kept on sending ball bearings to the Germans, and managed to skirt around the secret US deal by funnelling German-bound ball bearings via neutral Spain, Portugal and Switzerland. After the war, SKF resumed control of its plants in Germany, and no action was taken against executives von Rosen or Batt. Today, SKF is still the largest ball bearing manufacturer in the world, employing 48,000 people with an annual turnover of $US7.8 billion.

•

Henry Ford was an ardent Nazi in all but uniform. A pugilistic puritan who hated the demon drink and tobacco, Ford made no secret of the fact that he had a manic hatred of Jews, nor that he had admired Hitler long before he rose to power in Germany. He announced his fierce anti-Semitism as early as 1920 in the *Dearborn Independent*, a newspaper Ford printed at the home base of his Model T car plant. Every week Ford's paper churned out vicious anti-Semitic propaganda, long before Hitler did, with 700,000 copies a week handed to all employees and customers, proclaiming Jews were the cause of all international problems in articles such as 'The International Jew – the world's problem'.[52] Ford claimed Jews secretly planned World War I in order to profit from it, and Jews were plotting to dominate the world through a global bank.

It was great material for Hitler, and the hatred poured out in the *Dearborn Independent* was translated into German and sold as a booklet by the growing force of Brownshirts in Germany. At Hitler's trial in 1924 for treason, prosecutors said

Ford had given money to Hitler's fledgling National Socialists. In jail Hitler wrote *Mein Kampf*, in which he singled out Ford for praise. In 1927 Ford published his virulent anti-Semitic tract *The International Jew*, and it sold an enormous number of copies across South American and the Arab countries. Hitler erected a huge photograph of Henry Ford in his Munich Nazi headquarters. 'I regard Henry Ford as my inspiration,' Hitler told a *Detroit News* reporter in 1931 to explain why he kept the life-size portrait of the American next to his desk.[53] A large pile of Ford's book was stacked in Hitler's private office, to be handed to visitors to show that the great industrialist and he were on the same page as far as Jews were concerned. Ford returned the compliment, remembering Hitler's birthday and sending him 50,000 Reichsmarks a year.[54]

Ford proclaimed himself a pacifist and refused to build aircraft engines for the British Royal Air Force. But in the lead-up to the war, Ford's plants in France and Germany built five-ton military trucks that became the backbone of the German army. Despite rubber shortages in the US, Ford arranged to ship tyres to Germany. In 1938 Hitler showed his gratitude, awarding Henry Ford with the swastika-bedecked medal The Grand Cross of the German Eagle.

When Germany went to war with Britain and France, Ford's plant in Cologne was taken over by the Reich and converted to making military vehicles. The Ford plant in occupied France was also taken over. It made airplane engines in 1940 as well as trucks for the German army. Letters dated 1942 later emerged between Ford's son Edsel, who had responsibility for the company's international business, and the French factory boss, discussing profits made from manufacturing twenty trucks a day for the German

Army. Even though the US was now at war with Germany, Edsel said how 'delighted' he was at the production rollout of the French factory. These letters with the enemy were passed through US diplomatic channels.[55] In 1942 the RAF bombed the French plant at Poissy, fifteen kilometres outside Paris. The puppet French Vichy government paid Ford 38 million francs in compensation. In December 1941, just as the US entered the war with Germany and Japan, Ford-France established a new factory in Algiers to supply trucks to the German Afrika Korps. All directors were pro-Nazis.

The Ford company has since insisted that it had no responsibility for the operations of its German or French subsidiaries during the war. The company says it lost control of the subsidiaries once war began. However, on 20 October 1942, US Ambassador to the UK, John Winant, reported to Assistant Secretary of State Dean Acheson that 2000 German army trucks were authorised for repair by the Ford Motor works in neutral Switzerland.[56] A year later another US diplomatic report from Switzerland stated that spare parts from the Ford plant in Zurich were being shipped to the Ford plant in Cologne.

When American troops liberated Ford plants in Cologne and Berlin they were shocked to find starving and ragged foreign workers confined behind barbed wire. Company documents extolled the genius of the Führer. US military investigator Henry Schneider wrote in a report dated 5 September 1945 that the German branch of Ford served as 'an arsenal of Nazism at least for military vehicles' with the 'consent' of the parent company in Dearborn, US.[57] *The Washington Post* reported that German researchers found documents showing that, after the war, Ford US received dividends from its German subsidiary worth about

$60,000 for the war years 1940 to 1943. Managers at Ford's Cologne plant during the war were given new jobs at the plant a few years after the war was over. Ford even asked for compensation from the US government for losses due to bomb damage to its German plants.

•

Ford wasn't the only automobile company with links to the Nazis. The extremely wealthy Du Pont family dominated General Motors, and the firm's president from 1919 to 1925, Irénée Du Pont, was another great admirer of Adolf Hitler and an anti-Semite, even though he had Jewish blood. In 1926, in a speech to the American Chemical Society, he postulated that a race of supermen could be achieved by injecting drugs into boys. Between 1932 and 1939 the Du Pont bosses of General Motors poured $US30 million into IG Farben plants.[58]

When American troops invaded Europe in June 1944, they did so in trucks and tanks manufactured by Ford, General Motors and Chrysler only to find confronting them was an enemy driving trucks manufactured by Ford and Opel – the 100 per cent German subsidiary of General Motors US. In the air, Allied fighters faced German warplanes built by Opel. GM Germany built more trucks for the German army than Ford, including the 'Blitz' troop transport truck which would soon carry German troops into the Rhineland, Czechoslovakia, Austria, Poland and the Soviet Union. Researcher Bradford Snell told the *Washington Post* that Nazi armaments chief Albert Speer told him in 1977 that Hitler 'would never have considered invading Poland' without synthetic fuel technology provided by General Motors.[59]

•

In 2015, Coca-Cola ran an advertisement in Germany with the line 'Good Old Times' to mark the seventy-fifth birthday of its spin-off soft drink Fanta. The ad campaign went on to say, '75 years ago resources for our beloved Coke in Germany were scarce. To celebrate Fanta we want to give you the feeling of the good old times back.'[60] It wasn't the smartest marketing move. Simple maths told consumers that Coke's 'good old times' must refer to 1940, when times weren't good at all. Coca-Cola quickly pulled the advertisement and removed the words 'good old times'. A company spokesman said Fanta was invented in Germany during World War II but insisted the brand had no association with Hitler or the Nazi Party.[61] Once war was declared, Coke's German plant lost access to the sweet black syrup it needed to make Coca-Cola. So the firm's chemists used apple and whey to produce the new soft drink, Fanta. The German plant kept on making it, and German troops lapped up this new German Coke, just as the American GIs they were shooting at were lapping up good old American Coca-Cola.

German Coke was hugely successful and made huge profits during the war using the slogan 'Mach doch mal pause' – Take a break. Coke ads were on billboards across Nazi Germany, and German Coke was very much a part of Nazi life. After the war, the German branch of Coca-Cola turned over all its wartime profits to the American parent company in Atlanta.

It should come as no surprise that big business makes big profits from war. Somebody has to supply the weapons, communication equipment, uniforms, vehicles, food, medicines, accommodation and the myriad other necessities to equip a nation's military. But it should come as a shock that some corporations we know today as household names made money from both sides during World War II. It should come as a shock that some industrial giants that are part of our everyday lives made a fortune secretly trading with the enemy. It should come as an even greater shock that some of these multinational behemoths grew during the war on the tortured backs of slave labour, hundreds of thousands of whom died in horrendous conditions.

7

PROFITS ÜBER ALLES

'It was said both by the victims who survived and Krupp staff that the screams from the cellar could be heard all the way to the fifth floor of the building.'

The heavy black iron gates of Buchenwald concentration camp still carry the words '*Jedem Das Seine*'. It translates to the double meaning 'everyone gets what they deserve' or 'to each his own'. The words face inward so that only those inside the camp could read them. Using it on the gate of one of Nazi Germany's first concentration camps was some sort of twisted Nazi attempt at gallows humour. The phrase had a long German cultural association. Martin Luther used the phrase to argue his case for Reformation. Bach used it to name one of his cantatas. It was a title for several German nineteenth-century comedies. The tens of thousands of prisoners kept at the camp could only read the words as they left the camp, force-marched to nearby slave-labour factories, horrific places from which many never returned.

Next to the entrance gate are the wings of the camp administration building where prisoners were kept in tiny cells in isolation, and tortured. On some of the cell doors are explanations of who was kept there, for how long, how they were tortured and when they were killed. They included priests, pastors, communists and pacifists. Displayed in the last cell of the row are the torture instruments that were used.

The block huts where prisoners were kept during the war were razed long ago. Gravel crunches under your feet as you walk along paths between the stone-filled sites where the huts once stood. Up to 250 people were crammed inside each hut in horrendous conditions. At its peak in January 1945, the camp held 120,000 prisoners – 85,000 men, 25,000 women and 10,000 children. They were Jews, Gypsies, political prisoners, homosexuals, communists, so-called anti-socials, Jehovah's Witnesses, German deserters, pacifists, and prisoners of war, the latter mostly from the Soviet Union. Each category of prisoner was marked with a different coloured triangle on the sleeve of his or her striped pyjama-style uniform.

A group of 168 Allied airmen were transported from Gestapo cells in France to Buchenwald in September 1944. They were mostly Americans but included airmen from Australia, New Zealand, Canada and the UK. Nine Australians were recorded in Buchenwald records. In breach of the Geneva Convention, the POWs were ordered to strip and were then deloused, and forced to wear prison stripe uniforms instead of their uniforms.[1] The Allied airmen were treated in the same cruel manner as the rest of the prisoners. They were starved and forced to carry corpses to the busy crematorium. Around forty British commandos were executed at Buchenwald. Soviet POWs were usually executed soon after arriving – 7000 of them were shot in a special kill zone, their bodies burned and buried in mass graves. After several months in Buchenwald, the Australians were part of a group of Allied airmen that were moved out to a POW camp. They were the lucky ones.

In the first 100 days of 1945, 13,000 Jews died in Buchenwald. By then even the most fanatical Nazi knew they would soon lose the war. Their response was to speed up the killings and executions. Buchenwald was liberated by the US Army in April 1945. The horror the American soldiers found was unspeakable. It took some time to collate the scale of the atrocity. Statistics piled up. In all, about 250,000 people passed through Buchenwald before being sent to slave labour factories or extermination camps such as Auschwitz. Inside Buchenwald more than 56,000 people were murdered, starved to death, tortured to death, had medical experiments conducted on them till they died, were beaten to death, or were simply shot.

German army medical laboratories were set up to explore the limit a body could endure of starvation, torture, and beatings. Prisoners were injected with diseases such as typhoid fever in human experiments done for the giant IG Farben chemical and pharmaceutical concern. More than 1100 people died in these human experiments in Buchenwald.[2]

This horrific history envelopes you like a fog as you walk around the now-empty camp. A modern museum spares no details. There's a guard's uniform, here are the life stories of some of the executed, over there are torture instruments. One poignant exhibit is a group of carved wooden farm animals in a shoebox. Prisoner Otto Roth carved them for his toddler son Artur, and a guard who knew Roth from before the war agreed to deliver them to the boy when he went home on leave. Otto Roth survived the camp and Artur donated his precious possession to the museum. It is the one bit of kindness and humanity that can be found in this terrible place.

Stop walking through the camp for a moment to examine a small plaque or posy of flowers left among the stones for lost loved ones, and the silence is overwhelming. No one talks here. No one meets other people's eyes as they pass. Cold winds whip across the vast open space. There is shelter from the wind in the one original building that still stands. For many, it is too unbearable to enter. It is the crematorium. A dark-brown brick chimney stack towers over the innocuous-looking khaki building. The chimney is the tallest object in the camp. A fence blocks the view to spare passers-by who do not wish to see what is inside.

Visitors enter the crematorium through the white-tiled pathology laboratory. A sign in German, French, Russian and English says that on a nearby white slab, gold teeth were removed from corpses. Doctors also sliced off large rolls of skin from corpses to present as souvenirs to SS Death's Head guards. Some human skins were used as lampshades. Heads were shrunk to fist size, then used as paperweights by camp officers. A black and white photo of a pile of starved corpses hangs from a peeling white-washed wall. Dark stains in the concrete floor that couldn't be erased reveal where the bodies lay.

SS guards had an efficient system for handling the huge number of executions. When still alive, or half alive, victims were shoved down a metal chute from outside the crematorium building into the cellar, where brutish guards smashed them over the head with an axe or hammer till they were dead. The bodies were then hung up on butcher's hooks along the walls to drain the blood. When the incinerator on the floor above them had space, the corpses were thrown onto a platform and raised to the next floor. There they were put in rows and shoved into the highly efficient furnaces. Underneath the furnace, coarse ash containing bits of bone was shovelled onto carts. These carts were then wheeled outside the camp, where prisoners shovelled the ashes into deep holes. The greasy human ash that went up the chimney could sometimes drift as far as the picturesque town of Weimar, eight kilometres away. After the camp was liberated, General Eisenhower ordered every German living in Weimar to walk through the camp to see what had happened there.

Weimar, a university town, was the centre of German culture, home to Goethe, Schiller and Liszt. Goethe used to love walking through the forest of Buchenwald, a huge part of which was later to be destroyed to clear space for the concentration camp. One old oak tree was left standing in the centre of the camp. Folklore had it that Goethe used to sit under this tree with his wife. For the prisoners, the Goethe Tree was the only bit of nature in the camp. It burned down during an Allied bombing raid in 1944. The stump is still there – the highs and depths of German history in one tiny spot.

Buchenwald Museum states that between 1937 and 1945 at least 9000 SS guards served at Buchenwald and its nearby sub-camps where prisoners died in forced labour works. Only 148 guards and officers were ever charged with war crimes committed at Buchenwald. Between 1945 and 1987, fifty-nine trials of war crimes connected to Buchenwald concentration camp were held. A total of forty-six guards and officers at Buchenwald received the death penalty, sixteen got life sentences and sixty-four received sentences up to twenty years.

•

The furnaces for the Buchenwald crematorium were specially designed and built to streamline the burning of as many bodies as possible in as short a time as possible. Like a factory treadmill, bodies were loaded onto trolleys and rolled into the furnaces. The firm that developed and made the incinerators for Buchenwald proudly placed their company's black metal shield right beside the entrance to the furnace. It's still there today – Topf & Sons. It was a local firm at Erfurt, twenty-four kilometres from Weimar. The family company was founded in 1878 and made furnaces for breweries. Business grew in World War I making incinerators for municipal crematoria. When owners Ludwig and Ernst-Wolfgang Topf heard the SS were building a concentration camp just a few kilometres away at Buchenwald, they had a look and saw the huge number of inmates. They offered their services to the SS, saying they could get rid of lots of bodies quickly and easily. There was no pretence, no coyness about the purpose of the furnace. In their proposal to the SS, Topf made it clear that they were well aware the furnaces would be disposing of murdered human beings.[3] By 1938, bodies started piling up in Buchenwald, and Topf & Sons were in business.

Buchenwald wasn't established as an extermination camp for Jews. It was intended to hold political prisoners, homosexuals and 'undesirables' so long as they could be used as slave labour in factories and mines around the camp. Jews started arriving in 1939, and the murder rate accelerated. Topf & Sons put their mind to the problem of what kind of ovens would be needed to burn thousands upon thousands of corpses around the clock, and to do it in an energy-efficient manner with a minimum of smoke and grease. Topf's top engineer, Kurt Prüfer, came up with a sophisticated version of an agricultural oven that Topf used for the incineration of animal carcasses.

By 1941, Topf ovens were in such demand by the SS that the Topf & Sons brand name was on ovens in concentration camps across Germany, Poland and Austria – at Buchenwald, Dachau, Mauthausen, Gusen and Auschwitz. The firm had to construct the ovens on site, be in the camp when they began operation, and return to the camps for servicing and repair. According to the Buchenwald Memorial Foundation's Volkhard Knigge, the Topf people weren't fanatical Nazis or raging anti-Semites. The Topf brothers had joined the Nazi Party in 1933, but in those years anyone who wanted to do business in Nazi Germany virtually had to join the party. Knigge said the Topf staff of 1000 included members of the communist party and some 'half-Jews'. 'There is no indication that they differed from millions of other Germans of the time, or were in any way predisposed to aid the purposes of the Holocaust and mass murder,' writes Knigge.[4] In many ways that's even more horrifying than thinking they were all rabid Nazis.

The Topf technicians who frequently visited concentration camps to service the incinerators came up with ways to improve the efficiency and speed of the furnaces. There was no threat or coercion from the SS on Topf to work harder or faster. Documents reveal the sole objective of the Topf technicians was to find a solution to the technical problem of 'burning as many corpses as possible in as short a time, using as little fuel and leaving behind as little evidence as possible'.[5] The SS needed furnaces that could dispose of 80,000 corpses a month. Topf's senior technician, Fritz Sander, drew up plans for a four-storey oven – corpses would slide down a zigzag array of slanted grates, catching fire from the burning corpses below them. The corpses were the fuel, and the ovens could run non-stop. Topf applied for a patent on the high-rise oven, but it was never put into operation. Topf engineer Kurt Prüfer helped get the Auschwitz gas chambers running smoothly by devising an efficient gas exhaust to clear the chamber once the victims were dead.

While Topf saw nothing wrong in building better burners, the SS realised as enemy forces advanced that they were probably going to face mass murder charges. The guards started exploding Topf ovens at Auschwitz and other camps. But at Buchenwald the prisoners rose up and overpowered the few remaining guards, and held them for two days till American troops arrived. The Topf ovens were captured intact, company nameplate and all.

American troops captured Topf technician Prüfer, but released him. Two weeks later he was back working at Topf. Three weeks after Germany surrendered, company owner Ludwig Topf committed suicide rather than face arrest. In a farewell letter he claimed he was guilty of nothing and was being wrongly persecuted. 'I never consciously or intentionally did anything bad . . . there is no law, no decency left in this world . . . I was always decent, the opposite of a Nazi,' he wrote.[6]

After the war, Erfurt, Buchenwald and Weimar were in the Soviet occupation zone and became part of the German Democratic Republic – communist East Germany. Just before the borders closed, Ernst-Wolfgang Topf managed to slip across to West Germany. He was never arrested or prosecuted by British or American occupation forces. He re-established Topf in the industrial town of Wiesbaden. He stayed in the same line of business, building furnaces for crematoria and garbage incinerators. It went well for ten years until 1957 when a new book on the SS published evidence that Topf & Sons had supplied furnaces to the SS for the mass exterminations of the Holocaust. Ernst-Wolfgang Topf responded with a multi-page denial. He maintained, 'in our company no one was guilty, either morally or objectively'.[7] He argued that Topf ovens were misused by the SS in a way that couldn't be foreseen. Topf ovens were innocent, he insisted. Customers didn't buy it, and by 1963 he was bankrupt. He died in 1979, aged seventy-four.

Topf technicians stuck in the Soviet zone weren't so fortunate. In March 1946, four of Topf's senior technicians were charged with war crimes by Soviet investigators. Prüfer didn't deny that he was key to the efficient running of the death camps and he showed no guilt whatsoever. He insisted that he was just doing his job. In 1948 he was sentenced to twenty-five years in a penal colony. He died of a stroke in 1952. Sander also got twenty-five years and died a few weeks after Prüfer of a heart condition. Two other Topf technicians, Gustav Braun and Karl Schultze, were released from jail in 1955.

Topf & Sons kept going in East Germany, but not with incinerators. Crematorium furnaces were made by a state-owned firm. Topf & Sons in Erfurt instead made field kitchens. After several years the company changed its name to VEB Erfurter Mälzerei. It fell into ruin in 1996. In 2011 a memorial and wartime education centre was opened on the Erfurt site of the former Topf & Sons factory. Schoolchildren learn how technicians became part of evil by just doing their job and ignoring the consequences.[8]

It is vital that people remember what happened in those terrible places. Memories can be short. The Finnish firm Nokia got into trouble in 1998 for using the slogan *'Jedem Das Seine'* and had to withdraw it from thousands of billboards after the Nazi link was pointed out to the firm.[9] In 2009 ExxonMobil ran an advertising campaign for coffee in its German petrol stations with the same slogan. The ads were withdrawn after complaints from the Council of Jews in Germany. Exxon said its marketing department was unaware of the Nazi association.[10]

●

The Krupp family were the aristocrats of German steel, artillery and tanks. The Krupp dynasty began in 1587, proudly supplying arms for the Thirty Years War, Napoleonic Wars, Prussian wars and World War I. Krupp held the world patent for artillery shell fuses that were used in the Great War. In 1926, British artillery maker Vickers had to pay Krupp royalties on all the shells it had fired on German troops. Krupp steel built railways around the world and provided the shiny steel top for New York's Chrysler Building. Krupp was the largest industrial steel concern in Germany, and one of the largest in the world, with eighty-seven factories.

Krupp company chairman Gustav Krupp was an avowed monarchist, but as soon as Hitler was appointed chancellor in 1933 he became a fervent Nazi. In 1932, Krupp financially backed Hitler. Once Hitler became chancellor the firm pumped even more money into the Nazi Brownshirts and black-uniformed SS. Profits rolled in as Hitler beefed up Germany's arms industry, and when Hitler invaded Poland in 1939 it was with Krupp tanks, artillery and machine guns.

Shortly after the outbreak of war, Gustav's son, Alfried Krupp, inherited the massive steel concern. In 1942 Alfried Krupp personally approached Hitler and SS chief Himmler to point out that with all the men being conscripted for the army, his steel and iron factories in the Ruhr were left short of staff. In the earliest days of the war, Krupp management decided they could only expand production to meet the demands of the Nazi war machine by taking workers from the newly conquered lands of Czechoslovakia, Poland and Austria. Thousands of captured civilians and soldiers were forcibly put on trains and taken west to work in harsh conditions in Krupp factories. Eighteen months on, Krupp was still desperately short of slave labour. Krupp proposed a solution to Hitler. He suggested a contract between Krupp and the SS, who ran concentration camps such as Buchenwald, for the SS to supply camp inmates to the Krupp factories in the Ruhr and elsewhere. In return, Krupp would pay a daily rate to the SS – three Reichsmarks a day per unskilled worker, one and a half Reichsmarks for a child. Himmler liked the idea. It killed two birds with one stone – he pocketed more funds for his SS, and at the same time got rid of camp inmates he was going to murder anyway.

The wretched inmates, including many Russian and Polish POWs, were forced into railway cattle cars at the camps. Many died on the way to the Krupp factories. A German railway worker at the Essen yards described Krupp overseers beating and kicking the prisoners as they stumbled from the train, many of them too weak to walk. An estimated 100,000 Krupp slave workers were condemned to unadulterated misery and cruelty. It made no difference whether they were man, woman, teen or child. Everyone in Krupp's slave workforce was condemned to work until they dropped dead. Food was minimal. Krupp managers constantly complained about the cost of the thin watery soup they dished out once a day. SS guards simply shouted 'No work, no food'.[11]

Despite some complaints from the German military that Krupp's high death rate of slave workers meant that they had to constantly send more prisoners back from the Eastern Front, in 1943 and 1944 conditions in Krupp's slave work factories only worsened. Conditions were so shocking that even one of Krupp's medical staff, Dr Wilhelm Jäger, complained to his senior: 'Upon my visit I found these females suffering from open festering wounds and other diseases. They had no shoes and went about in bare feet. Their only clothing was a sack with holes for head and arms . . . a person could not enter the prisoners' quarters without being attacked by fleas. I myself left with huge boils from them on my arms and the rest of my body.'[12]

If slaves didn't die of starvation, disease, exhaustion, beatings or random murders from SS guards and Krupp supervisors, Allied bombing raids would probably get them. Slave workers were forbidden from taking cover in air-raid shelters, even if there was space. They were blown apart by falling bombs along with the Nazi machinery the Allied bombers had come to destroy. They were also bombed in the open as they were force-marched by the SS through the streets of Essen, right under the windows of Alfried Krupp's office, from their barracks to the factories for twelve-hour shifts. Those too weak to work were sent to be gassed to death at the nearest extermination camp. Krupp's German workers also beat the prisoners. Dr Apolinary Gotowicki, Polish army doctor and inmate of the Krupp factory camp in Essen, witnessed this: 'Every day at least ten people were brought to me whose bodies were covered with bruises on account of the continual beatings with rubber tubes, steel switches or sticks. The people were often writhing in agony. Dead people often lay for two or three days on their palliasses until their bodies stank so badly that their fellow inmates took them outside and buried them somewhere.'[13]

Krupp had a torture chamber in the basement of his main administrative office. It was said, both by the victims who survived and by Krupp staff, that the screams from the cellar could be heard all the way to the fifth floor of the building.[14]

As the Allies advanced on Essen, Krupp feared the liberated slaves could become trial witnesses to his atrocities. Company management knew the SS guards planned a last-minute mass extermination of surviving prisoners to stop them being rescued. Krupp's senior director, Max Ihn, told the board that the furnaces couldn't cope with such a rush of hundreds of corpses. According to minutes of the board meeting in March 1945, 520 female prisoners were marched eighteen kilometres to the train station at Bochum for transport to Buchenwald. They were crammed into a train with 1500 other women. In the confusion at Bochum, five women escaped and lived to testify at the trial of Alfried Krupp.[15]

Krupp was a fanatical supporter of Hitler and the Nazi cause to the very end. As American troops advanced on Essen, the factory furnaces were flat out burning incriminating company documents. When American soldiers seized the Krupp headquarter buildings, they found papers showing that Krupp had still been sending laudatory messages to Hitler days earlier. Alfried Krupp and eleven directors of his firm were charged with war crimes for the use of slave labour, and stood trial with other major German industrialists at the Nuremberg Trials.

•

From the early days of the rise of Hitler and the Nazi Party, one of the chief financiers and supporters was IG Farben. Formed in 1925 as a massive chemical and pharmaceutical conglomerate from eight German firms – including Hoechst, Bayer, BASF, and Agfa – IG Farben was the largest chemical concern in the world, with tentacles stretching around the globe – including America's Standard Oil. It had a monopoly on the booming chemical industry in Germany, and was the country's single biggest exporter.

The firm and its bosses worked hand in glove with Hitler and his cronies. IG Farben wanted guaranteed government commissions, and funded the Nazi Party to ensure they'd get them. Hitler wanted German industry to be independent of imported raw materials and IG Farben could do that with its new, but very costly and labour-intensive, process of making synthetic rubber from coal or gasoline. On 20 February 1933, leading German industrialists held a high-powered meeting with Hermann Göring, Heinrich Himmler and Reichsbank president Hjalmar Schacht. IG Farben bosses handed over 400,000 Reichsmarks for the Nazi Party's election campaign, the biggest single donation that evening, which all up raised more than 3 million Reichsmarks – a fortune at the time. It far outstripped the financial funds of Hitler's political opponents.

Business boomed once Hitler seized total power and put Germany on a war footing. As German troops advanced into

Austria, Czechoslovakia and Poland, all captured chemical plants were handed over to IG Farben. Captured soldiers and camp inmates were forced to work at IG Farben plants, but the company wanted even more cheap labour. On 6 February 1941, IG Farben's executive director Carl Krauch told Göring and Himmler that the company wanted to build a chemical plant next to a concentration camp in order that it could be supplied with a constant stream of workers to make synthetic rubber. That was the death camp Auschwitz in Upper Silesia, chosen by IG Farben because it was near a coal mine and railways ran nearby. IG Farben paid the SS (at the same rate as Krupp) to supply 10,000 workers to build its new synthetic rubber plant.

IG Farben was to have another profitable link to the Auschwitz camp. The company owned forty-five per cent of a firm called Degesch that made the lethal gas Zyklon B, used in the camp's gas chambers. The gas was prussic acid and already had a commercial use as a pesticide. All IG Farben had to do was remove the warning saying it was not safe to be used near humans and to be careful using it in enclosed spaces. When the Auschwitz gas chambers went into around-the-clock operations in 1942, IG Farben's dividends from its investment in Degesch more than doubled.[16]

IG Farben's new building site, called IG Auschwitz, was outside the barbed wire of the fast-growing concentration camp, so SS guards divided the work site into ten-square-metre blocks. Anyone who stepped outside the block was shot without warning for attempting to escape. Sometimes an SS guard would order a prisoner to fetch some object outside the square and then shoot him just for fun. Prisoners had to run from the camp to the building site, and anyone who fell out of line was shot. Anyone killed at the plant had to be carried back to the camp by other prisoners so they could be accounted for at rollcall. Anyone who could not keep up with the crushing workload was sent for 'special treatment' in the gas chambers.[17]

To speed up the work in March 1941, Auschwitz camp commandant Major Rudolf Hoess agreed with the IG Farben managers, including general manager at the construction site Dr Walter Dürrfeld, to assign to the building site more of the hated 'capos' – brutal inmates who acted as enforcers among inmates for the SS. Every twenty slave labourers would have one capo to keep them in line. 'These Capos are being selected from amongst the professional criminals and are to be transferred from other concentration camps to Auschwitz,' noted Dürrfeld.[18]

Weekly reports from the Auschwitz plant to IG Farben headquarters in Frankfurt noted that the constant cruelty and bashing of prisoners by the capos was having a demoralising effect on the German workers. Company managers asked the capos to inflict punishment once they got back to the concentration camp instead. However, the managers agreed that 'only brute force has any effect on these people'.[19]

IG Auschwitz's factory was operating by mid-1942. The SS picked out the most healthy-looking arrivals at the camp's railway station and marched them off to the camp especially constructed for IG Farben's slave work force. Slave workers were now prisoners of IG Farben, kept behind electrified barbed wire fences with watchtowers, armed guards, attack dogs and searchlights. Prisoners were kept in unimaginable conditions, starved and disease ridden. The plant had a punishment cage in which the victim could neither stand upright, kneel nor lie down. The factory gallows nearly always had a couple of cadavers hanging from it. Many were literally worked to death. Bodies were stacked up in full view of the prisoners and taken to the huge crematorium and Topf furnaces at the Birkenau part of the massive Auschwitz camp. The Auschwitz motto *'Arbeit Macht Frei'* (work sets you free) was repeated on the IG Farben factory gates.[20]

Camp survivor Rudolf Vitek, a physician, later described the horror of the IG Farben camp: 'The prisoners were pushed in their work by the Capos, foremen, and overseers of the IG in an inhuman way. No mercy was shown. Thrashings, ill-treatment of the worst kind, even direct killings were the fashion. The murderous working speed ended with many prisoners collapsing, turning blue, gasping for breath, and dying like tortured animals. It was no rare occurrence that detachments of 400 to 500 men brought back with them in the evening five to twenty corpses. The dead were brought to the place of rollcall and counted as being present.'[21]

On 27 July 1943 Krauch wrote to Himmler asking if the SS could build another concentration camp similar to Auschwitz so that IG Farben could make use of the slave labour force and build another synthetic rubber plant. 'I would be grateful if you would continue sponsoring and aiding us in this matter.'[22] From the sparse records available, an estimated 300,000 slave workers passed through the gates of IG Auschwitz. Around 25,000 were worked to death.[23]

When Soviet troops finally approached Auschwitz in January 1945, the Nazis forcibly sent 58,000 of the surviving prisoners on a long death march. One in four died. The 7500 left in the camp were liberated by Soviet troops on 27 January 1945. Six hundred corpses were stacked in a long pile. The guards fled. Soviet troops discovered clothes for a million people and 7.7 tonnes of human hair.

Auschwitz commandant Rudolf Höss was captured on 11 March 1946 by British Intelligence agents near Flensburg on the Danish border. He faced trial in Warsaw, and confessed to war crimes. He was hanged on 16 April 1947. Around twelve per cent of the 6500 Nazi guards and staff at Auschwitz were caught and put on trial. Auschwitz was now in Polish territory, and Poland prosecuted 673 of the total 789 guards and staff put on trial. In December 1947, twenty-three were hanged, seven received life sentences, and nine received sentences up to fifteen years. Other Auschwitz staff faced war crime charges at the Dachau and Belsen trials.

The owner and the chief executive of the firm that supplied the poison gas Zyklon B, Bruno Tesch and Karl Weinbacher, were tried by the British as war criminals for killing an estimated one million people in gas chambers. They were found guilty and executed.

The senior executives of Krupp, IG Farben and other firms that used slave labour to support Hitler's war machine were brought to trial in late 1947, two years after the end of the war and long after the top Nazis had been dealt with. Lesser war criminals who committed atrocities were being put on trial in other parts of occupied Germany. A sense of atrocity fatigue was setting in among the public, and the prosecutors knew they could face an uphill battle to get widespread support to jail businessmen who made profits, but hadn't used their own hands to carry out the beatings, executions and murders.

The young American prosecutors at the Nuremberg Industrialists trial, led by Josiah DuBois, were keen to nail these senior executives. Senior British government officials, however, were decidedly cool on putting Germany's leading industrialists in jail and breaking up their massive firms.

Sir Patrick Dean, senior legal adviser to the British Foreign Office, had advised Conservative Foreign Secretary Anthony Eden in October 1944: 'It is not a war crime for anyone to have financed and assisted the growth of Hitlerite power, and the industrialists and others who may have done this cannot be indicted as war criminals.'[24] That attitude continued throughout the Nuremberg Trials. As the trials of top-level Nazis such as Göring dragged on through 1946 and 1947, Dean recommended a legal go-slow as far as the industrialists' trials were concerned. He expressed doubt as to whether Alfried Krupp and other industry bosses could have been aware of what happened to the work slaves on the factory floor. He seemed to deliberately ignore much of the evidence. 'I cannot help feeling that there is much to be said for going very slowly on this matter,' he said in an internal memo. Sir David Scott-Fox, head of the British War Crimes Executive, described it in public servant language as 'masterly inactivity'.[25]

DuBois was also coming in for some ugly attacks back in the US for his enthusiasm to prosecute Germany's industrial bosses. By 1947 the Cold War had begun and the former enemy Germany was now seen as a necessary bulwark against Soviet Union aggression. A strong capitalist western Germany was needed to fend off godless communism from the east, regardless that just two years earlier the Soviets had been valuable allies. Congressman George Dondero of Michigan accused DuBois of being part of a communist conspiracy. The fact that Dow Chemicals, which had links with IG Farben before the

US entered the war, was based in Dondero's Congressional district might have had something to do with his attack on DuBois. Mississippi Congressman John Rankin chose to suggest a Jewish conspiracy when he said on the floor of the House of Representatives on 27 February 1947: 'What is taking place in Nuremberg, Germany, is a disgrace to the United States. Every other country now has washed its hands and withdrawn from this saturnalia of persecution. But a racial minority, two and a half years after the war closed, are in Nuremberg not only hanging German soldiers but trying German businessmen in the name of the United States.'[26]

There were to be three trials of Nazi industrialists before the Nuremberg War Crimes hearings – that of the giant Krupp, IG Farben and Flick concerns.

Flick was first to face trial in 1947. Friedrich Flick, coal magnate and director of the Dresdner Bank, was Hitler's first major financier and a rabid anti-Semite. He argued that the SS gave him no choice and he had to take thousands of slave workers sent to his coal mines to speed up production. However, documents proved Flick had pleaded with the SS for more Russian prisoners to work his mines. He was found guilty of crimes against humanity and was sentenced to seven years' jail. That included time already served, and by 1951 Flick was out of jail and reunited with his fortune. He promptly bought forty-five per cent of Daimler-Benz shares, and by the mid-1950s he was the richest man in the new nation of West Germany and the fifth richest man in the world. Flick was fêted for the rest of his life and died leaving a billion dollars to his family in 1972. Flick never paid compensation to the families of those who died making him wealthy.

Next to face the judges at Nuremberg were twenty-four directors of IG Farben. With a mountain of evidence gathered by investigators showing that the firm had financed the Nazi Party, been intimately involved with Nazi extermination camps and used extensive slave labour, prosecutors expected easy convictions and stiff sentences. The IG Farben trial began in August 1947. The prosecutors were well aware of pressure from British and American conservative politicians to quickly wind up the trials. The prosecutors presented horrific accounts from eyewitnesses of the conditions in IG Auschwitz and other forced labour factories. Several German lower-level IG Farben employees testified that their seniors were well aware of what went on in Auschwitz and the treatment of the slave workers at IG Farben plants.

British POW Eric J Doyle, who was held in the town of Auschwitz, testified: 'The condition of the concentration camp inmates was deplorable. I used to see them being carried back at night, dead from exposure, hunger or exhaustion. The inmates did heavy manual labour, such as carrying steel girders, pipes, cables, bricks, and sacks of cement weighing about 100 pounds. As a rule the inmates weighed less than the cement sacks. I have seen the inmates shuffle, trying to make it in double time, but unable to do it, and I have seen them collapse . . . we would see the chaps hanging up in the gate of Lager IV, and the prisoners had to walk underneath them. I saw those bodies myself . . .'[27]

Another British POW held in the town of Auschwitz, Charles Joseph Coward, testified: 'The population of Auschwitz was fully aware that people were being gassed and burned. On one occasion they complained about the stench of burning bodies. Of course all the Farben people knew what was going on.

Nobody could live in Auschwitz and work in the plant or even come down to the plant without knowing what was common knowledge to everybody.'[28]

The defence argued that German company managers had no choice but to go along with SS demands for increased output using slave labour or they would be arrested themselves. Defence lawyers questioned whether executives of companies like DuPont in America or Imperial Chemical Industries in England wouldn't also have to do their utmost for their nation's war effort. They argued that German industrialists supported the Nazi Party in the 1930s because the country faced being taken over by communists.

The trial ended on 12 May 1948 after 189 witnesses, 6000 documents, 2800 affidavits and a transcript that stretched across 16,000 pages. A month later the judges gave their verdict: of the twenty-four IG Farben defendants, only thirteen were found guilty of crimes against humanity and war crimes. The highest sentence given was eight years. Chief prosecutor Josiah DuBois was disgusted. He condemned the light sentences as 'light enough to please a chicken thief'. Four years later he published a damning book, *The Devil's Chemists*.[29]

Carl Krauch, by then IG Farben chairman, was sentenced to just six years and was released in 1950. He continued to deny all knowledge of events at IG Auschwitz. He died in 1968.

Otto Ambros, a production chief at Auschwitz who had tested poisons and chemicals on inmates and worked on the production of the nerve gas sarin, was sentenced to eight years. He had argued that the lives of concentration camp inmates were saved by working in the IG Farben plant. On his release in 1951, Ambros was employed by Dow Chemicals and the US Army

Chemical Corps. He advised the Grunenthal company on the development of thalidomide. He became an economic adviser to Friedrich Flick and German Chancellor Konrad Adenauer. He lived until 1990.[30]

Fritz ter Meer, the head of IG Auschwitz, was sentenced to seven years. At the trial he argued that it made no difference whether prisoners suffered at IG Farben's plant as they would have died in the concentration camp anyway. On his release for good behaviour in 1950, ter Meer got a senior position at Bayer AG, becoming chairman of Bayer in 1956. He retired in 1961, a highly respected businessman on the boards of several major companies. He died in 1967.

Walter Dürrfeld, head of construction at IG Auschwitz, was sentenced to eight years but was out of jail in 1951. He was appointed to managerial positions at several chemical firms and died in 1967.[31]

The Krupp trial was the last of the industrialist trials at Nuremberg. It began in December 1947 and lasted until 31 July 1948. Twelve Krupp directors were accused of war crimes. Gustav Krupp had earlier faced the prospect of being charged with war crimes for financing the Nazi Party, but his trial was abandoned as the seventy-five year old was senile and in poor health. He lived until 1950.

Alfried Krupp denied everything. He told the three American judges that he didn't care about politics and, like any businessman, was only interested in having a system that allowed the firm to prosper. The judges were less sympathetic to his argument that he had no choice but to work with forced labour under the Nazis. Alfried Krupp was stunned when he was sentenced to twelve years' jail for crimes against humanity. On top of that, the Krupp family fortune was to be forfeited. Other Krupp directors received between twelve and three years. Only one was acquitted.

By all accounts, the jailed industrialists locked up in Landsberg Prison near Munich had a reasonably pleasant time. Flick managed to keep his business interests alive through weekly visits from his lawyer, who brought business partners with him. Conditions were far better than they had been for their slave workers.[32]

The American High Commissioner for Germany (a civil post set up to govern the US military-occupied zone of western Germany), John J McCloy, was under pressure to normalise relations with what was about to become the Federal Republic of Germany. The US, Britain and West Germany wanted to put an end to the punishment of German war criminals in order to clear the way to building up West German industry and economy to face the threat from communist Russia. In 1951 McCloy pardoned Krupp, Flick and the IG Farben bosses, and they all walked free. Krupp and Flick had all their wartime wealth restored to them. McCloy pardoned several other convicted war criminals, including diplomat Ernst von Weizsäcker, Waffen SS Colonel Joachim Peiper and Waffen SS General Josef Dietrich.

After the war, IG Farben was broken up into its original components; Bayer, BASF, Hoechst and Agfa went back to their former entities and became giant corporations. (Hoechst recently became Sanofi-Aventis after merging with a French firm.) Alfried Krupp died in 1967, leaving his entire fortune and the company to a philanthropic foundation named after him. In 1997 Krupp merged with Thyssen and is now a multinational steel and technology conglomerate known as ThyssenKrupp. The Alfried Krupp Foundation is still the largest shareholder.

Many other German business leaders and industrialists collaborated with the Nazis and made extensive profits from the war and the cheap labour that came from slave workers of the concentration camps. Many of the firms are still around today. They include electrical appliance giant Siemens, which had an agreement with the SS to be supplied with slave labour for its factories at Auschwitz, Buchenwald and Ravensbruck.[33] Engineering giant Mannesmann was chaired by Nazi Party activist Wilhelm Zangen during the war, and the company used slave labour in its German factories. Zangen served four months in jail for his involvement then remained a leading figure at the firm until his retirement in 1966.[34] BMW drew slave labour from the nearby Dachau concentration camp.[35]

Hugo Boss had a small clothing company in a village near Stuttgart and, like many other small firms, struggled to survive the Great Depression. But his fortunes changed when he joined the Nazi Party in 1931 and designed the smart SA Brownshirt and Hitler Youth uniforms. After the war he was barred from running a business and fined 100,000 Deutschmarks. Hugo Boss died in 1948 and his company continued making uniforms for police and postal workers. It branched into high fashion with smart business suits and today is a global brand. In 2011 the fashion house issued a formal apology when it was revealed that the founder of the firm not only designed Nazi uniforms but also used 140 Polish and forty French prisoners, mostly women, as forced labour.[36]

In 1999 the German government and business leaders agreed to pay $US5.1 billion in reparations to people who were used as slave labour during the Nazi regime. German President Johannes Rau made a formal apology: 'I pay tribute to all those who were subjected to slave and forced labour under German rule and, in the name of Germany, beg forgiveness. Their suffering will not be forgotten.'[37] Financed equally by business and government, the fund was to be used to compensate slave labourers and Jewish people whose property was stolen by the Nazis. It ended legal class actions launched by Jewish groups in the United States. In 2013, Germany agreed to pay 772 million Euros to survivors of the Holocaust. The money was dedicated to paying for the health care of around 56,000 Holocaust survivors who are still alive.[38]

8

IGNORE WAR CRIMES OF THE USEFUL

'His file said he was "an excellent German scientist"
and no indication he was pro-Nazi or pro-communist
– despite him once being a member of the SS.'

The 3000 determined and technically skilled men and women of T Force don't get much of a mention in heroic action war movies. Nor does the name of their top-secret mission inspire awe and excitement. But Operation Paperclip was one of the most extraordinary projects of World War II, a mission that took its elite and highly educated agents deep behind enemy lines and at the forefront of the fighting. They were experts in all fields of science, engineering, aeronautics and weapons of mass destruction, from chemical and biological warfare to atomic bombs. Their high-level military IDs gave them top priority classification. They had the authority to commandeer planes, ships, trains, vehicles, huge amounts of money and even entire military units. Their helmets bore a distinctive red 'T', and they were supervised and assigned their targets by a 230-man Anglo-American mobile headquarters.[1]

The targets of T Force were 9000 of Nazi Germany's top scientists, engineers and technicians. The operation had been planned since late 1944 as fears grew among the Allies that Nazi scientists were close to creating their own atomic bomb and biological weapons. Hitler's Aryanisation program had forced many Jewish scientists out of scientific projects, however, and Germany's race to the atom bomb slowed as a result. Half of Germany's top scientists – including Albert Einstein – fled as Hitler took power in 1933. Many ended up working to create an atomic bomb for the Allies, including Enrico Fermi, Edward Teller, Klaus Fuchs, Victor Weisskopf and John von Neumann. But as the war was coming to an obvious conclusion, the Allies had a new concern. They feared that German scientists who had made astounding breakthroughs in jet engines, V2 rockets, biological weapons and superior tanks such as the Tiger might be captured by the Soviet Union and put to work for the communists in what many saw as a looming conflict with the wartime ally.

The question of whether these scientists were war criminals, responsible for the deaths of tens of thousands through the weapons they created, was not a consideration for T Force.

Operation Paperclip was given the official green light by the US Defense Department in July 1945, but operations had secretly begun a year earlier. As the Allied victory approached, the US Joint Intelligence Committee (JIC) – which reported directly to the military Joint Chiefs of Staff – set up the Joint Intelligence Objectives Agency (JIOA). It was set up specifically to recruit Nazi scientists at war's end and put them to work on Allied weapons projects and scientific programs with the navy, army, air force and secret intelligence agencies. If the German scientists whom T Force recruited had been too close to Hitler to be allowed out in public in the US or UK, they were to work secretly at military facilities inside occupied Germany. The JIC was convinced that war with the Soviets was inevitable. Within one year of the atomic bombs being dropped on Hiroshima and Nagasaki, the JIC warned the Joint Chiefs of Staff that the United States needed to prepare for 'total war' with the Soviets, including atomic, chemical and biological warfare. They set the estimated start date for the new world war as early as 1952.[2] So, on 29 August 1949, when the Soviets exploded their first atom bomb, Western military and political leaders were shocked.

However, they had a head start. By the autumn of 1944 a veritable boffins' brigade of British, American and Commonwealth scientists, engineers, technicians, biologists, chemists and weapons experts had been given elementary commando training. They had to know how to stay alive behind enemy lines – not as fighting men, but to get past German guards to reach their target. Hundreds were given assignments that entailed dropping behind enemy lines with commandos to find individual scientists and persuade them to come back with them to safety on the other side of the Allied lines. Other people in the unit were sent to find the scientists' families and escort them to safety. Sometimes the boffins of T Force risked their lives to reach their targets, not knowing whether the German scientist would willingly defect. Many times Allied agents pointed guns at unwilling scientists and their families to help persuade them to switch sides and work for their former enemy.

One such mission took place in November 1944 in the historic university city of Strasbourg, where the Allies had just pushed out the German army. The city was shaking from the force of a German counterattack, bringing grand old buildings crashing down. In a deserted apartment in the historic centre of the city, American particle physicist Samuel Goudsmit and bacteriological warfare specialists Bill Cromartie and Fred Wardenburg were searching the deserted apartment of German virus expert Dr Eugen Haagen. Haagen was thought to be a key figure in a secret Nazi biological weapons program which was being developed at Strasbourg University. Haagen had fled just a day earlier as the Allies fought their way into the city, leaving many of his papers behind. Ignoring the sound of explosions getting closer, the three scientists, normally accustomed to working in a lab rather than in the centre of a battle, poured over the documents. They had to find out just how close Germany was to waging war with weapons of mass destruction – be they atomic, biological or chemical. There could be a clue among Haagen's papers. Commandos protecting the T Force scientists took up positions at windows and doorways. As night fell they lit candles to continue their search work. It was close to midnight when Goudsmit let out a yell.

'We had found papers that suddenly raised the curtain of secrecy for us. Haagen had left behind an apparently harmless communication that contained secret information available to anyone who understood it,' Goudsmit later told author Annie Jacobsen.[3] Dated a year earlier, Haagen's memo stated that of the 100 prisoners he had just received, eighteen died in transport and 'only twelve are in a condition for my experiments'. Haagen asked for 100 more prisoners aged twenty to forty in a 'physical condition comparable to soldiers'. Goodsmit realised he had discovered evidence that Nazi doctors were conducting medical experiments on healthy humans, and, as Haagen was a specialist in viruses, the Nazis were probably developing biological weapons.[4] The T Force men noted the names of German scientists Haagen worked with, and added them to the target list. But T Force never got Haagen. He was captured by the Soviets and ended up working for them.

Other T Force missions were more successful. Missile designer Professor Herbert Wagner was found by an American T Force unit in Oberammergau in the Bavarian Alps on 1 May 1945. Hitler was dead. His war was lost. Wagner faced prison for designing missiles that had rained destruction down on London. A smart man, he recognised a good deal when he saw it. Wagner showed the T Force specialists where he had hidden crates of blueprints of his work. A mere fifteen days later, Wagner was in a requisitioned Washington hotel room designing glide bombs for the US military to use against Japan.[5] His FBI file said he was 'an excellent German scientist' and there was no evidence he was pro-Nazi or pro-communist – despite his once being a member of the SS.[6] Wagner worked for US defence contractors and died in 1982 aged eighty-two.

Competition to beat the Soviets to the German scientists was intense. In one lightning raid, an American T Force unit moved an entire lab full of forty-nine chemists and their families – at gunpoint – from Leuna, a town in Soviet-occupied eastern Germany, into the American zone. The Soviets had their own scientist snatch operation, called Osoaviakhim. In one operation, Russians forced a whole trainload of German scientists east to Russia. They were given an ultimatum – work for the Soviet Union or sign a paper declaring they were unwilling to assist in the reconstruction of the Soviet Union. The scientists knew that the second option couldn't lead to a good result, so they signed up.[7]

The Western Allies and the Soviets also raced to grab German scientific and factory equipment and take it back to their lines. American T Force shipped an entire brand-new German submarine back to the US along with a 2500-horsepower turbine. An entire IG Farben pilot plant for the production of synthetic fuels was crated up and sent west, just as the Soviets were stripping every German machine and railway track and taking it east.

Paperclip's greatest success was the capture of more than 400 scientists who had worked on the revolutionary V2 rocket. From September 1944 more than 3000 V2 rockets were launched on London and on the advancing Allies from Peenemünde on the Baltic coast. For V2 project leaders Wernher von Braun, Arthur Rudolph, Georg Rickhey and the hundreds of engineers, technicians and aeronautic experts involved in the massive rocket project, the prospect of falling into the hands of America or Britain was far preferable to being enlisted by the Soviets.

Shortly after the American 3rd Armoured Division liberated Buchenwald they discovered a concentration camp nearby, called Dora. Three thousand bodies were stacked up inside buildings or lay rotting in tunnels. Thirty thousand corpses had been shoved into furnaces at Dora in the last months of the war. The forced labour prisoners died from beatings, starvation, disease and overwork. There were 23,000 survivors to tell of the horrors of the slave labour camp. They had been forced to dig the tunnels by hand, to provide secure places for the construction of parts for V2 and other rockets.

A T Force unit with the 3rd Division saw the horror differently, describing in their report what they'd found as a 'magician's cave'.[8] Within hours they commandeered the healthier men amidst the newly liberated slave workers to clear a mile of the main tunnel and drag the equipment out of the mountain. They requisitioned a fleet of trucks from all over the region to load the equipment up and take it to a railway siding, where it was loaded onto trains. A US combat engineer group had to rebuild a damaged bridge for the trains to head west. In eight days, 400 tons of machinery was moved from Dora to Antwerp for shipment to the United States.[9]

Wernher von Braun had been the top scientist at Dora and had been fully aware of the use of slave labour to build the tunnels and factories for his rockets.[10] As the Americans closed in, von Braun escaped to the mountains of Austria. He eventually handed himself in to the Americans, along with his blueprints. The rocket scientist had been a member of the Nazi Party and the SS, but once he was working for America he played that down. He argued that he couldn't have been part of the V2 rocket program without being in those organisations. He insisted that he was only doing his duty to his country by helping build the deadly V2 rockets that rained destruction on London. Von Braun knew slave labour was used to build the underground bases for the rocket bases, but he insisted that during the war he was unable to do anything about slave labour atrocities. Tens of thousands of concentration camp inmates died hacking out the insides of mountains to house the rockets. Von Braun said that if he had protested or intervened he would have been shot.[11] He pointed out that during the war he was held for two weeks by the Gestapo for uttering 'defeatist' remarks. However, von Braun was too important for the Gestapo to do their normal dirty work. At war's end US intelligence wiped von Braun's Nazi past from the records. With other German scientists from the

V2 program, von Braun was immediately put to work building rockets that eventually took Americans to the moon.

There were many other T Force recruits.

Theodor Benzinger was chief medical officer in the Luftwaffe's technical division where experiments were done on prisoners to see how long they could survive in frigid waters. He was listed as a defendant in the Nuremberg Doctors' Trials, but was mysteriously released and went to work for the US Naval Medical Research Institute in Bethesda, Maryland.

Kurt Blome, a senior Nazi, deputy surgeon general of the Third Reich and head of bioweapons facilities, refused to live in America but worked for the US Army at labs in Germany.

Kurt Debus was a V2 rocket flight test director and SS officer. Within months of the war ending he was working with the British, conducting tests on V2 rockets from an abandoned test range in Germany. The US recruited him as a special employee of the US Army, and he worked on space rockets with von Braun. He became the first director of NASA's John F Kennedy Space Center. A crater on the far side of the moon was named after him.

Major General Walter Dornberger was in charge of the V weapons and the slave labour tunnels. The British arrested him for war crimes, but he was released to the Americans. He worked for the US Air Force, then Bell Aircraft Corporation and as consultant to the Joint Chiefs of Staff.

Richard Kuhn was a Nobel prize-winning chemist who developed the nerve gas soman for the Third Reich. During the war he always started lectures with 'Sieg Heil'.[12] He worked for the US Army in Heidelberg.

Georg Rickhey was the general manager of the slave labour operation at Nordhausen, near Dora concentration camp. Operation Paperclip recruited him to work for the US Air Force. His abuse of slave labourers was exposed by a fellow scientist and he faced war crimes charges at the concentration camp trials. Acquitted due to lack of evidence, he was never taken to the US.

Arthur Rudolph was the operations director at Camp Dora who oversaw slave labour allocation. In the US he worked on the Pershing missile and the US Saturn rocket program until 1980, when he was investigated for war crimes. He renounced his US citizenship and left the US for Germany in return for not being prosecuted. He died in 1996.

Dr Siegfried Ruff conducted medical experiments at Dachau but then worked for the US Air Force Aero Medical Center in Heidelberg. He was tried at Nuremberg and acquitted. He worked for Lufthansa as an expert in the medical effects of flying. He became a professor at Bonn University and died in 1989.

SS Brigade leader Walter Schreiber was chief of Reich armaments supply, responsible for the production of tabun and sarin gas. He went on to work for the US Army in Heidelberg, working on sarin production.

Dr Hubertus Strughold was director of the Reich Air Force medical research institute for ten years and was listed as a war criminal for conducting human experimentation at Dachau. Recruited to be co-director of the top secret US Army medical research program at Heidelberg, and then by the US Air Force in Texas, he was referred to as the father of space medicine. Honours bestowed on him were withdrawn after his links to human experiments became public with the release of his wartime files.[13]

Nazi military intelligence officers, especially those who had spied on the Soviet Union, were heavily recruited for UK and US intelligence.

There was no such dedication to catching Nazi war criminals, no equivalent of a T Force to hunt down those who had committed mass murder. War crimes investigations were hampered by lack of staff and resources, limited access to secret military files, and a government policy that trials would be limited to the most senior and obvious Nazi war criminals. There was only a cursory questioning of the German scientists sought by T Force – ignoring how many people had died so they could conduct their work. Instead, these scientists of destruction were urged to keep on making weapons of mass destruction, this time for the West against a future war with the Soviets.

Justice did catch up with some, eventually, but many more scientists who were integral to the Nazi machine flourished with the open connivance of the Allies. It was, said British historian Richard Aldrich, 'one of the biggest transfers of specialists and knowledge from one country to another that the world has ever seen'.[14]

•

Australia didn't miss out in this rush to seize the best scientific minds that constructed Hitler's war machine. At least 127 German scientists and technicians were quietly recruited by the Australian government between 1946 and 1951. Declassified files marked top-secret at the National Archives of Australia[15] reveal the names and careers of the German scientists, engineers and technicians. Up to a quarter of them were known to have been members of the Nazi Party. Some of those party members had been in the SA, the brownshirted militant thugs of Hitler's supporters.[16]

Early in 1947 the British Dominion Office in London said it had a list of 200 German scientists and technicians, most of them specialists in munitions production, 'for whom it is considered desirable that employment should be found outside Germany'. Australia wanted to take around seventy of them.[17]

A special ten-man committee of civil servant department heads, security chiefs and university and industrial research groups was set up by the Australian government in December 1946 to handle the recruiting of German scientists. It was called the Employment of Scientific and Technical Enemy Aliens Committee (ESTEA). The committee was supposed to weed out any scientist who had been a hardcore Nazi, especially with links to the SA or SS, and certainly anybody implicated in Nazi atrocities. In reality, Australia turned a blind eye to the scientists' political backgrounds and whatever roles they had played in Hitler's war machine. ESTEA relied on the British and Americans to vet the scientists destined for Australia. Australia's intelligence service had the final say on their admission to Australia, but again they largely assumed that British and American military intelligence had weeded out the worst of the war criminals. The US and Britain had already taken their pick of German rocket engineers, atomic scientists, chemists and biologists, some of whom had worked on weapons of mass destruction. Australia was urged to act swiftly to take its pick of the German scientists, as the Soviets had abandoned an agreement not to recruit scientists with Nazi backgrounds and were kidnapping leading scientists from Western occupation zones. A top-secret memo from London said both the US and UK were planning to prevent the movement of German scientists eastward 'since it would increase significantly the war potential of Russia'.[18]

The head of Australia's Scientific and Technical Mission in London said an estimated 1500 scientists would have to be permanently moved out of Germany to Western countries. Australia was keen on getting German experts in mining, energy and agriculture as well as the chemical and biological industries. Some were earmarked for work on the giant Snowy Mountains scheme, and the committee said there was intense interest from private industry to sign up the German experts. A key member of the ESTEA committee selecting German scientists for Australia was Professor Victor Trikojus, head of Melbourne University's Biochemistry Department. Trikojus had toured Germany in 1936 and praised Hitler's economic progress in a speech to the Australian Institute of International Affairs in 1937. Against all evidence to the contrary, Trikojus asserted that any Jews who were of use to the Nazis were kept in their positions. In 1941 Trikojus was interned as an enemy alien, but released thirteen weeks later after a court appeal and protests from the scientific community. Trikojus worked for the Australian Army's medical research unit on anti-malarial drugs that were controversially used on Australian servicemen during the war. Jewish refugees arriving in Australia after the war were experimented on with malaria injections.[19] In 1948 the doors were opened for German scientists and their families to come to Australia, well before general immigration from Germany began in 1952. The scientists and their families had to move through Switzerland and Italy to board foreign ships to reach Australia.

In the early days of the scheme, Eric Longfield Lloyd, director of the Commonwealth Intelligence Service – the forerunner of ASIO – wasn't as accepting of the Allied screening process for the scientists as the committee. In May 1948, Lloyd protested to the attorney-general that scientists had arrived before his service had been able to conduct security checks. Lloyd said there was no documentary evidence that the scientists had been cleared by US or UK authorities. He warned that scientists who had worked in the Soviet occupation zone, or who had family still in the Soviet zone, could be pressured to conduct espionage. No alien from Soviet satellite regions should be allowed in defence-related work, he said. The British High Commission in Canberra wrote to the prime minister saying the recruitment of German scientists was a crucial matter for the entire Commonwealth, and suggested that even if a scientist were a possible security risk, employment should be found for them in a non-defence industry to prevent the Soviets recruiting them.[20]

Lloyd was a highly decorated Gallipoli veteran who had been an intelligence chief during World War II. He was one of the few who tried in 1938 to warn the Australian government that the Japanese were preparing for a long war expanding southwards towards Australia – at the same time Menzies was insisting Australia sell pig iron to Japan.[21] As a respected old soldier, Lloyd had little time for Canberra bureaucrats. In May 1948 he wrote a blistering letter to the attorney-general protesting at the wartime activities of some of the scientists who were being welcomed to Australia. He singled out three scientists as unsuitable: two who had worked for IG Farben and a radar expert who had proudly said he had worked on defences to shoot down Allied night bombers and to jam British radar so that German battleships could escape the Royal Navy blockade.

'There should not be any tolerance as that which enables such men as these to enter Australia. They should be sent away again at once,' Lloyd wrote to the government. The radar expert 'may be assumed to have been largely responsible for the loss of many Allied lives,' Lloyd thundered, ignoring the fact that since the war the radar expert had worked for the US Air Force. 'It is unwise to overlook past affiliations and activities upon the part of an enemy alien and every security instinct is aroused. It is not reasonable for potentially dangerous aliens to have been brought into Australia without prior security cognizance,' Lloyd said.[22] His protests fell on deaf ears. The ESTEA committee decided there 'could be no grave objection raised' to these German scientists having been used in 'war work'. There was an element of hypocrisy here from the intelligence service. Lloyd's moral concerns didn't prevent Australia's secret services from recruiting war criminal ex-Nazis and atrocity-committing anti-communists as spies from as early as 1950.

Nevertheless, Australia's archive files reveal that key German military scientists were welcomed as part of the influx of wartime scientists. At least twelve – six of them former Nazi Party members – were employed in government defence and aeronautical laboratories in Victoria and South Australia, but not on anything classified as secret. In 1951, after seven of the German scientists protested that they were not being treated with the respect they believed they deserved, several were cleared for work on secret military projects.[23] They included the former head of the top-secret Messerschmitt jet aircraft works at Peenemunde, where slave workers were forced to dig the deep underground bunkers for the V2 rockets; the radar expert who helped jam Allied radar so Germany's battleships could break out to sea in 1942; a designer of electric controls for the V rockets; the manager of the Reich's biggest explosive factory; the manager of an aviation fuel plant that was dug underneath the Harz Mountains (which used slave labour);[24] one of the developers of the helicopter; an expert in bomb-proof concrete; a poison gas researcher; a developer of an aircraft night bomb aiming device; and the German High Command's chief cartographer.

ESTEA got the Australian Treasury to make a special deal for the scientists to exchange their old Reich currency for current currency to help support their families. After one scientist 'disappeared' in Berlin while waiting for a flight, ESTEA arranged for the scientists to get priority seating on the crowded civilian planes out of the ruins of the old German capital.

Also welcomed to Australia were at least ten chemists who had worked with IG Farben. It is not clear from the files whether they had worked at the company plant at Auschwitz or at other sites where prisoners were literally worked to death, gassed with the company's lethal product Zyklon B, or were experimented on. Some went to Defence Research Laboratories, CSIRO and the Post Master General's Department. ESTEA said their employers expressed 'complete satisfaction' with their new German scientists.[25]

The scientists recruited to come to Australia were asked to submit a letter spelling out their expertise and life history. Most just skimmed over the war years without detailing what they had done. Others candidly stated that they had been members of the Nazi Party and the SA. The committee appeared to be concerned primarily about security risks only so far as the Soviets were concerned. In May 1950, in a file marked 'Secret', the director of the committee wrote to the secretary of the Attorney-General's Department urging ASIO to sit in on committee meetings to let them know of any security concerns with the scientists they were bringing in. In the letter, the director cited the case of German physicist Klaus Fuchs who had worked on the Manhattan Project and who had just been exposed as a communist spy who supplied details of the atomic bomb mechanism to the Soviets.[26] 'The Fuchs case in England shows that enemy alien scientists be regarded as safe and no doubt there are Nazi "Fuchs" as well as communist ones,' the director wrote.[27]

The recruitment of German scientists wasn't kept a secret. After all, ESTEA had to ask university and industrial research groups if they would employ the scientists. They were all deemed by ESTEA as 'politically unobjectionable' and any Nazi background or questionable wartime role the scientists had were buried in files and not mentioned publicly. In March 1948 a confidential memo was sent from London to the head of the committee, George Sharwood of the Division of Industrial Development, about one German scientist on his way to Australia who had been a squad leader in the SA in 1933. The memo said the man's Nazi past 'is not a matter which is desirable to give too much prominence [to] because of the chance of misinterpretation by those who desire to depreciate the scheme by innuendoes . . . It is as well to be forearmed in case by mischance this information becomes public property and twisted in the wrong form.' The scientists' contracts banned them from talking to the press, and any journalists who wanted to talk publicly had to seek permission from the relevant government minister.

They were normally refused. The committee would not disclose to the public where the scientists were working or who they were employed by. But ASIO did inform the committee that the scientists should be 'quietly and unobtrusively' kept under observation, their movements and associations away from their jobs noted.[28]

The existence of the Nazi scientists was kept from the government's Special Investigations Unit looking into war criminals living in Australia. Professor Konrad Kwiet, a special investigator to the SIU, said fifteen of the scientists would have been of interest to the war crimes investigation. 'I am quite certain now there was deliberately a kind of protection around these people so the SIU didn't get hold of [them],' Kwiet said.[29] The 1986 report on war criminals in Australia by Andrew Menzies gave all the German scientists a 'clean bill of health', so they were not even looked at by the SIU. Kwiet said it wasn't clear whether there was a deliberate cover-up to prevent embarrassment to the Australian government, but he said it was 'definitely in the interests of politics to cover up that story'. An ASIO spokesman replied: 'We would have no reason . . . why would we hide from an official government inquiry information on our files?'[30]

ESTEA was shut down in 1954. Committee officials in London were instructed to destroy all files relating to applications from German scientists and 'any files you consider necessary'.[31] Some scientists returned to West Germany at the end of their contract. The vast majority stayed on to enjoy their new life in Australia.

9

THE EVIL OF JAPAN'S UNIT 731

*'I don't know what those sons of bitches
gave me but I feel like crap.'*

Australian doctor Captain Desmond Brennan thought there was something very strange about the white-coated Japanese in surgical masks who marched into the prison camp's makeshift hospital in 1943. In faltering English they said they were doctors inspecting camp conditions, and they waved their clipboards to prove it. Japanese army officers hovered around, bowing and saluting them as senior and honoured superiors. Brennan watched them closely. He suspected from the way they went about their inspection and the questions they asked that they weren't there to ensure the prisoners were well cared for.

Conditions in the camp were truly atrocious. The 1500 prisoners kept in the Japanese Mukden (today it is the Chinese city Shenyang) prisoner-of-war camp on the harsh plains of southern Manchuria – 1400 Americans, eighty-one Britons, sixteen Australians and three New Zealanders – were barely surviving on the meagre food they received. After two years of imprisonment, the men weighed on average less than forty kilos. When they arrived at the camp in November 1942, the POWs were sprayed in the face with some chemical by men in surgical masks, and given injections. Over the course of that first winter in Mukden, temperatures plunged to minus 40 degrees Celsius. Around 300 American prisoners died from cold, disease and malnutrition. The Americans were already terribly weak when they arrived at the Mukden camp after their horrific 110-kilometre Bataan Death March in the Philippines. The freezing Manchurian winter killed many of them. The ground was too frozen to dig graves, so hundreds of bodies were stacked up in an open, unheated building on the camp site until the spring. Each frozen cadaver was tagged with the prisoner's identity.

In the spring, as temperatures rose and the earth thawed, 'Doc' Brennan watched as the Japanese took hundreds of the POW bodies away to conduct autopsies before burial. He wondered why they bothered. The cause of death was obvious.

US POW Frank James later told a US Congressional inquiry into Mukden that he was one of two POWs ordered to work with the Japanese medical team conducting the autopsies. 'Our duties were to lift the bodies off the tables, those bodies that had been selected. These were identified by a tag tied to their big toe which listed the POW's number. The Japanese then opened the bodies – the head, chest and stomach – and took out the desired specimens which were placed into containers and marked with the POW's number. The specimens were taken away by the Japanese medical group.'[1]

Doc Brennan thought the leader of the Japanese medical team, Dr Taniguchi, behaved professionally. Taniguchi had shown him the report on camp conditions he had written, and it noted the terrible state of prisoners in the camp. At the time, Brennan believed the autopsies were normal medical practice for the Japanese. However, Brennan thought the second medical team inspecting the camp a year later without Taniguchi was nowhere near as competent, even though they tried to big-note themselves. 'They rubbished Taniguchi and the work he had done,' Brennan later recalled.[2] One tried to strike up a discussion with Brennan, saying in his stilted English that soon Japan would occupy Sydney and he would be able to read the medical text-books Brennan had used during his studies at Sydney University. Brennan muttered under his breath that the Japanese doctor may try to read the textbooks, but he wouldn't understand them. The doctor tried to impress Brennan, telling him: 'There will soon be an inspection by very big Japanese genitals.' He meant generals. Brennan had to stop himself bursting out laughing.[3]

This second Japanese medical team visited the Mukden camp three times during the course of the war. This was highly unusual. Most Japanese POW camps never had a visit from medical teams. But at Mukden there were many strange and unique occurrences.

Mukden was the northernmost Japanese POW camp, far from the battlefields where the men had been captured. The prisoners, especially the Americans, were forced to work in a nearby former Ford factory where they made engines. The POWs went to considerable efforts to sabotage the machinery in small ways, and proudly claimed after the war not one machine that left the factory worked properly. Mukden had an unusual structure in that American POWs were mainly kept separate from the British and Australian POWs. On arrival at the camp, Doc Brennan had agreed with the two American medical officers that he would take care of the infectious diseases ward – essentially just a sparsely furnished hut close to the British barracks. Here he fought a long and hopeless battle to save lives in terrible conditions. The hospital hut was suitable for forty patients but it usually contained between ninety and a hundred. Men had to lie two or three to a cot, feet to head.

There was no help for Brennan from the visiting Japanese 'medical' teams. No medicines, no medical equipment, no clean sheets or bandages. Brennan and the other POW medical officers were therefore puzzled when the Japanese team started measuring selected American POWs with callipers, recording sizes of skulls, chests, arms and legs. The Japanese injected the men with drugs from unusually large needles, explaining to POW doctors that they were inoculations against typhoid, smallpox and dysentery. Blood samples were taken from the healthier prisoners, then taken again when the Japanese team returned months later. Tests were conducted with oral and rectal smears. They inspected welts that the injections had caused. All the results were noted down on the clipboards the team carried. Brennan had managed to smuggle a small diary to the camp and recorded in code everything that happened. He kept it buried under the makeshift mattress of the sickest man in the ward. No Japanese guard ever searched there.

Several strange things happened to the prisoners, which aroused suspicion about what the Japanese medical teams were really up to. US Private Greg Rodriquez was lying sick in bed late at night when one of the Japanese medical men came over and placed a mirror under his nostrils. Rodriquez later recalled: 'At the time I thought he's just checking to see if I am still breathing. But after a little bit he came back again with a feather. He ran that feather up and down under my nostrils. Later on I discovered this was one of the methods used to get prisoners to ingest bacteria.'[4]

US Army Sergeant Paul Lankford was one of the prisoners singled out for thorough body inspections. 'Blood samples were taken by slitting our ear lobes to reduce the pain. We were given shots – they didn't say what for. Very few of the Japanese doctors spoke English. After the shots many men got sick and a lot died.'[5]

US Corporal Wilson Bridges described how the men slept close to each other for warmth and how one night he was in the middle when Japanese doctors crept in and gave injections to the two men sleeping on the outside. 'In the morning both would be dead.'[6] Max McClain got injections with his bunk mate George Hayes. Two days later Hayes told him, 'Mac, I don't know what those sons of bitches gave me but I feel like crap.' That night McClain heard that 'the boys at the morgue' were cutting his friend up.[7]

US Army Staff Sergeant Arthur Campbell was picked out with eight other American POWs in what seemed like a random selection and ordered to an isolated barracks at a far end of the camp. They were kept there for two weeks. On one occasion the Japanese medical team took blood, urine and saliva samples. 'The next day they brought a basket full of oranges. We all lacked in vitamins and suffered from scabies, inflammation on mouth corners and stomatitis. We were told to take a half orange each with vitamins [and it] would solve the problems caused by the shortage of vitamins. We happily ate those oranges.'[8] Afterwards they all fell sick. They had stomach cramps, diarrhea, fever. 'One thing we thought was odd – they gave us tooth powder in grey cans and crude toothbrushes with wooden handles. They made us brush our teeth morning and night. We thought this especially odd since we had no other medical treatment for the past year.'[9] The Japanese took more blood samples and conducted more tests before returning them to their fellow POWs.

US Sergeant Herman Castillo was singled out by the Japanese team and taken to an empty barracks. He was forced into a steel cage that was fifteen metres long, one metre wide, one metre high at one end and just thirty centimetres at the other. Castillo was kept in this cage for nearly two weeks. He had to defecate and urinate in the cage, and couldn't wash or change his soiled clothes. He didn't know why he was forced to undergo this torture. During his incarceration in the cage, Japanese doctors sprayed something into his mouth, waved a feather under his nose, injected powder into his mouth and inserted a glass rod into his anus. He broke down with fever, shaking, chills, vomiting and dysentery. When he was eventually released a guard said: 'Now you are a carrier for life.'[10] Castillo was too weak to ask what he was a carrier of. He was a wreck. He couldn't bring himself to tell other prisoners or the POW doctors what had happened to him. He was terrified of being put back in the cage. After the war he couldn't face talking about it with military intelligence, his family or doctors. It wasn't until 1995 when he was approached by a documentary-making team from Japanese television that he felt able to tell of his ordeal. 'At the time I felt I was being used as a human guinea pig. I knew the Japanese medical team came from outside [Mukden camp] but I didn't know who they were or where they came from.'[11]

Officially this medical team were from the innocuously named Sanitation and Water Supply Branch of the Japanese Kwantung Army. In reality they were from a mysterious top-secret military research facility called simply Unit 731. The unit had a small base near Mukden, but the headquarters were at a large, specially built complex at Ping Fan, 566 kilometres north of Mukden near the Manchurian city of Harbin. The well-financed Unit 731 was headed by General Ishii Shiro, a brutal, arrogant, highly connected, imperialist fanatic. Ishii was also a brilliant medical scholar who had been promoted to army surgeon general at a young age. Ishii made a name for himself among the top echelons of the Japanese army chiefs as early as 1930, as he argued that bacteriological weapons should be used as part of regular Japanese armaments. As a student in the 1920s he'd travelled around the world – including the United States, the Soviet Union, France and Germany – studying the use of chemical and biological warfare in World War I. He acquired a reputation as a fast-living heavy drinker who spent up big in Tokyo's red-light geisha houses, especially on girls under the age of fifteen.[12]

In 1931, Japan invaded Manchuria, a divided region of northern China that Japan had been trying to colonise for decades. The Japanese army quickly quelled resistance from the splintered Chinese nationalist army and set up the puppet state of Manchukuo.

In 1932, Major Ishii got himself posted to Japan's new Manchurian colony and quickly convinced the high command that bacteriological weapons were the only way Japan's forces in China could hold back an attack from the Soviet Union. The army gave Ishii 300 men and an open cheque to begin his work. He took over an old prison at Ping Fan in northern Manchuria. It was a six-square-kilometre fortress – perfect to conduct his human experiments. Ishii got the Japanese army to send him thousands of Chinese prisoners, mostly resistance fighters but also criminals and any citizens who stood in the way of the Japanese invaders. Ishii got to work. By Japanese standards, the prisoners were treated quite well at first. They were fed, then had blood taken for testing every three or four days. They were also injected with Ishii's growing variety of test vaccines. Once in the hands of Unit 731, the prisoners rarely lived longer than a month. When prisoners died the bodies were dissected and disposed of in the prison crematorium. Ishii concentrated on three contagions – anthrax, glanders and plague.[13] In one test conducted on three prisoners, Ishii took fleas from rats caught in plague areas of northern China and extracted a virus that was injected into the prisoners. Within days, all three went down with high fevers. They were dissected while unconscious.[14] Ishii set about expanding the plague virus to use on the Chinese as a weapon. When Ping Fan ran short of human victims, local police simply grabbed vagrants off the streets.

Unit 731 also conducted human experiments on the effects of frostbite. Ishii's researchers repeatedly froze and defrosted limbs of living prisoners. In the extreme cold winter months, prisoners dressed in warm clothing were taken out into the open, their arms bared and dunked into a barrel of ice-cold water. They then had to shove their arm into a pile of snow and hold it there for a long time. Unit 731 staff then blasted the arm with cold air from a strong fan. Medical orderlies tapped the frozen arm with a short stick – when it sounded like striking a piece of wood they were satisfied that the arm was frozen solid right through. The doctors then tested various methods of defrosting the arm to see which was the most effective. After an extensive number of tests they found that soaking the frozen arm in warm water at exactly 37 degrees Celsius worked best. All test subjects were then killed – or 'sacrificed', as the unit members described outright murder.

Some other experiments included prisoners being hung upside down to see how long it took them to die; prisoners being injected with air to see how long it took before the onset of embolisms; horse urine being injected into human kidneys to see what happened. The experiments were all carefully recorded and written up. Members of the unit were medical researchers and doctors who had the attitude that Chinese were inferior humans whose 'sacrifice' was for the greater good. Addressing his team, Ishii said the superior Japanese race would benefit from the sacrifices of people who were of little value.[15] The names of the Chinese prisoners were never recorded. On entering the Unit 731 facility they were given a number from 1 to 150. When all those prisoners were dead, the unit members started numbering fresh prisoners again from 1. That way the records could not reveal how many prisoners passed through the facility. They were not even recorded as humans. The Japanese called them *maruta* – 'logs'. It was a Japanese in-joke. The Ping Fan facility was officially designated a timber mill to explain the endless stream of smoke coming from chimneys of the three crematoria. Chinese townsfolk were told the smoke was from burning off-cuts from the logs. More than 3000 prisoners were experimented on and murdered by Ishii's team at

Ping Fan. Thousands more died at other facilities operated by Unit 731 across China and even in Japan.[16]

Ishii was promoted to colonel in 1935 and was on the way up. His research staff now numbered more than 500, and they had a fanatical loyalty to him. Ishii liked to parade around in an immaculate colonel's uniform. He lived with his wife and seven children in a commandeered local mansion and was driven daily to Ping Fan in an armour-plated limousine. His plan to cause mass murder with biological weapons was going well. It was to be carried out on a massive scale. Unit 731 was producing pathogens for plague, cholera, typhoid, dysentery, anthrax, tetanus and gas gangrene. All were tested in experiments on humans. Once peak production was reached, the gigantic autoclaves would be able to produce many billions of microbes, or thirty kilograms of deadly disease mass per month. Captured Japanese later boasted cultivators built across China had the capacity to produce up to 600 kilograms of anthrax germs, 900 kilos of typhoid or 1000 kilos of cholera germs a month. They didn't ever make that amount, but they were proud that they could do it.[17]

By 1941 Ishii was investigating the best method to deliver the deadly disease microbes in order to inflict maximum destruction. First they tried artillery shells. Gunners fired into a compound holding Chinese prisoners, but it was found that the force of the explosive charge was too great for the anthrax spores they wanted to spread. In 1941 and 1942, Unit 731 experimented with various types of disease-laden bombs. Anthrax was considered useful as it was still deadly once it dispersed and settled on the ground. The unit also experimented with aerial sprays but could not perfect a system for widespread dispersal. The team also conducted human experiments on how to best use clothes, food or eating utensils as germ carriers. Prisoners were given food laced with germs, including chocolate laced with anthrax and biscuits containing plague bacteria. It was all very scientific. They would take twenty healthy prisoners, inject half of them with various strains of vaccine against cholera, then make them all drink cholera-infected milk. They watched and waited to see who lived the longest, carefully noting the results. Survivors were executed.

The unit devised ways to spread disease into villages. Chinese prisoners were dressed in disease-infused clothing and told they were free to return to their village. The unit monitored what happened. In another exercise, anthrax-laced biscuits and sweet cakes were 'accidentally' left near playgrounds, schools and parks. Particularly targeted was the southern Chinese coastal resort town of Hangchow (today's Hangzhou). Ishii wanted to strike at Shanghai's wealthy who holidayed there. It was probably a coincidence that Hangchow was also the birthplace of Chinese nationalist leader Chiang Kai Shek. In yet another exercise, plague-infected rats were released into Chinese cities to weaken the population before Japanese troops arrived. In July 1940 Ishii sent seventy kilograms of typhus bacterium, fifty kilos of cholera germs and five kilos of plague-infected fleas to a Japanese-controlled airfield near Hangchow. Japanese planes dropped disease-laden bombs on the city and monitored the effect. The most effective method appeared to be the distribution by air of plague-laced grain. Starving civilians raced out and gathered up the grain to use for bread or chicken feed. Plague spread throughout the city. More than 1000 fell ill and 500 died. The city only managed to save itself by walling in the infected zone and burning it to the ground. Plague continued to ravage the city until 1947. Outbreaks occurred sporadically as late as 1959.[18]

In 1942 Ishii was promoted to surgeon major general and posted to Nanking (today's Nanjing), the scene of atrocities in 1937 that earned the title The Rape of Nanking. Ishii set about constructing bacteriological weapons that would destroy the remainder of the Chinese armies under Chiang Kai Shek and the communists. Ishii's human experiments expanded in Nanking and he amassed large numbers of plague-infected fleas. His ambition was to take the fight to the home soil of the United States and Australia with his army of fleas.

One of the more bizarre weapons the Japanese worked on in 1944 was the 'Cherry Blossom' bomb. The plan was for Ishii's plague fleas to be packed into bombs that could be carried by small planes launched from 108-metre long B1 submarines. The planes would then fly over Sydney or Seattle and drop the Cherry Blossom bombs. At the same time, Unit 731 frogmen from the sub would sneak ashore and release cholera and plague bacteria. The plan was approved by the military chiefs of staff in March 1945.[19] But it never got off the ground due to the fact that the giant Japanese B1 subs were in short supply by then. However, the plan was viable. On 29 May 1942 the Japanese had launched a small spotter plane over Sydney from a large B1-class submarine to mark targets in the harbour for an attack by midget submarines the next night. They could easily have dropped a plague flea bomb on Sydney during their flight.

Ishii had other plans to drop his fleas on the US. His team released 9000 hydrogen-filled balloons from Honshu to ride the jet stream winds across the Pacific Ocean and come down in the United States and Canada. Altimeters on the balloons released sandbags to keep them to the right altitude to reach the North American continent in about three days. Suspended from the ten-metre-wide balloons was a gondola carrying incendiary bombs. The idea was that they would land and start fires, causing panic along the West Coast. Some made it as far east as Michigan. A pastor and his family on a fishing trip in Oregon saw one come down and went over to examine the strange object descending from the heavens. It exploded, killing five children and his wife – the only known victims of the balloon bombs.[20] Japanese propaganda falsely claimed that the balloon bombs killed 10,000 Americans and started fires that were raging across the continent. The US imposed a news blackout on the balloons for more than a year until the number of people finding balloons grew too great to keep it secret. The US feared the Japanese could stick disease bombs on the balloons. Ishii had the same thought, but his attention was on using bacteriological warfare against Chinese resistance fighters and against Soviet territory.[21]

The use of human experiments by the Japanese wasn't limited to China. In May 1945, a US B-29 Superfortress bomber crashed in northern Kyushu Island after being rammed by a kamikaze Japanese fighter. One of the twelve crew died when another Japanese plane slashed his parachute cords. Another one shot himself before being captured, and villagers killed another. The senior officer of the surviving nine was taken to Tokyo for questioning. The remaining eight were subjected to horrific medical experiments at Kyushu Imperial University. One airman was injected with seawater to see if it worked as a substitute for sterile saline solution. Other airmen had organs removed in live vivisection experiments. Doctors took out an entire lung of one airman to gauge the effects of surgery on the respiratory system. Doctors drilled through the skull of a live prisoner to determine whether epilepsy could be treated by removal of part of the brain. The International Military Tribunal for the Far East – popularly known as the Tokyo War Crimes Trials – later heard claims from US lawyers that the liver of one victim was removed, cooked and served to officers in a warrior ritual. All charges of cannibalism of the Kyushu prisoners were dropped due to a lack of evidence, even though allegations of cannibalism by Japanese emerged in other places.[22] A young first-year medical student at the time, Toshio Tono, told *The Guardian* newspaper in 2015 that he was told to wash the blood from the operating theatre floor and prepare seawater drips where US airmen were experimented on. All the US airmen died, their remains preserved in formaldehyde for future medical students. At the end of the war, the remains were destroyed by Japanese doctors to cover up these horrific experiments on living prisoners.

Thirty Kyushu University doctors stood trial in 1948. Of the twenty-three found guilty of war crimes, five were sentenced to death. The death sentences weren't carried out. The Supreme Commander for the Allied Powers in Japan, General Douglas MacArthur, commuted the death sentences to life. Four received life imprisonment and the rest shorter jail terms. By 1958 they were all released from jail. Tono said in 2015: 'The experiments had absolutely no medical merit. They were being used to inflict as cruel a death as possible on the prisoners.'[23]

Many other Allied prisoners were subjected to live experiments by the Japanese. At Shinagawa a senior doctor injected into prisoners caprylic acid, soybean extract, sulphur, castor oil, serum from malaria sufferers, and urine. He bled men to death for plasma.[24] On Ambon, a prison camp doctor took nine groups of ten prisoners, ranging from fit men to hospital cases, and injected them with what he told them was vitamin B. Fifty of them died soon after. A senior Japanese naval doctor killed eight prisoners in an experiment – tightening tourniquets for hours followed by a shock death when they were suddenly removed. Others were speared with infected bamboo to cause blood poisoning. The bodies were then dissected, the heads cut off and boiled. On Guadalcanal two prisoners were shot in the feet to stop them from escaping, and then a medical officer dissected them live, cutting out their livers.[25]

Unit 731 had doctors and agents scattered across Japanese-conquered territory in South East Asia and the Pacific to conduct human experiments on captives. One such human experiment was at Rabaul in New Britain, where thousands of Australians and Americans were kept in terrible conditions in POW camps. Australian Army Captain John J Murphy testified in 1947 that he had been part of a group of POWs kept in Tunnel Hill Camp above the town. Murphy said that for six months they were given differing amounts of food, a mix of cassava root and rice, with the changes to their weight and health carefully recorded. The ration changed every thirty days. They were weighed, and when POWs died of malnutrition their corpses were taken away by the doctor's team for examination. There were only nine survivors from the thirteen who were forced on the diet experiment, and they were all very weak. Murphy said a Dr Hirano then injected the surviving prisoners with blood taken from Japanese patients suffering from malaria. Murphy testified to war crimes investigators that Hirano said he hoped to develop a serum that would render people immune to malaria. 'He added he had experimented on Japanese, Chinese and native blood types, but not on white men,' Murphy recalled.[26] Murphy said that during the malaria experiment they all additionally suffered beri-beri, dysentery and starvation. Two American prisoners died after being injected with malaria-infected blood.

Murphy's account was supported by US Air Force Lieutenant James McMurria, who testified to US war crimes investigators in 1948 that: 'About every three days these five men gave a few ounces of blood to the doctor and we in turn were given an equal amount of blood taken from Japanese soldiers, who were visibly and noticeably suffering from malaria. This exchange of blood occurred several times and lasted over a period of about a month. During this time an orderly was stationed near our compound and he made three or four smears each day, I suppose to determine whether or not we were contracting the malaria thus injected. These experiments were performed over our protests. Such protest being taken very lightly and, of course, disregarded. We made no physical effort to prevent these experiments. Dr Einosuke Hirano offered bribes, e.g. medical treatment later, perhaps an improved diet, etc. Such promises were never fulfilled.' McMurria said two men died as a direct result of these experiments – naming them as Ensign David Atkiss and Seaman Richard Lanigan. Many more POWs died because Japanese doctors refused to provide any medical assistance. Outside their cell, a bottle holding some clear liquid smelling like acid smoked and fumed. The fumes drifted across the POWs and they all suffered malignant skin diseases such as tropical ulcers. Sometimes the guards doused the prisoners in the acid solution, 'the whole display being highly entertaining to the guards', McMurria told the investigators.[27]

What happened to two Australian members of Z Force commando unit demonstrates that human vivisection by the Japanese wasn't limited to scientists and doctors. Lance Corporal Spencer Walklate, twenty-seven, and Private Ron Eagleton, twenty, disappeared during a dangerous mission on Mushu Island just twenty kilometres off the north coast of Papua New Guinea. They were part of a Z Force mission to map gun emplacements on the island. The operation went disastrously wrong and the squad agreed to split up, with half of them trying to reach help on makeshift rafts. On 11 April 1945 Eagleton and Walklate, a former St George rugby league player and policeman, paddled out to sea on their raft, and were never seen again. Sixty-eight years later the charred bones of two men determined to be Walklate and Eagleton were found on neighbouring Kairuru Island by Australian Defence Force Unrecovered War Casualties Office researchers in the dump of a wartime Japanese military camp. A forensic examination of the bones revealed that they had been tortured. Moreover, buried in the files of war crimes investigators held in Australian archives were reports from local natives and Japanese soldiers that after beatings and torture the two men were cut open while still clinging to life. 'One prisoner whilst awaiting his execution was beaten about the feet and legs to such an extent that he could not stand. He was thereupon executed where he was sitting by being struck a heavy blow on the back of the neck. Shortly afterwards an incision was made in the chest and abdomen and the walls of the flesh were drawn apart to expose organs underneath. The heart and lungs were seen to be still pulsating. The skull was then sawn with a surgical saw and the brain was removed and several lumps of flesh removed. The second POW was then executed by shooting and liver and portions of the flesh were removed.'[28] None of the seventeen Japanese known to be involved in the war crime ever faced trial. The Japanese commander on the island, Rear Admiral Sanjuro Sato, killed himself, his wife and two children the night before he was due to be questioned over the crimes. The case against the others was quietly dropped in the early 1950s after the Australian government bowed to pressure from the United States to wrap up war crimes trials. The case was reduced to a G classification. This meant the accused, if convicted, would not face the death penalty. The horrific details of the Australians' deaths were removed from the men's files and buried deep in the archives to spare their families. The remains of the men were buried at Port Moresby War Cemetery.

Japanese scientists didn't shrink from publicly admitting that they were conducting immunological experiments. In fact, they were proud of their achievements. Unit 731 members published more than a hundred scientific papers during the war. They demonstrated a bit of discretion in their papers by substituting the word 'monkey' for human. Japanese medical scientists knew that these experiments were really conducted on humans. This made the results extremely useful, unique even, in immunology research. But as soon as Japan surrendered, no one in authority had ever heard anything about biological warfare. They insisted that Emperor Hirohito couldn't possibly have known about it, even if it did happen, which it didn't.

Ishii did his best to destroy the evidence of his crimes. As Soviet troops advanced on his Ping Fan facility he ordered it blown up and all bacteria stores burnt. More than 400 prisoners still held at the camp were murdered. It took three days to burn all the bodies.[29] However, not everything was destroyed. Ishii filled a train with crates of documents and research material and transported it to Pusan in Korea. It was then shipped to Japan along with most of Unit 731's senior personnel. Ishii had embezzled a small fortune from the army and bought a mini fortress in Chiba Province, forty kilometres east of Tokyo. Many of the crates were secretly buried in the garden of Ishii's manor house or put in the safekeeping of trusted colleagues. For months after the war, Ishii hid out in his fortress. He got friends and military colleagues to spread the story that he was dead, killed somewhere in Manchuria. Local villagers even staged a fake funeral for him.

American war crimes investigators didn't buy it. US military intelligence had known for the past two years that Japan had an advanced bacteriological warfare program and that Ishii was the leader of the program. They were keen on talking to him. In late 1944, President Roosevelt was informed of captured Japanese documents that listed 'various bacillus bombs' and that attempts had been made to spread plague in China.[30] Ampules of an anthrax vaccine had been captured in New Guinea. 'There appears to be little doubt that Japan is preparing defensively and offensively for biological warfare', the 1944 report concluded.[31] The intelligence agencies didn't share their knowledge with war crimes investigators. The investigators were generally young and rather naïve former scientists and lawyers recruited to the military for the task of gathering evidence to prosecute war criminals.

Frustrated with the lack of action against Ishii and the senior ranks of the Japanese military for war crimes, on 14 December 1945 the Japanese Communist Party presented a dossier on Ishii, human experiments and Japan's bacteriological warfare to the US intelligence agency. Intelligence reports summarising the dossier said Unit 731 had 'succeeded in cultivating pests which were applied to Manchurian and several American citizens captured during the war' and named dozens of leading scientists who had been involved in the program in Japan.[32] One Japanese veteran, disgusted at what he'd seen, wrote directly to MacArthur detailing Ishii's experiments on Chinese and Allied prisoners. When nothing happened after several weeks, the Communist Party slipped a copy to Tokyo-based American journalists. On 6 January 1946 the American Armed Forces newspaper *Pacific Stars and Stripes* carried a United Press (UP) story attributed to Japanese communist sources that Americans were among Ishii's human victims injected with plague virus. *The New York Times* also carried the UP story on the same day, saying POWs were injected with bubonic plague virus.[33] US Colonel Thomas Morrow, principal assistant to the US chief war crimes prosecutor Joseph Keenan, got a copy and immediately requested Ishii be questioned. Six days later the *New York Times* reported that war crimes investigators had ordered Ishii be brought in for questioning.

The bacteriological warfare issue was out in public and military intelligence was not happy. They hoped to secure Japan's knowledge of bacteriological warfare for themselves. Military counterintelligence unit G2 acted quickly to kill the story spreading further. United Press Tokyo bureau chief Ralph Teatsworth received a visit from G2 agents who demanded the source of his Ishii story. Teatsworth gave the name of his source, the editor of Japan's communist newspaper *Red Star*. The agents 'requested' the UP news agency not reveal that US intelligence was interested in finding Ishii, and not 'write any stories which would indicate to Ishii that the American Army is desirous of obtaining further information on the experiments'. Teatsworth agreed.[34] War crimes investigator Colonel Morrow, who had moved to arrest Ishii, was suddenly reassigned to desk duties in Washington. The cover-up of human experiments on POWs had begun.

There was no doubt that the most senior US authorities in Japan, including MacArthur, knew all about Ishii. Yet Ishii remained comfortably ensconced in his mansion while other war criminals were arrested and interrogated and brought to face justice at the Tokyo War Crimes Trials. Ishii was being treated with kid gloves. US command declared to the press and war crime investigators that they didn't know where Ishii was.[35] The CIA knew exactly where he was and had even drawn up a map for agents to find his mansion.

US military intelligence set about trying to get all they could from Ishii and began a series of excruciatingly slow interviews with the Unit 731 commander in his mansion. Ishii denied he had conducted tests on POWs, and portrayed himself as a brilliant scientist just doing his duty. Ishii showed the agents anonymous death threat letters he had received and demanded protection. Counterintelligence believed that the threats may have been from Soviet agents trying to silence Ishii. The Soviets had been denied permission to interview Ishii for their own War Crimes Trials. US intelligence forces provided armed security around Ishii's mansion. Ishii said he would not reveal the most crucial data from his experiments until he had a written guarantee of immunity from prosecution for war crimes. The interviews dragged on through 1946 and 1947. Ishii knew he had something the Americans desperately wanted and felt he had them over a barrel. Frustrated US war crimes agents kept investigating, and in April 1947 produced a damning report on Ishii's wartime activities, including twelve testimonies that Ishii had experimented on POWs.[36] There was more than enough evidence to put Ishii on trial for his abhorrent human experiments and the murder of hundreds of thousands of people. He would have been a Class A war criminal, one facing the death penalty.

However, the US had other ideas. Just as they had protected Nazi scientists for their own war machine for the Cold War, they would embrace Japanese mass murderer scientists to gain their deadly knowledge – or at least to prevent the Soviets from getting their hands on it. In May 1947 MacArthur asked Washington to give Ishii and his Unit 731 associates what they wanted – full immunity. He even cited the living human dissections performed at Ping Fan as a particular bonus for America.[37] 'Request for exemption [from prosecution] of Unit 731 members. Information about vivisection useful,' MacArthur wrote.[38] In June 1947 MacArthur ordered 'all information obtained in this investigation would be held in intelligence channels and not used for War Crimes programs'.[39] An intelligence report to Washington emphasised that Ishii's information was of 'vital importance to the security of the nation' and 'far outweighs the value accruing from war crimes prosecution'.[40]

The question of bacteriological weapons was very briefly raised at the Tokyo War Crimes Trials. It was quickly crushed. The presiding judge was Australian Sir William Webb, a distinguished judge of the High Court and the Queensland Supreme Court. The tribunal consisted of eleven judges, one from each of the Allied powers. It was a mammoth task, with twenty-eight major war criminals indicted, 419 witnesses, 779 affidavits and 4336 documents. Proceedings took two and a half years and it was clear from the start that the tribunal could only scratch the surface of Japanese atrocities. If there was any justice, thousands of Japanese military figures should have faced trial for war crimes, but Webb knew he had to somehow limit the court action.

But that wasn't on Webb's mind on 29 August 1946 when David Sutton, an American lawyer assisting China's prosecutors, rose in the court and said 'the enemy took civilian captives to the medical laboratory where the reactions to poisonous serum were tested. This detachment was one of the most secret organisations. The number of people slaughtered by this detachment cannot be ascertained.' Sutton's declaration hit the court like a bombshell. Lawyers on both sides were stunned. Sutton had mentioned the unmentionable. He'd pointed his finger at the elephant that wasn't even allowed in the room. Webb ordered a brief recess to restore order. When they returned, Webb asked Sutton from the bench: 'Are you going to give us further evidence of these alleged laboratory tests for reactions to poisonous serums? This is something entirely new we haven't heard before. Are you going to leave it at that?' Webb fixed Sutton with a stare. Sutton backed down. 'We do not at this time anticipate introducing additional evidence on that subject'.[41] An American defence lawyer for two Japanese generals objected to the allegation being raised in the court, pointing out that the serums might just be regular inoculations. Another American defence lawyer representing Japanese defendants protested that it was a slanderous charge and should be stricken from the record. Webb agreed, saying tests on Chinese with poisonous materials was a mere assertion that was unsupported by any evidence. And that was it. The subject of experiments on living humans was never again raised in the Tokyo War Crimes Trial. What happened during that brief recess can only be guessed at. But there had to have been some reason Sutton backed down so quickly from raising human experiments in the trial.

Three years later the only war crimes trial of Unit 731 members took place in the Soviet city of Khabarovsk. It would be difficult to find a more isolated spot for a major war crimes trial – thirty kilometres from the border with China and 800 kilometres north of the port of Vladivostok. The trial of twelve Unit 731 doctors and military leaders captured by the Red Army was remarkable for the ready confessions of the Japanese to their crimes. As there were no Western journalists or observers at the 1949 Khabarovsk trial, it is difficult to discern the accuracy of transcripts and summations later released in English by the Soviets. But the statements they made confirmed evidence gathered by US intelligence and testimonies by Chinese and Allied survivors of the Unit 731 terror.

Major General Kawashima Kiyashi told the Khabarovsk trial that he served with Unit 731 in 1941 when plague fleas were dropped from planes over the city of Changde in central China, which caused an epidemic to break out. Kawashima said Unit 731 'experimented widely in the action of all lethal bacteria on human beings – we used imprisoned Chinese patriots and Russians whom the Japanese counterintelligence service had condemned to extinction'.[42] Kawashima said Unit 731 killed civilians on a massive scale – he personally saw 600 a year die from experiments. Nishi Toshihide testified that he saw Lieutenant Colonel Ikari, chief of 2nd Division of Unit 731, order ten Chinese prisoners be tied to stakes ten to twenty metres apart and a bomb exploded near them. 'All ten were injured by shrapnel contaminated with gas gangrene germs and within a week they all died in severe torment.'[43] Another saw prisoners of Unit 731 with all the flesh stripped from their fingers, leaving just the bone – the result of freezing experiments. Mitomo Kazuo confessed to injecting Russian prisoners with various poisons until they were too weak to take anymore, then injecting potassium cyanide to kill them.

The Commander in Chief of the Kwantung Army, Yamada Otozoo, testified at Khabarovsk on 17 November 1949 that Japan planned to use Ishii's bacteriological bombs against enemies such as the US and 'England' (more likely Yamada meant Australia, which was seen by Japan as an outpost of England) using plague-infected fleas. Yamada said the plans were approved by the Japanese General Staff, and Unit 731 was ordered to proceed with the mass production of the necessary epidemic bacteria. The army at each front were to have at their disposal special bacteriological detachments stemming from Unit 731. 'Bacteriological weapons would have been used against the US, England [Australia] and other countries if the Soviet Union had not taken action against Japan and the swift advance of the Soviet Army into the heart of Manchuria deprived us of the possibility of employing the bacteriological weapon against the USSR and other countries.'[44]

The Soviets imposed unusually light sentences on the Unit 731 captives, ranging from two to twenty-five years imprisonment. No one was sentenced to death. All were back in Japan by 1956, except for one who committed suicide the day before his departure home. There is little doubt that they told the Soviets all they knew about bacteriological weapons.

MacArthur dismissed the Khabarovsk Trial as communist propaganda. In an outright lie, his staff issued statements that no evidence could be found in US records that POWs were ever used for live experiments. Surviving American Mukden POWs had been warned before they were flown home to the US that they would be court-martialled if they ever spoke to anyone, including their family, suggesting that the Japanese engaged in experiments on American POWs.[45] A thick blanket of secrecy had been thrown over the entire episode.

The Cold War was raging. Enemies of just a few years ago were being embraced as new allies against communism. In 1947 America launched the Marshall Plan to rebuild Western Germany so it would not fall to the Soviets. In 1948 communists took over Czechoslovakia and the Berlin airlift began to beat the Soviet land blockade of West Berlin. On 29 August 1949 the Soviet Union tested its first atomic bomb – three years earlier than Washington expected. On 1 October 1949 Mao Tse-Tung won the Civil War and China went Red. In June 1950 communist North Korea invaded capitalist South Korea, starting a war that is still formally going. MacArthur saw the need for Japan to rebuild in order to resist the communist advance. Emperor Hirohito was crucial to that recovery, and he had to be preserved in a place of power for stability. Never mind that he had been integral to launching Japan's war of aggression.

Ishii got his immunity from prosecution, a decision that went all the way to the top in Washington. Ishii dug up his garden and provided US intelligence and military bacteriologists with all his research from Unit 731. He became a recluse in his mansion, living on a general's military pension granted by the Japanese government. He rarely ventured out, possibly because he feared Japanese communists and Soviet agents would seize him. Some of those who later investigated Ishii were told by reliable sources that he made a secret trip to the US in the 1950s to lecture at the US military biological warfare centre at Fort Detrick in Maryland.[46] The reports can't be dismissed, as German scientists with Nazi SS backgrounds were employed in US military research labs. Two Nazi doctors – Dr Kurt Blome and Major General Dr Walter Schreiber – had conducted death camp experiments on prisoners with plague, typhus and tuberculosis, yet were hired by the US Army Chemical Corps after the war to lecture and conduct research. Schreiber worked for the US military in Texas.

America was building up its biological warfare capability and the knowledge accrued by Ishii and Unit 731 members was keenly sought after by US military scientists. Many Unit 731 veterans rose to prominent positions in post-war Japan and had honours and wealth bestowed on them. Over the next forty years, every director of the Japan National Institute of Health – with just one exception – had served in a bacteriological warfare unit. Four of the eight men appointed to the key medical body between 1947 and 1983 had conducted human experiments.[47] Unit 731 senior officer Masaji Ryoichi founded Japan's leading pharmaceutical company, Green Cross, and employed many unit veterans.[48] (Green Cross merged with other firms and today is called Mitsubishi Pharma Corporation.) Unit veterans occasionally gathered at Ishii's mansion to honour the man they considered innocent of any crime. In 1959 Ishii contracted throat cancer. He converted to Catholicism before he died, aged sixty-seven. By the 1970s, Unit 731 scientists were the most active veterans group in Japan. They called themselves Seikonkai, the association of refined spirits, and built a memorial tower to Unit 731 veterans in a Tokyo cemetery.[49]

Despite its horrific history, Ishii's research was picked up by the US. In 1952 North Korea, China and the Soviet Union claimed the US was using germ warfare on a large scale in the Korean War. China claimed bubonic plague, smallpox and cholera were being spread in North Korea from US bombs that released infected fleas. The respected Reuters newsagency reported Ishii and several other Unit 731 veterans had been taken to South Korea in 1951 to assist in the bacteriological attack.[50] Australian journalist Wilfred Burchett, the first journalist to enter Hiroshima after the atomic bomb, reported in the French leftist journal *Ce Soir* that he'd found a large patch of insects not native to the region just after an American plane had flown overhead.[51] China invited an international team of scientists to inspect the infected zones, and the scientists concluded that bacteriological weapons had been used on North Korea. US officials strongly and indignantly denied the allegation that it was committing biological warfare. The US denial was backed up by its United Nation allies in the Korean War, including Australia.

But the reports persisted. In 1952 American journalist John W Powell wrote in the English language *China Monthly Review* that the US had systematically spread smallpox, cholera and plague in North Korea using bacteriological warfare and employing Japanese Unit 731 war criminals. In 1956, when Powell returned to the US, he was charged with sedition, and copped the full fury of McCarthy era accusations that he was a communist agent. After his defence lawyers started demanding access to secret documents they argued would prove the US had used bacteriological weapons, the case slowed to a crawl. In 1961 President John F Kennedy finally ordered the charges be dropped.[52] The files remain closed. It wasn't until 1982 that Japan officially admitted Unit 731 had existed.[53]

10

WHY JAPANESE WAR CRIMINALS ESCAPED JUSTICE

'Chin up girls. I'm proud of you, and I love you all.'

'On a morning like this it's hard to believe there's a war on,' nurse Vivian Bullwinkel remarked wistfully to the merchant navy officer leaning on the railing next to her. They gazed at the hazy outline of the Sumatran coast gliding by in the distance, lit softly by the orange light of dawn. The flat sea slipped by, the small cargo ship carving a wide wake as it steamed south at maximum speed.

'Yeah, but I'd rather it was pelting down in a heavy storm,' replied the officer. 'This stillness makes it too easy to find us,' he muttered, looking around the sky overhead. He smiled at the pretty, dark-haired nurse, and left for the bridge.

•

Australian army nurse Sister Vivian Bullwinkel was aboard the 1670-ton British cargo ship SS *Vyner Brooke* together with

181 passengers, mostly women and children, evacuated two days earlier from Singapore. They'd made it out just in time as Japanese forces were advancing into the outskirts of the city. The *Vyner Brooke* was one of the last ships to get out, and the last nurses still in Singapore were ordered to get on board. The sixty-five nurses were reluctant to leave, as there were many wounded to attend to, but the army commanders didn't want the women falling into the hands of Japanese troops.

It was the morning of 14 February 1942. Back in Singapore the surrounded Australian and British forces were fighting a desperate rearguard action. Japanese ships and planes were hunting for any ships that had escaped Singapore Harbour. Bullwinkel joined the other nurses tending to the wounded and frightened passengers. Aged twenty-six, she'd been an army nurse for just four months, but the horrors of war had created a strong bond among the young women who'd volunteered. Bullwinkel had trained as a midwife in Broken Hill, and shortly after war broke out she'd tried to join the air force as a nurse. They'd knocked her back for having flat feet. The army didn't care and she was shipped off to Singapore. Now she and the other nurses were fleeing, desperately trying to stay ahead of the unbelievably fast Japanese advance.

The previous morning the skipper of the *Vyner Brooke* had nosed his ship into a sheltered bay, taking it in as close as possible to overhanging trees to disguise the outline of the ship with branches. As night fell they edged out into the ocean and turned south, racing down the coast, hoping to reach the port of Palembang at the southern end of Sumatra. Shortly after noon their luck ran out. A stream of Japanese fighter bombers suddenly roared out of the sun, firing down on the little ship.

Bombs fell to the side of *Vyner Brooke*. Water cascaded on to the deck. Anti-aircraft guns fitted on the deck of the old cargo vessel fired back. The Japanese planes came in low, strafing the ship from stern to bow. Then they were gone. Maybe they were low on ammunition. Perhaps they'd been called to a bigger target. Everyone on the plucky little ship let out a cheer. They'd survived.

An hour later another squadron of enemy planes roared down, dropping bombs that fell close to the ship. One bomb went straight down the funnel and exploded in the engine room. A second bomb crashed through the deck and blew up below, where the passengers huddled. Many were killed instantly. It was carnage. The sea rushed in. The ship was going down fast. Panic set in among the civilian passengers. Despite their wounds and shock, the nurses showed incredible discipline. They helped the wounded to the lifeboats. More bombs exploded on the deck. The ship listed steeply, tipping people and lifeboats into the ocean. Bullwinkel looked down and saw dozens of people struggling in the water, then leaped into the churning chaos below. The fall sent Bullwinkel deep under the surface. When the cork jacket brought her up into the air she almost collided with the ship's hull, it was leaning over so far. Nurses and struggling passengers were hauled into the one surviving lifeboat and onto floating rafts. Several quick-thinking nurses had leaped into the water carrying medical packs. They tossed them into the lifeboat. They turned as they heard the roar of a plane coming low over the water towards them.

'Out, get out of the boat now!' shouted one of the ship's officers. He guessed what was coming and shoved everybody he could reach into the water.

'Get down under the water, quick!' he shouted. The Japanese pilot opened fire on the women and men struggling in the water, strafing them as he flew over so low that they could see him in the cockpit looking down at them. Spouts of water blasted into the air as he ploughed through the helpless civilians who had abandoned ship. The ocean ran red with their blood.

Somehow the plane's bullets missed Bullwinkel. As the warplanes rose into the sky and flew away over the horizon, their murderous rampage complete, Bullwinkel grabbed onto an upturned boat. Screams filled the air around her. She recognised a few of the horrified faces dripping blood nearby. At least some of her fellow nurses had survived. There was a loud metallic grinding noise and she turned to see the *Vyner Brooke* roll over, her stern rise into the air and then slide down into the deep. Air pockets burst the surface, along with the ship's floatable gear. Bullwinkel was horrified to see the bodies of babies and children bob to the surface; then, too small for life jackets, they slipped below. Battered bodies still kept afloat by life jackets drifted away. Silence descended over the horrific scene. Survivors, too shocked even to cry, clung to floating wreckage.[1]

The ship's officer had taken stock of where land was before he'd abandoned ship. He got everyone paddling towards the shore that had to be just over the horizon. Slowly the tops of palm trees poked above the flat sea, and the group of survivors felt encouraged. It was starting to get dark and they were afraid of losing track of where the land was. Then they saw a light, a fire on the beach. They paddled on. Finally they could feel sand under their feet. Their spirits soared as they dragged themselves up the beach. Exhausted, they collapsed on the sand.

As their strength slowly returned, Bullwinkel, a crewman and several other nurses decided to explore the beach to find other survivors, and whoever had lit that fire. To their joy, around a bend they saw the fire and around it was Matron Drummond and other survivors who had managed to reach shore by lifeboat. Altogether on the beach there were now twenty-two nurses, several members of the crew, including first officer Bill Sedgeman, and some civilians – men, women and, miraculously, a handful of children. The wretched survivors gathered together in one group and decided to wait till daylight before sending inland for help. Sedgeman figured that they were on Bangka Island, just north of Sumatra. It was some distance from Allied forces, and it was by no means certain whether local islanders would help them or curry favour with the invading Japanese by handing them over.

Around 1 am they saw huge flashes far out to sea, then the sound of explosions rolled in. The Japanese had sunk another ship. Hours later, a lifeboat pulled into the beach. It contained forty servicemen, some of them wounded. There were now around eighty survivors on the beach. At first light Sedgeman led a group inland to seek help. The group comprised five sailors and five women, including Sister Bullwinkel. They met some old villagers who told them they couldn't help, as Japanese troops were already on the island. They returned to the beach and told the group the bad news. They agreed that they had no chance of escape. They had wounded among them, and they'd heard Japanese troops didn't take wounded prisoners; they just killed them. The group thought that with so many women and nurses present the Japanese would have no choice but to take them all prisoner.

Sedgeman set out with two sailors to make contact with a Japanese patrol and bring them back to the beach. Then they would all surrender. It was a horrible decision, but they had no choice. Bullwinkel and the nurses tended the wounded as best they could while Sedgeman was away. A large group of women and children decided to follow Sedgeman in the belief that it would help him convince the Japanese the group on the beach posed no threat. The nurses stayed behind with the wounded. They wouldn't leave them under any circumstances.

Around mid-morning Sedgeman emerged back on the beach with a large force of Japanese soldiers. The Japanese officer led his troops across the sand as the soldiers spread out, guns ready. Sedgeman said loudly that they all wanted to surrender and were now prisoners of war. The officer kept a stony face, barked something to his men, and they all cocked their weapons and brought them up to the firing position. There was an audible gasp from the nurses, and several leaned over to cover the wounded with their bodies. The Japanese troops advanced on the group, forcing the nurses away from the wounded at the point of their bayonets. All the sailors, merchant seamen and soldiers who could walk were forced at gunpoint to move off the beach and march up a jungle trail. Nervously the nurses watched them go, ears straining to hear anything.

Suddenly the crack of gunshots reverberated from the jungle. More shots, machine guns. Then silence. Five minutes later the Japanese soldiers reappeared, talking and laughing among themselves. They strolled back along the beach towards the nurses and the wounded. The nurses gasped in horror as they saw that many of the Japanese troops were wiping their bayonets clean.

'The bastards killed them,' one of the nurses muttered.

'They're not taking prisoners.'

'We're done for.'

Bullwinkel feared they were right. This was it. They were about to be murdered in cold blood. The red crosses on their grey uniforms denoting that they were nurses would be no protection. The Japanese troops casually lined up in a semi-circle around the nurses, herding them away from the wounded men still lying on the sand. They prodded their bayonets at them, forcing the nurses to walk into the sea. The nurses didn't plead for their lives. They knew it would be useless against these cold-blooded killers. They were Australian army nurses, and they weren't going to give any satisfaction to this barbarous enemy.

The twenty-two army nurses linked arms in the shallows. They supported two wounded nurses between them as they waded deeper into the water. Some turned around and saw a group of seven heavily armed Japanese casually stroll down the beach towards them. They carried machine guns. The nurses turned around and walked steadily into the waves. They turned to each other and smiled grimly. Each had their own thoughts of loved ones, family they would never see again. They knew what was coming.

'Chin up, girls. I'm proud of you, and I love you all,' called out Matron Irene Drummond.[2] The nurses all looked to her and then raised their chins proudly. The sun blazed down on them.

'Girls, take it, don't squeal,' urged Sister Esther Stewart.[3] The nurses held hands, facing out to sea. The sun's reflection off the water was almost blinding. It was still for a moment, gentle waves lapping against their legs.

The machine guns spat out their deadly bullets, slamming into each of the women, throwing them forward into the water that quickly turned red with blood. The machine-gun firing lasted only seconds. The soldiers then walked up and down at the edge of the water, firing into any nurse who was still moving. Bullwinkel waited for the impact of death. Her friends next to her had fallen, but for some reason she was still standing. It was only for a fraction of a second, then she felt a bullet slam into her lower back like a massive punch, throwing her forward into the bloody water.

'So this is what it is like to die,' she thought as the waves rolled over her head. She felt strangely relaxed, floating face down in the water, her body bobbing beside her friends. She blacked out for a bit, then came to, spluttering and vomiting up sea water. She turned her head slightly to suck in some air.

'Oh, I'm not dead,' she thought. She knew she'd have to stay absolutely still or they would shoot her again. She ignored the pain in her back and kept her body as still as she could, even as it bumped into the bodies all around her. She kept her head to one side to pull in a bit of air, careful not to swell her chest. She drifted in and out of consciousness as the gentle waves brought her body back towards the beach. She wondered if any of the others were still alive. She couldn't hear the Japanese, but she dare not move or risk a look. She dug her fingers into the sand below her so that she wouldn't wash up on the beach where it would be harder to disguise her breathing. She felt the drag of the water pulling her gently out to sea. She had to stay in this half metre of water or risk being swept out to sea or pushed onto the beach. The dark passage between death and life seemed to go on forever. After what seemed like hours she still hadn't heard any sign of the Japanese. She risked lifting her head a bit to look up and down the beach. Nobody was there.

She struggled to sit up and look around. The bodies of the other twenty-one nurses were gone, swept out to sea. She was alone.

She pulled herself into a sitting position. The pain was intense. She felt around and discovered she had been hit high on the left hip and the bullet had gone right through without hitting any vital organs. She struggled to her feet and staggered towards the cover of the jungle. She collapsed in the undergrowth and slipped into an exhausted sleep.

After what must have been several hours she was awoken by the terrifying sound of Japanese voices. She peered out from her hiding place and saw boots and guns with bayonets just a metre away. If they saw her they would certainly kill her. She held her breath as the soldiers passed by, chatting to each other. They kept on walking to the other end of the beach. Then they were gone.

Bullwinkel had to get water or she would die from dehydration. She pulled herself out from under cover and stumbled along the path until she came to a stream she had seen earlier when they walked to the village with Sedgeman. As she drank from the stream a soft voice came from the undergrowth, scaring her half to death.

'Where have you been, nurse?' She breathed a sigh of relief. He spoke English. After a whispered conversation she learned he was a British private called Cecil Kingsley, one of the wounded they had been tending on the beach before the massacre. Kingsley told her he'd seen the Japanese machine-gun the nurses in the water. They then came looking for the wounded men and bayoneted all those they found. He'd been stabbed twice but had managed to crawl into the jungle before they came back to check he was dead.

Bullwinkel examined his wounds and found they were infected. He would die without hospital treatment. She had managed to patch up her own wound but she knew she also needed medical help. She decided she had no choice but to ask the village elders for help. The village chiefs refused and told her to surrender to the Japanese. As she staggered back to where Kingsley was hidden, two village women came up behind her and silently handed her fruit and chicken meat bundled into leaves. Days later the women again defied the head men and provided food. After eleven days in hiding, Bullwinkel saw gangrene was setting in Kingsley's wounds. They had to give themselves up or he would die. They decided to get far away from the beach, hoping they didn't run into the same patrol that had carried out the massacre.

Luckily they ran into a truck driven by a Japanese soldier who had had nothing to do with the beach massacre. He drove them to a POW camp. Kingsley died before he reached a hospital. In the camp hospital Bullwinkel met up with other army nurses, but for the entirety of her internment she kept the beach massacre secret, confiding it to just a couple of officers so that someone would know, if she didn't survive the war. If the Japanese heard she'd witnessed such a monstrous war crime they would silence her for good. Only when the war was over did she make a full report on the terrible crime to senior army officers debriefing the freed POWs. The war crimes unit immediately started hunting down all those who had played a part in the Bangka Beach Massacre. On Bullwinkel's return to Australia she set about visiting relatives of all twenty-one murdered nurses to tell them what had happened to their loved one. She told of their incredible bravery.

War crimes investigators found out which unit was in the region at the time of the massacre, then set about tracking down every officer, sergeant, corporal and private in that unit. It was a huge task. Tens of thousands of Japanese were held in prison camps by Australia. Hundreds of thousands more were held in camps run by the Allies – principally Americans – scattered across South East Asian islands, Thailand, Burma, Laos, Cambodia, Vietnam, Singapore, Malaya, China, Manchuria, Korea and Japan itself. The Soviets also had huge numbers of Japanese prisoners after their short war against Japan.

But track them down they did. The commander of the 229 Infantry Regiment that was on Bangka Island at the time of the massacre was Lieutenant Colonel Iwabuchi. He was killed during the war. Two of his officers – 1st Lieutenant Ichikawa and 2nd Lieutenant Asai – were also dead. After Bangka Island, the regiment was involved in island fighting and were almost wiped out fighting Australians and Americans. Justice had already been delivered.

But two suspects for actually carrying out the massacre, Captain Orita and Lieutenant Takeuchi, were still alive.[4] Takeuchi was found in a prison camp in Malaya. A third suspect, Sergeant Major Taro Kato, was captured in New Guinea. Orita, promoted to Major, had been transferred to Manchuria where he fought the Soviet Red Army. Initial replies from Soviet authorities said Orita could not be found in prison camps.

In 1946 Bullwinkel testified at the Tokyo War Crimes Trial along with fifteen Australian witnesses to other Japanese massacres and atrocities committed at Ambon, Borneo, Singapore, the Burma–Thailand railway, Changi Camp and prison camps in Java, Japan, Formosa (today's Taiwan), Manchuria and Malaya.

Bullwinkel appeared in formal Australian army nursing uniform with her new rank of captain on her shoulders. The twenty-six Japanese accused of war crimes sat stiffly, with expressionless faces, on long benches, all signs of rank removed from their undecorated uniforms. One judge from each of the Allied nations engaged in the war against Japan sat on the high bench overlooking the court. The judges were led by Australian Sir William Webb.

One by one the Australian survivors of Japanese atrocities gave their testimonies, telling the court the horrors they had witnessed. Bullwinkel got her turn to tell her story to the court in mid-afternoon. For two long hours she recounted in great detail what happened four years earlier on Bangka Island. The faces of the Japanese prisoners remained set in stone, their eyes fixed on the wall opposite. They might not have pulled the trigger on the nurses at that beach, but they were prominent participants in a military regime that readily butchered prisoners and murdered countless innocents. Allied servicemen in the court looked grimly at them. Some women in the court quietly wept.

When Bullwinkel completed her testimony there was a period of stunned silence in the courtroom. Webb finally took a deep breath and said: 'You are a model witness, Sister Bullwinkel. You have given your evidence faultlessly.'[5] And with that, Bullwinkel was thanked and allowed to leave. Her story had been told and recorded. She had done her duty by her twenty-one friends and fellow nurses gunned down on the beach that terrible day.

Major Orita was later found alive in a Soviet stockade in Siberia. He was taken to Tokyo to stand trial for the murder of the Australian nurses. The day before Orita was due to appear in court he committed suicide in his cell.

Orita escaped having to face justice. He wasn't the only one to cheat judgement by taking their life at the last moment.

•

There were so many massacres and atrocities committed by the Japanese it would be impossible to recount them all: the Thai–Burma Railway; the Sandakan Death March; the massacre of hundreds of Australian prisoners; the torture and beheadings of so many prisoners; starvation, beatings and worse treatment in POW camps; bayonetting of wounded servicemen and civilians; the Rape of Nanking . . . the list goes on and on. While most Japanese probably didn't consider that they might some day face a judge for what they were doing, towards the end of the war, when it was clear Japan could not win, some took measures to ensure they would escape the victor's noose.

On 3 July 1945, nine Australians and one Briton, survivors of Operation Rimau, a disastrous Z Special Unit commando raid aimed at attacking Japanese ships in Singapore Harbour, were put on trial in Singapore. The raid was mostly made up of Australians, but led by British Major Ivan Lyon. They were part of an overly ambitious mission to repeat a successful canoe raid on Singapore Harbour, carried out a year earlier and called Operation Jaywick, that sank or damaged seven Japanese ships. All the Jaywick commandos made it back to Australia. Japanese commanders thought the raid must have been carried out by local saboteurs in Singapore as it was believed impossible for Allied commandos to reach Singapore. In reprisal, Japan executed hundreds of local Singapore people.

Rimau (Malay for 'tiger') was intended to be bigger and bolder, and it went wrong from the very start. Of the twenty-three men on the Rimau mission, ten were captured and imprisoned in Singapore's notorious Outram Road Jail. The rest, including Major Lyon, were killed in action or captured, tortured and killed.

Japan felt they had lost face, and they took their vengeance on this second commando group. For weeks, the ten captives of Rimau were beaten, tortured and starved in Outram Road Jail. They were kept separate from other prisoners.

By July 1945 it was obvious Japan would not win the war. US forces were island hopping all the way to Japan. US planes were bombing Tokyo and other Japanese cities. In April the Soviet Union had declared war on Japan and was advancing through Manchuria.

Japan's regional commanders wanted to make an example of these Australians for their audacity in attacking the heart of the Japanese military empire in South East Asia. They would be executed, but first they would go through a trial under military law to give the executions a veneer of justification. The victors might think that simply executing the prisoners was a war crime. The Japanese commanders feared they might face execution themselves when the Allies won the war.

Japan's Seventh Army HQ designated the commandos war criminals because they had violated 'international law and the convention of warfare'.[6] This came from a nation that refused to sign the Geneva Convention and breached all human moral codes in its treatment of prisoners and civilians. The trial was a sham. The Rimau men had no defence lawyer, witnesses could not be cross-examined, evidence could not be challenged and translations were dodgy at best. Prosecutor Major Kamiya set up the entire event. He was in a hurry; there was no time for statements from witnesses. Judicial Major Mitsuo Jifiku ordered the trial to start on 28 June. The actual charge against the ten was 'perfidy and espionage'. The Rimau men had allegedly confessed to the crime of spying,[7] but the confessions were extracted under torture. The military judge ruled they were all spies because they were not wearing uniforms during the action, and so could be executed in accordance with the law of warfare.

Three military judges sat on what was in reality a kangaroo court – Major Jifiku, Major Miyoshi Hasada, with Colonel Masayoshi Towatari presiding. The judges tried to dress up the executions as an honourable act in accordance with Japan's *Bushido* warrior tradition. The judges went to great lengths to praise the Australians for their bravery. 'The last moment of a hero must be glorious,' Colonel Towatari said, delivering the inevitable guilty verdict. 'It must be historic and dramatic. Heroes have more regards for their reputations than anything else. This is the feeling of the Japanese people. As we respect them, we feel our duty of glorifying the last moment of these heroes just as they deserve, and by our doing so, the names of these heroes will remain in the hearts of Australians and Britishers as real heroes eternally.'[8]

It was total rubbish. There was nothing honourable or heroic in what the judges were about to do. The Japanese judges slipped in something else they thought might help them if they were ever to face Allied war crime courts: they cited the honour and respect shown by the Australians to Japanese submariners killed during the midget submarine attack on Sydney in 1942. They didn't mention that the Japanese sailors were all killed in action; they weren't executed after being captured.

The execution on 7 July was void of even the most twisted notion of honour. The ten prisoners were ordered to kneel blindfolded in front of three large open graves while five burly guards walked forward carrying swords. These weren't skilled swordsmen. They weren't *Bushido* officer warriors given the 'honour' of beheading an enemy with one sweep of a coveted sword. These were thug prison guards, none above sergeant, with army-issue swords. The result was disgusting, even by Japanese standards. They hacked and hacked at the necks of the kneeling prisoners until their heads rolled off. Half the prisoners had to wait their turn while the guards chopped off the heads of their friends. The guards then pushed the bodies into the graves, one on top of the other. They were covered over with soil and left in unmarked graves. Each man had been stripped of all markings of rank so his body could not be identified. Honour be damned.[9]

The Japanese official record of the execution claimed British Major Reg Ingleton, the senior prisoner, thanked the Japanese for their kindness, courtesy and excellent treatment as well as the honourable words from the judges recognising their heroism. No one believes Ingleton made such a statement. The remarks were put in the official record to save the necks of all those involved in the execution.[10] Four weeks later, atom bombs fell on Hiroshima and Nagasaki, and Japan surrendered.

Three months after the end of the war, Australian war crimes investigators dug up the bodies and discovered the butchery. They wanted the judges and executioners to stand trial for war crimes. Higher powers had other ideas. On 7 January 1946 the British War Crimes command issued 'guidelines' at the request of Australian authorities to clarify the Allied legal position regarding Japan's 'trial' of the Rimau commandos. London advised that where a prisoner had been tried in accordance with Japanese law and sentenced to death, the people constituting the court or the executioner could not be regarded as war criminals. British lawyers stressed this held even if it were a sham trial. 'No hard and fast rule can be laid down as to what constitutes a fair trial as different countries adopt different codes or rules governing their trials,' the British said, adding that the policy of the British war crimes section was not to bring to trial any suspect unless the evidence was strong enough to make a conviction 'virtually certain'. London said there were so many cases of wartime atrocities that it would take a long time before they could be brought to trial. They also warned that even 'a very small percentage of acquittals would have a bad effect on public opinion.'[11]

The farcical trial of the Rimau commandos in Singapore in the dying days of the war achieved its aim. None of the judges nor the executioners were put on trial for war crimes. In 1947, the mother of 23-year-old Lance Corporal John Hardy, one of the Australians executed in Singapore, received this reply from the Minister for the Army, Cyril Chambers: 'By being dressed in non-military attire, these intrepid Australians voluntarily deprived themselves of the right to be treated as prisoners according to the custom and usage of war. Technically, therefore, the Japanese did not commit a war crime and, accordingly, there is no means of bringing them to justice in this particular case.'[12]

Justice did, however, eventually catch up with most of the judges and executioners of the Rimau men, even though it came in a circuitous manner. General Itagaki, who insisted on the death penalty, was hanged for other war crimes. Also meeting the hangman for other crimes was Major-General Otsuka, who was in charge of the prosecution. Commanders of Outram Road Jail – Major Kobayashi and Major Mikizara – were executed for other war crimes committed in the prison. Prosecutor Major Kamiya was sentenced to life imprisonment for another crime. Executioner Corporal Hirata committed suicide before he could be tried. His four fellow executioners were sentenced to between five and ten years jail for other crimes committed in the jail. Judges Jifiku, Hasada and Towatari never faced justice.

•

The Australian government knew from an early stage in the war that the Japanese were committing atrocities at a shocking rate. Australian troops and refugees who managed to escape and reach Allied forces told of the horrors they had witnessed being methodically carried out by advancing Japanese forces. These were not one-off incidents. Massacre, torture, beatings and utmost brutality were the norm for Japanese forces. It was obvious to Australians that codes of warfare did not apply in this Pacific War.

During 1942, when Japan overran Australian forces across the Pacific and was on the verge of invading the continent, consistent reports of Japanese atrocities alarmed military and political leaders in Canberra. In June 1943, after the first Allied victories over Japan, the government appointed Sir William Webb, the Queensland Chief Justice, to gather evidence of Japanese war crimes. The Webb Inquiry heard testimony from officers and troops from Australian and US forces as well as civilian refugees. Webb's investigators also examined captured enemy documents and interrogation reports of Japanese prisoners. In March 1944, Webb tendered his report with testimony from 471 witnesses. Among the atrocities Webb detailed were the January 1942 massacre of at least 123 Australian prisoners at Tol and Waitavalo plantations in New Britain; the August 1942 torture and slaughter of thirty-six Australians and fifty-nine native men and women around Milne Bay in New Guinea; the August 1942 massacre of eleven missionaries at Buna, Popondetta and Guadalcanal; the bayonetting of prisoners tied to trees; and the beheading of many prisoners of war. The war crime investigations even found that the 'widespread practice of cannibalism by Japanese soldiers in the Asia–Pacific war was something more than merely random incidents perpetrated by individuals or small groups subject to extreme conditions. The testimonies indicate that cannibalism was a systematic and organised military strategy'.[13]

Australia's Foreign Minister, HV 'Doc' Evatt, was aghast at the extent of Japanese war crimes. He asked Webb to conduct a continuous inquiry to be ready at war's end to bring charges against Japanese war criminals. In 1944 Webb gathered further eyewitness testimonies of atrocities, such as the torpedoing of the hospital ship *Centaur* by a Japanese submarine off Brisbane on 14 May 1943, the extremely brutal treatment of prisoners on the Burma–Thailand railroad, and the many massacres of prisoners and civilians. In February 1945, Webb presented both his reports to an Allied war crimes committee in London. Before victory over Japan was on the horizon, the Allies already had arrest warrants for seventy-three Japanese and more than ten Japanese army units listed for interrogation for war crimes. The Allies agreed that each nation could arrest and try suspected enemy war criminals.

Japan surrendered on 15 August 1945 and Emperor Hirohito formally signed the surrender on 2 September. Australia and the Allies were ready to swoop on Japan's suspected war criminals. On 11 October the Australian parliament passed the War Crimes Act under which Australian military courts over the next couple of years would put on trial 814 Japanese military servicemen, of whom 644 were convicted and 148 executed. Two died in custody before their death sentence was carried out.

Rabaul, scene of some of the largest massacres of Australian prisoners, was also the site of the greatest number of war crime trials. Between December 1945 and August 1947 a total of 390 Japanese faced the Australian military court in Rabaul. Two hundred and sixty-six were convicted, 113 received the death sentence (but twenty-six of those were commuted to life imprisonment), eight were sentenced to life in jail, two got twenty-five years, forty-nine got between eleven and twenty-four years and ninety-eight received under ten years. Around twenty were transferred to face trials elsewhere or their charges were dropped, and 124 were acquitted. None of them served out their complete sentence. Other Australian military trials were held in Labuan, Morotai, Manus Island, Hong Kong, Singapore, Wewak and Darwin. The last trial was held on Manus Island in April 1951.[14]

Close to 3000 Australians and 11,000 other Allied prisoners died as forced labour on the notorious Burma–Thailand Railway, but only forty-four Japanese faced trial for their crimes in Australian military courts. Sixteen were hanged – six officers, three NCOs, one private and six Korean guards. Twenty-four were given jail sentences – seven for life, and eight for up to twenty years. None served their complete term.

Only six Australians survived the Sandakan Death Marches in which 2345 sick and weak Australian and British prisoners were murdered when they couldn't continue. Just seven Japanese were sentenced to death for this war crime – mostly officers, but also Formosan guards who tortured a prisoner for four days. Around thirty lower ranks received jail sentences for murdering prisoners. They argued they were only following orders. Many had jail sentences commuted to lesser terms by the Australian Confirming Authority, the final arbiter for appeals and disputes in military courts.

Many Japanese never faced justice for their war crimes. In March 1943 the Japanese destroyer *Akikaze*, en route for Rabaul, took on board around fifty civilian internees. They included a child, Australian and European plantation owners, a large group of Catholic priests and nuns of German origin, and American protestant missionaries. While at sea the crew bound their hands behind their backs then escorted them one by one to a platform under the starboard side of the ship's bridge, where they were blindfolded. In 1946 one of the *Akikaze* officers told Australian war crime investigators: 'On the execution platform, they were faced toward the bow, suspended by their hands by means of a hook attached to a pulley, and at the order of the commander, executed by machine gun and rifle fire. After the completion of the execution the suspension rope was slackened and it had been so planned that when the rope binding the hands was cut, the body would fall backwards off the stern due to the speed of the ship. Moreover, boards were laid and straw mats spread to keep the ship from becoming stained. Thus, in this way, first the men and then the women were executed. The child going on toward five years old was thrown alive into the ocean.'[15] The Australian War Crimes Section completed its investigation into the massacre on the *Akikaze* on 18 July 1947. There was a US citizen among the executed group, so the Australians handed the matter over to American authorities in Tokyo. Historian DCS Sissons found the Americans took no action regarding the *Akikaze*.[16]

All Japanese sentenced to jail by Australian military courts were eventually transported to Sugamo Prison in Tokyo. Once there it got even better for the war criminals. In 1951 the Australian government of Robert Menzies authorised 'good conduct remissions' of one quarter of the sentence for those serving long sentences. It meant that the first Japanese war criminal prisoners sentenced in 1946 to twelve years were out of jail in January 1955. Jail time kept on being reduced so that on 4 July 1957 the last of the convicted Japanese war criminals – even mass murderers sentenced to life in jail – were released as free men. None served their full prison sentence. None, not even the worst war criminal, spent more than ten years behind bars. Justice for the thousands of victims was simply discarded by the Menzies government.

In 1948 the Allied Council in Tokyo – which was controlled by MacArthur – had recommended that war crime trials should not continue beyond 30 June 1949. Britain announced it would end its investigations into new war crime cases at the end of 1947, but those already charged by that time would still face trial into 1948 and 1949. The Australian Labor government instructed that every endeavour should be made to complete its war crime trials by the end of 1948. Two days before the deadline, the issue of the scheduled wrap-up of the trials was discussed by cabinet. Evatt and other ministers vehemently protested that the trials should continue. When the US refused to hold more trials in Tokyo, Evatt suggested holding them in Darwin or Manus Island off the north coast of New Guinea, an Australian protectorate. He argued that war crime suspects already being held awaiting trial should not be released but kept locked up until the trials could be held.

On 16 September 1949, MacArthur's HQ in Tokyo notified the Australian mission that, in the absence of any plan for their immediate trial, the eighty-seven Japanese war crimes suspects being held in Sugamo Prison on Australia's behalf would be released on 1 November. MacArthur's office cabled Canberra that the eighty-seven suspects had already been held without charge for more than four years after war's end, and holding them longer would be a breach of the concept of justice. After considerable pressure from Canberra, MacArthur reluctantly agreed to keep the suspects in jail until the end of the year. On 19 October MacArthur released all Sugamo prisoners being held under US authority. MacArthur told the Australian mission that he had examined the files on Australia's eighty-seven suspects and concluded that only fifty-one suspects deserved a trial.

Menzies won the December 1949 election and took office on 19 December. At his first cabinet meeting on 20 December, he ordered that the suspects singled out by MacArthur should go to trial as soon as possible. That would end Australia's war crime trials. Cabinet ordered that all further war crime investigations be terminated. Of the 91 Japanese who faced trial in these hurried and final trials on Manus Island and Darwin, thirteen were sentenced to death. Only five of the death sentences were carried out. This infuriated Australian veterans and much of the public. The New South Wales president of the Returned Services League, Mr Nagle, told the *Daily Telegraph* that if the government was having trouble finding executioners, 'I know plenty of ex-prisoners of war who would willingly do the job for free'.[17]

The Australian military courts convicted 644 Japanese and brought down a total 214 death sentences, from which 137 executions were actually carried out. The rest were commuted to lengthy prison sentences, which were never fully served. Australia's military courts were not the most severe of similar Allied military courts conducted outside the Tokyo Trials. A total 4488 Japanese faced trial in these Allied military courts, of which number 1041 (twenty-three per cent) were given the death penalty. American military courts convicted 1229 and sentenced 163 to death (thirteen per cent); Britain convicted 811 and sentenced 265 to death (thirty-three per cent); Holland convicted 969 and sentenced 236 to death (twenty-four per cent); China convicted 504 and sentenced 149 to death (twenty-nine per cent); France convicted 198 and sentenced sixty-three to death (thirty-one per cent); and the Philippines convicted 133 and sentenced seventeen to death (thirteen per cent). Soviet convictions are unavailable, apart from the Khabarovsk trial of Unit 731 members, none of whom was executed.[18]

•

The big question that the Tokyo War Crime Trials steered well clear of was whether the Emperor himself should be facing trial. It was a battle behind the scenes that Australia lost. The Labor government's attorney-general and foreign minister, Doc Evatt, had long been convinced that Emperor Hirohito must be charged as Japan's number-one war criminal. Britain argued that the post-war occupation of Japan would be better worked through the existing power structure in Japan, and that included the emperor. Australia's Labor government reacted with outrage. 'The Emperor as Head of State and Commander in Chief of the Armed forces [must] be given no immunity for Japan's act of aggression and war crimes which in evidence before us are shown to have been of the most barbarous character,' Canberra cabled to London.[19] Australia urged Britain to resist any move to grant the emperor immunity from punishment. Australia argued that Hirohito should be deprived of any authority to rule. 'Any other course would prevent the emergence of a democratic and peace-loving regime in Japan,' the government of John Curtin warned.[20] But London insisted it would be a 'capital political error to indict him [Hirohito] as a war criminal. We desire to limit commitment in manpower and other resources by using the Imperial throne as an instrument for the control of the Japanese people and indictment of the present occupant would, in our view, be most unwise.'[21]

Behind the scenes the US was urging Britain to get its upstart dominion, Australia, under control. The US wanted Australia to back away from demanding dozens of top-level Japanese officials face war crime trials in Tokyo, especially the emperor. The US and Britain feared that the remnants of the Japanese army and masses of civilians would rise up in revolt at any move against Hirohito, who still commanded God-like reverence. MacArthur warned that if the Emperor were indicted 'it is quite possible that a minimum of a million troops would be required which would have to be maintained for an indefinite number of years'.[22]

Nevertheless, Canberra's Labor government had drawn up a list of sixty-four top politicians, bankers and industrialists it wanted to face trial in Tokyo, with Emperor Hirohito at the very top of the list. This flew in the face of the US and Britain who wanted to restrict the Tokyo trials to top military officers and one or two war-mongering politicians. (The commanders of the horrific biochemical warfare experiments, such as Ishii, had already been secretly isolated so their names wouldn't get anywhere near the Tokyo trials.) Canberra sent its list to Webb in Tokyo. Webb replied that a decision about the emperor had to made at the top levels of the Allied powers, but he would put

Australia's list to the newly formed United Nations committee that was drawing up plans for the Tokyo trials.

'The Emperor's authority was required for war,' Webb argued to the UN committee. 'If he did not want war he should have withheld his authority. It is no answer to say that he might have been assassinated. That risk is taken by all rulers who must still do their duty. No ruler can commit the crime of launching aggressive war and then validly claim to be excused for so doing because his life would otherwise have been in danger.'[23] In reality MacArthur ran the Tokyo trials, and he was adamant that Emperor Hirohito would not be put on trial or punished in any way for the war. The UN war crime trial committee met and voted almost unanimously not to include the emperor, and limit the list of war crime defendants in the Tokyo trials to just twenty-eight. Only Australia voted to include the Emperor and dozens more senior Japanese officials and businessmen, unsuccessfully arguing that Hirohito started the war and could have ended it at any time, as his power over the military was absolute.

The trials of Japanese war crime suspects were divided into three categories: A for war crimes by the most senior Japanese who conspired to wage aggressive war, and B and C for men who ordered atrocities, allowed them to happen, or actually committed them. With Emperor Hirohito excluded from the A-class list, at the top of the trial list was General Tojo Hideki, prime minister from 1941 to 1944, war minister and home minister, mastermind of Japan's war, the man who ordered the surprise attack on Pearl Harbor. Tojo had said that any POW who did not work should not eat. Tojo knew all about atrocities committed on the Burma–Thai Railway, the Bataan Death March and the executions of POWs, yet did nothing to stop any of them.

Two weeks after Japan's surrender, US military police went to arrest Tojo at his palatial home. It was a highly publicised event, with press photographers at the ready outside the mansion. Inside, Tojo got a doctor to mark the exact spot on his chest where his heart was, aimed a service revolver at the spot, and fired. But there was no samurai death for Tojo. He missed the spot and was still alive when American military police stormed in. Press photographers heard the shot and were hot on the heels of the MPs. They took pictures of Tojo with blood pouring out of a frothing chest wound. Some of those present dipped pieces of paper or handkerchiefs in the blood as souvenirs.[24] Tojo recovered in hospital with transfusions of blood from US marines. On 8 December 1945 he was transferred to Sugamo Prison to await trial. Guards were ordered to keep him under close observation twenty-four hours a day to avoid another suicide attempt. He was manacled to guards whenever he walked in the prison yard. When Tojo had terrible toothache and couldn't speak in court, an American dentist was brought in to give him dentures. The dentist secretly inscribed a message in morse code on the false teeth: *Remember Pearl Harbor.*[25]

Others charged included Koki Hirota, prime minister from 1936 to 1937, Hiranuma Kiichiro, prime minister in 1939, Shigenori Togo, foreign minister from 1941 to 1942, and six other government ministers. Tojo was the most senior military officer on the list, but also charged were Generals Tomoyuki Yamashita, Masaharu Homma, Seishiro Itagaki and sixteen other high-ranking officers.

Seven were sentenced to death by hanging for war crimes and crimes against humanity. Tojo removed his dentures before his hanging with the six others at midnight on 23 December 1948.

MacArthur refused to allow the executions to be recorded on photograph or film.

Sixteen received life sentences. Three died in prison, while the remaining thirteen were paroled between 1954 and 1956. Shortly after Tojo and the others were sentenced, a large group of high-ranking prisoners who were still awaiting trial were released from Sugamo Prison. The last hanging at Sugamo Prison took place in April 1950. By 1952, prisons around South East Asia holding Japanese war criminals were almost empty. Those prisoners with long sentences still to be completed were all transferred to Sugamo Prison. The prison administration was handed over to the Japanese government. With repeated commutations and clemencies, the longest prison sentence actually served behind bars by any Japanese war criminal was less than thirteen years. The last Japanese war criminal behind bars, military affairs bureau chief General Kenryo Sato, was released from Sugamo Prison a free man in December 1958.

•

Tojo's body was cremated and the ashes scattered so no shrine could be built. A commemorating tomb at Nishio was later built for him, however, and his spirit is enshrined in Tokyo's controversial Yasukuni Shrine, which honours all those who died in the service of the Empire of Japan. More than two million names are listed as heroes of the nation. It includes an estimated one thousand convicted war criminals.

Many Sugamo inmates went on to fortune and fame after the war. Ryoichi Sasakawa, a wealthy fascist supporter of the war, was freed from Sugamo without facing trial, then worked with the CIA and the *yakuza*, Japan's organised crime syndicate, combating Japan's communists. He went on to be elected to parliament and made millions out of a gambling monopoly. In 1995 he was the last of the Sugamo Prison A-class inmates to die.

Yoshio Kodama, an ultra-nationalist and drug runner, was one of the richest men in Asia before the war. He was also freed from Sugamo without trial, then worked for the CIA using *yakuza* thugs to fight communists and unionists in Japan. He died a very rich man in 1984.

Wartime politician Shigemitsu Mamoru served seven years in jail. Just a few years after his release he became deputy prime minister and foreign minister of Japan.

Nobusuke Kishi was held in Sugamo for three years but never went on trial for his brutal rule in occupied Manchukuo in north-east China, a period which earned him the moniker the 'Showa Monster'. He was not included in the Tokyo War Crimes Trials charge list because the US thought he would make a good pro-American, anti-communist Japanese leader. Soon after his release from Sugamo Prison, Kishi entered politics with a new moniker thrust upon him: 'America's favourite war criminal'.[26] By 1957 he was prime minister of Japan and lasted in the post until 1960. His grandson is Shinzo Abe, prime minister from 2006 to 2007 and from 2012 until the present (2017).

The second-in-command of Unit 731, Surgeon General Kitano Masaji, was never arrested or charged for war crimes. After the war he set up the pharmaceutical company Green Cross and made millions out of commercial blood. He was accepted as a member of the New York Academy of Sciences, a rare honour.

Lieutenant Colonel Masanobu Tsuji was regarded by many as an extreme warmonger, responsible for the massacre of thousands of Chinese and the killing of Allied prisoners, doctors and nurses at Alexandra Hospital in Singapore. He was never arrested and lay low until 1952, when he was elected to Japan's parliament advocating renewed militarism.[27] In 1961 he disappeared during a trip to Laos and was never seen again. His supporters erected a statue to him in Kaga City.

Today Japan seems intent on wiping away all shreds of its history of atrocities in World War II. Sugamo Prison was demolished in 1971. Japanese schools skip over the details of World War II, with nationalists fighting to remove any trace of the atrocities Japan's troops committed. War crimes such as the Rape of Nanking, human experiments by Unit 731 and the massacre of prisoners are deliberately excluded from Japanese school textbooks. Public discussion of Japan's war crimes is taboo.

Prime Minister Shinzo Abe sparked anger in the US, China and South Korea when he visited the Yasukuni Shrine in 2013. He sought to make amends by being the first Japanese leader to visit the Pearl Harbor memorial in 2016, declaring, 'We must never repeat the horrors of war'.[28] The next day, however, Japan's right-wing Defence Minister, Tomomi Inada, who was with Abe for the historic Pearl Harbor ceremony, made a surprise pilgrimage to the Yasukuni Shrine.[29]

Japan's ongoing attitude to World War II and the atrocities their military committed has been completely the opposite to that of Germany. While all German schoolchildren must study the concentration camp horrors and visit the camps that still stand as memorials, Japan's youth are kept ignorant of the terrible acts of their forefathers.

Perhaps this was part of the legacy of the way their war criminals were brought to justice after the war. (In Germany,

some are still facing trial in their 90s.) Germany was shocked
into facing up to how their nation could fall in behind a maniac
like Hitler and seek to exterminate an entire race of people.
The nation lives with that guilt. That Japan had been allowed to
ignore its monstrous wartime atrocities is an immense betrayal
of all those who suffered under those atrocities.

11

TRAITORS AND OTHER
TWO-FACED VILLAINS

*'Der Führer performed quite well in bed despite
the loss of a testicle in the trenches.'*

Was Errol Flynn a Nazi spy? Could the dashing Tasmanian
heart-throb, the swashbuckling hero of the silver screen, the
rascally rapscallion and handsome lover of many a Hollywood
beauty of both sexes, really have been a secret Nazi who spied
for Hitler? It's a hotly contested question, one that hasn't been
completely resolved despite decades of argument.

The furore over the political allegiance of the Australian
screen idol began in 1980 with the release of a new biography
of Flynn by journalist Charles Higham.[1] The British-born journalist knew Australia well, having spent fifteen years working
in Sydney at the *Sydney Morning Herald, Daily Mirror* and *The
Bulletin.*[2] Higham moved to America in 1964, where he became
Hollywood correspondent for the *New York Times.* He wrote

potboiler Hollywood biographies, but also scholarly investigative works including a groundbreaking investigative book on Allied multinational corporations that traded with Nazi Germany during the war. So, when Higham shone his light on the Aussie star, he had plenty of experience digging into the murky world of Nazi spies, traitors and two-faced villains. Higham's book caused a sensation. He wrote of Flynn's scandalous bisexual sex life in great detail, including his lifelong pursuit of beautiful women and underage girls – as well as of men and boys. Higham claimed Flynn counted leading men Tyrone Power and Bruce Cabot, as well as young writer Truman Capote, among his male Hollywood lovers, and enthusiastically joined orgies with young rent boys.

But the real scandal caused by Higham's book was the claim that he had uncovered enough evidence to establish that Flynn – the hero of *Captain Blood* and *Robin Hood* – was a closet Nazi sympathiser who worked undercover for Hitler. Flynn was certainly an anti-Semite. In 1933 he wrote to a friend describing a business associate as 'a slimy Jew ... I do wish we could bring Hitler over here to teach these Isaacs a thing or two. The bastards have absolutely no business probity or honour whatsoever.'[3] But the core of the allegation that Flynn was a Nazi centred on his long friendship with a mysterious Austrian called Dr Hermann Friedrich Erben. They met in 1933 when Flynn was a tearaway 24-year-old who had just shipwrecked himself on New Britain in a stolen yacht. Erben was an adventurer, a Nazi Party member and enthusiastic Hitler supporter who travelled the world as a ship's doctor. Erben had contacts with medical and German communities in the Pacific and in both South and North America, including the movie industry. At the time, young Flynn was a drifter and he became fascinated by Erben, who took him under his wing. They travelled throughout Asia together and Erben introduced Flynn to a circle of rich and powerful fascists. Flynn eventually landed in London, where he got bit parts on stage. His good looks brought him to the attention of a Hollywood agent and he got small parts in westerns.

Flynn got his big Hollywood break in 1935 with *Captain Blood* and, when Flynn's fame rose, Erben turned up on his doorstep. Higham maintains that FBI files on the mysterious Austrian suggested he was involved in the 1934 assassination of Austrian Chancellor Engelbert Dollfuss.[4] In 1937 the Spanish Civil War was in full swing, with Nazi Germany backing General Franco's fascist rebels against the Loyalist troops of the elected socialist government. Flynn and Erben planned to make a goodwill mission to the Loyalist troops in Spain. But Higham claimed it was secretly an undercover mission for the Gestapo to get the names and addresses of Germans fighting for the Loyalists. Erben would travel as a doctor and take down the names of wounded German Loyalists, while Flynn, already a movie star, would spread goodwill and promise to write home to the troops' families in Germany. They would then pass the names and addresses on to Nazi intelligence.[5]

Higham said that when Ernest Hemingway met the pair in Spain he became suspicious. 'Hemingway knew at once that Errol was a fascist. He warned Errol not to spy for the fascists or to cross to the fascist line or his career as a star would be finished.'[6] Allegedly, this made Flynn determined to do just that. But Flynn was struck on the head by falling debris before he reached the fascist lines and ended up in hospital. He woke to read newspaper headlines declaring he was dead. It was the greatest publicity possible, but it also increased the Allies' focus on Flynn.

Years after the controversial biography was published, Higham claimed he had received new information revealing that Flynn had gone to Bavaria in 1938 and secretly met Hitler at his mountain retreat.[7] However, there is no hard evidence of this alleged meeting, such as a photo or official record. The FBI were keeping a close eye on Flynn, logging everyone he met, noting that Flynn attended a dinner party in 1940 at the Washington home of the Brazilian Ambassador that was 'full of Nazis'.[8] Higham claimed Flynn had affairs with a string of femme fatale Nazi agents in the lead-up to the war. These included, Higham says, Swedish singer and Nazi sympathiser Gertrude Anderson, and American Nazi Tara Marsh who, Higham claims, had formerly been involved with Goebbels and boasted to Flynn that she had been to bed with Hitler himself. She proudly proclaimed Der Führer performed quite well in bed despite the loss of a testicle in the trenches.[9]

Meanwhile, Erben had risen to the rank of chief Nazi agent in Mexico and was spying on US installations on the west coast and the Panama Canal. The FBI was keen on revoking his US residency visa and kicking him out of the country. Higham claims that Flynn persuaded the president's wife, Eleanor Roosevelt, to get the government to allow Erben to stay.[10] While Flynn was filming *The Sea Hawk*, the FBI questioned him about his relationship with Erben. Flynn told the FBI that Erben was opposed to Nazism. 'It seemed Errol was the only individual on earth who did not know Erben was a Nazi,' Higham wrote.[11] The FBI allowed Erben to sail through the Panama Canal in April 1940, filming everything as he went, even though Germany was at war with Britain and the dominions. When the FBI eventually decided to detain Erben as a Nazi spy, Higham claims Flynn smuggled him out of the US to Mexico on board his yacht *Sirocco*.

In the early 1941 film *Dive Bomber*, Flynn played a US Air Force officer flying off aircraft carriers. The film was shot at naval bases in Honolulu and San Diego and on board the aircraft carrier *Enterprise*. The film was directed by Hungarian-born Michael Curtiz, who began directing films in the 1920s and early 1930s in Germany. *Dive Bomber* contained such enormous detail of the naval installations at Pearl Harbor that Higham says it must have been extremely useful to Japanese planners for their devastating surprise attack later that year. Higham said the film's producer, Robert Lord, wrote many years later that Flynn had personally shot lots of aerial footage of Pearl Harbor for a semi-documentary on America's power in the Pacific. A print was sent to the studio's representative in Japan in the late summer of 1941.

While he was a teenager in Sydney, Flynn had a friend called Freddie McEvoy. They got up to loads of mischief around the harbour, joy-riding on stolen boats and getting up to other teenage pranks. Flynn was expelled from the prestigious Shore School after he was caught *in flagrante delicto* in the coal shed with the laundry maid's daughter, and left Sydney for adventures in New Guinea. But, over the years, Flynn kept in touch with his chum McEvoy. As dashing and handsome as Flynn, Freddie McEvoy moved to England and in the 1920s and early 1930s was a sporting playboy who climbed rapidly up London's social ladder by bedding the most strategically well-placed aristocrats.

McEvoy competed at the 1936 Winter Olympics in the British bobsled team, winning a bronze medal. The event at

Garmisch-Partenkirchen led him to mix with the Nazi hierarchy, and McEvoy made no secret of his admiration for Hitler. As war loomed between Britain and Germany, McEvoy moved to Hollywood where he renewed his friendship with Errol Flynn. Higham claims FBI reports show that before the US joined the war, McEvoy tried to convince rich American industrialists to invest in Germany and support the Fascist cause. McEvoy saw Flynn as the key to open that door, and together they attended dinner parties where McEvoy proclaimed Hitler was doing great things for Germany. Higham also said he had seen US intelligence reports that McEvoy scouted possible sites in Central America and the Caribbean for German U-Boat refuelling bases.[13]

In 1950, McEvoy was the best man at Flynn's wedding to starlet Patrice Wymore. McEvoy drowned in mysterious circumstances the following year in a boat accident off the coast of Morocco, aged forty-four. Nine years later, hard living caught up with Flynn when he died aged just fifty.

Several historians disputed Higham's claim that swashbuckler Errol Flynn was a secret Nazi spy. Australian movie historian Alan Royle wrote that the head of British Intelligence during the war, Sir William Stephenson, looked into the claims and concluded 'in my professional opinion Mr Errol Flynn was not a Nazi spy.'[14] Mind you, British Intelligence missed super Soviet spies Burgess, McLean and Philby. World War II historian James Holland told Britain's *Daily Mail* the notion was 'totally ridiculous . . . he had a dubious past but I don't think he was a spy. He went to Spain because he was an adrenaline junkie.'[15] Flynn's family were outraged at the claim. They acknowledged he may have been a scoundrel who dipped his wick wherever he could, but denied he was a Nazi agent.

It may be that with all the hard drinking and leaping into as many beds as he could (to earn his moniker 'In Like Flynn'), the swashbuckling sexaholic mightn't have had time to be a dangerous and deadly Nazi spy.

•

As the US rolled towards joining World War II McEvoy and Flynn seem to have found receptive ears at those swank dinner parties with American billionaires On 3 May 1941, FBI boss J Edgar Hoover sent a memo to President Roosevelt's office declaring that he had received information from a 'socially prominent' source that Joseph Kennedy, former US Ambassador to England (and father of John F Kennedy), and Ben Smith, a Wall Street 'operator', had met with Göring in Vichy, France. Soon after that they 'donated a considerable amount of money to the German cause'. Hoover said: 'They are both described as being very anti-British and pro-German.'[16]

Mandarins of several huge American industrial dynasties not only admired Hitler for what he was doing in Germany, but also put their money behind him. Some even harboured desires to pull off a fascist coup of their own in Washington.

After the rise of Hitler, America's Du Pont family, owners of the giant chemical corporation bearing their name, started financing fascist groups in the United States including the pro-business, ultra right-wing American Liberty League. The league was opposed to President Roosevelt's New Deal that increased social welfare and imposed regulations on the financial system. It was intent on branding him a communist, claiming he was dominated by Jews. Together with millionaires at the top level of JP Morgan Bank, 3 million dollars was poured into the Liberty League – a vast amount at the time – to fund thugs and street brawlers to battle unions and supporters of President Roosevelt. The aim, incredible as it might seem, was to mount a coup in Washington that would have the government run by a tight committee of men from Big Business. Roosevelt would have to take orders from this committee or he would be jailed, even executed.

In August 1934, just days after Hitler took dictatorial powers in Germany, the group decided to approach popular and highly respected retired Marine Corps Major-General Smedley Butler. They believed 'Old Gimlet Eye' Butler would have the public support to replace Roosevelt in the treasonous act they were planning. Butler had twice been awarded the Medal of Honor and was a legend across the nation. When he retired from the marines, he had been critical of Roosevelt's New Deal. He had campaigned for military veterans who had missed out on pensions, and spoke out for more aid for thousands of veterans who still suffered from wounds received in World War I. Butler was a man of the common soldier who had spent a career bucking military bureaucracy. At his retirement speech to farewell his marines, he handed each of them a map showing where his home was and urged them to come and see him if ever they needed help or wanted a chat. Many did.

Butler gave a speech to veterans titled 'War Is a Racket', one of the great anti-war and anti-war profiteering tracts by any military man in history. It was later printed as a booklet. 'WAR is a racket. It always has been,' Butler starts. 'It is possibly the oldest, easily the most profitable, surely the most vicious. It is the only one international in scope. It is the only one in which the profits are reckoned in dollars and the losses in lives . . . It is conducted for the benefit of the very few, at the expense of the very many. Out of war a few people make huge fortunes.'[17]

The Du Ponts and millionaire industrialists behind the league must have seen the title of the speech and not read any further. They believed that in Butler they had found a kindred soul, even though Butler was condemning people just like them who profited from war. In August 1934 the backers of the bizarre league plot asked Wall Street attorney Gerald MacGuire to quietly approach Butler to see whether he would accept the post of president if Roosevelt were suddenly forced out. MacGuire visited Butler at his home in the steamy Washington summer heat. The smooth-talking MacGuire told Butler that he had just returned from Europe where he was impressed with the way thousands of angry, unemployed military veterans joined Italy's Blackshirts and Germany's Brownshirts. MacGuire said it was these people who had got the two economies working again and dragged their nations out of the Depression. He said the fascists had suppressed the communists and brought in law and order, and he pressed on Butler that America needed just such an organisation.

Butler was no dummy and twigged instantly to what was being suggested. He was horrified, to say the least. He kept a poker face and didn't reveal his shock to MacGuire. Instead, Butler feigned interest and said he would like to hear more. MacGuire went back to his bosses and they were thrilled at Butler's reaction. MacGuire returned to Butler, this time with details of millions of dollars ready to fund a mass movement of 500,000 veterans to march on Washington to force out the president. MacGuire said the Liberty League's backers could

raise 300 million dollars for the march and he presented plans
that included Butler taking the role of assistant president, who
would really run the country, leaving the role of president as
a mere symbolic figurehead.[18] Butler again feigned interest,
and insisted that if this plot was serious and he were to agree
to take part, he would have to know who was putting up the
money. MacGuire told him financiers of the JP Morgan bank
were at the centre of the plot. He told Butler the bankers had
favoured General Douglas MacArthur, but MacGuire said he
had argued that MacArthur was too unpopular with veterans.
MacGuire said he'd convinced the bankers that Butler had the
veterans' support and would be the best to run the government.
MacGuire's flattery was followed by a threat: if Butler didn't take
the offer, they would have to approach MacArthur.

MacGuire told Butler that the league planned to launch the
march in about three weeks. It would be depicted as a march
to 'maintain the constitution'.[19] The Democrat Governor of New
York, Al Smith, was on board, MacGuire added proudly. Butler
knew Smith was in the pockets of the Du Ponts. His shock was
deepening. He asked himself how many more people at the top
of American industry were involved in this industrialist-financed
fascist plot to mount an American coup. He kept his demeanour
curious, and pretended to be flattered without committing
himself.

As soon as MacGuire left his home, Butler investigated this
strange organisation calling itself the American Liberty League.
He discovered that its founders were the heads of US finance
and industry – including people at the top levels of JP Morgan,
Andrew Mellon, Rockefeller and General Motors – and that
it had affiliations with fascist groups including the Ku Klux

Klan. Butler was stunned to realise that the threat of a looming American fascist coup was very real. He knew he would need evidence before he took this any further. He asked an old friend, Tom O'Neil, editor of the *Philadelphia Record*, to help him find proof of what the Liberty League was up to. O'Neil knew the story was dynamite, and one they couldn't get wrong or the industrialists would be able to destroy him and the newspaper.

An investigator for the Congressional Committee on Un-American Activities (the first such committee with that name, it investigated both left- and right-wing extremists, unlike the notorious post-war committee of Senator Joseph McCarthy) got wind of the plot and asked Butler whether he had heard anything. Butler decided to tell everything to the committee. He had supporting evidence from O'Neil's inquiries. Butler felt the league might launch its coup attempt at any time. On 20 November 1934, Butler gave his testimony to the Congressional Committee in a closed session in New York City. The same day, the *Philadelphia Record* and its sister paper the *New York Post* published its sensational story of the planned coup under the screaming headline: '*$3,000,000 Bid for Fascist Army Bared*'. The papers opened their sensational scoop with: 'Major General Smedley D Butler revealed today that he has been asked by a group of wealthy New York brokers to lead a Fascist movement to set up a dictatorship in the United States.'[20]

The *New York Times* reported the next day that Butler told the committee the plot by 'Wall Street interests' was to assemble half a million veterans in Washington in the autumn of 1935 and that 'such a show of force would enable it to take over the government peacefully in a few days'.[21] *Philadelphia Record* reporter Paul Comly French, who had been assigned the story by his paper, said he interviewed MacGuire and that MacGuire had openly said American needed a fascist government, that veterans had the patriotism to save the country from communists, and that a million men would rise up and follow Butler once the movement started. French said MacGuire told him the plotters could obtain guns from the Remington Arms Company on credit through the Du Ponts, who owned a controlling interest in the arms manufacturer.

The committee summoned MacGuire, who denied everything. Newspapers such as the *New York Times* ran denials from just about everybody named in connection with Butler's testimony. 'It's a joke, a publicity stunt, it's made up, I deny the story completely,' MacGuire told the *New York Times*. The Mayor of New York, Fiorello La Guardia, mocked the story as a 'cocktail putsch' dreamed up on the party circuit. 'Plot Without Plotters', ridiculed *Time* magazine.[22] The public mocking of Butler was getting more press than the content of his allegations. Powerful forces were at work to destroy the old general. None of the big industrialist names cited by Butler were called before the committee to answer questions. It seemed all over and buried. But there was one big surprise left in this extraordinary tale.

On 15 February 1935 the committee reported its findings to Congress. Most observers expected something vague and inconclusive, but the committee dropped a bombshell. 'Your committee was able to verify all the pertinent statements made by General Butler,'[23] it declared. In other words, there was indeed a plot to form a veteran army to march on Washington and force a fascist government on the United States. But the committee added that this verification didn't include Butler's suggestions of the creation of the organisation – a rider that dismissed allegations against the big industrialists. It was an unexpected vindication of Butler, but it was barely reported in the nation's press. No one was prosecuted over the plot.

The battling *Philadelphia Record* slammed those behind the planned coup. 'The folk who want Fascism in this country are the same folk who made profit while others bled and who would rather see the veteran starve than unbalance the budget,'[24] the paper thundered in an editorial.

Others got wind of the planned coup and had the courage to speak out. In 1937 US Ambassador to Germany, William E Dodd, resigned in protest at the lack of opposition to the Nazi regime from the Roosevelt administration. He told the *New York Times* there were US industrialists with ties to Nazi Germany who wanted an American dictatorship. 'There are politicians who think they may gain powers like those exercised in Europe. One man, I have been told by friends, who owns nearly a billion dollars, is ready to support such a program and, of course, control it.'[25] On his return to the US, Dodd gave a shipboard press conference and said 'a clique of US industrialists is hell-bent to bring a fascist state to supplant our democratic government and is working closely with the fascist regime in Germany and Italy. I have had plenty of opportunity in my post in Berlin to witness how close some of our American ruling families are to the Nazi regime.'[26]

Butler continued to speak out against war, urging the US to only go to war to defend the home shores from invasion. The man who could have been the first dictator of the United States of America died on 21 June 1940, the day France surrendered to Nazi Germany. *The Philadelphia Record*, the newspaper that investigated the fascist plot and found it to be true, went broke and closed down in 1947.

•

In early 1941, FBI director Hoover told President Roosevelt's office he had received reports that the Duke of Windsor – the abdicated King Edward VIII – had secretly met Göring, even though the duke's own nation was at war with Germany. This alone was an act of treachery, but Hoover had learned the duke had struck a deal that if Germany won the war, Göring would overthrow Hitler and reinstall the Duke of Windsor as King of England – and Australia.[27] If Hoover was right, the duke's preparedness to get back his throne by collaborating with his nation's mortal enemy in a time of war is absolutely extraordinary, and one of the greatest treasons of the war.

It wasn't the only indication that the former monarch was in cahoots with the Nazis. The year after he abdicated in 1936, he and his wife publicly met Adolf Hitler in what the Nazis described as a 'State Visit'. There were smiles all round and the couple were treated like royalty. The duke was grateful for the welcome and impressed that German aristocrats bowed and curtseyed to his wife, Wallis Simpson – something she never received in England. A friendship was struck. The question was, how deep did it go?

According to German foreign ministry records, in February 1940 the Duke of Windsor was said to have revealed to a Nazi official that the Allied War Council meeting in London had discussed in detail what would happen if Germany invaded Belgium, and that the most favoured option was not to defend Belgium at all but to set up a resistance effort further behind the Belgium–France border.[28] Such a leak was enormously useful for German invasion plans and it was taken straight to Hitler.

The FBI regarded Wallis Simpson as, at best, a Nazi Fifth Columnist, at worst a fully fledged Nazi agent with extremely close associations with Hitler and his cronies.[29] British intelligence kept the duke and his wife under close observation out of concern that they might be enticed or kidnapped to Germany, where they could be held up as a king and queen in waiting for a German victory. After war broke out, the duke and his wife were shuffled from France to neutral Spain and Portugal, from where the duke was sent to the Bahamas in a cushy job as governor. But even there it was feared the duke and his wife could fall into the welcoming clutches of Nazis. Also living in the Caribbean was Swedish multimillionaire businessman Axel Wenner-Gren, a suspected Nazi and personal friend of Hermann Göring, whose wife was Swedish. Errol Flynn had been a frequent guest at Wenner-Gren's wild and lavish parties before the war. Wenner-Gren fancied himself as a go-between for Germany to keep the United States from joining the war. Suspicions about his Nazi links led him to be black-listed by both the US and Britain. That didn't stop the duke from befriending him. They had long talks about Hitler and the good things he was doing for Germany. Another close friend of the duke's, French millionaire Charles Bedaux, was a Nazi collaborator who was captured by US forces and charged with trading with the enemy. Bedaux killed himself before coming to trial.

Even though British troops had been slaughtered in France, in December 1940 the duke said in an interview with the editor of *Liberty* magazine, Fulton Oursler, that it would be tragic if Hitler were overthrown. 'Hitler is the right and logical leader of the German people,' the former king said. 'It is a pity you never met Hitler, just as it is a pity I never met Mussolini. Hitler is a very great man.'[30] The duke then asked a stunned Oursler whether the US president would be prepared to act as mediator between Germany and Britain to end the war between 'two stubborn peoples' when and if the proper time came. 'It sounds very silly to put it this way but the time is coming when somebody has got to say, you two boys have fought long enough and now you have to kiss and make up.' The duke warned that if the US entered the war, the fighting would go on for another thirty years. He even bragged that the German army had never been defeated on the battlefield. The duke told the influential editor not to print what he had said, but made it clear that he wanted Oursler to convey his words directly to President Roosevelt. Oursler did so in a seventeen-page memo. Oursler later said that Roosevelt was aware of the duke's plot and how close he was to US industrialists, who wanted the US to stay out of the war so that they could trade with both sides. Roosevelt also suspected that the duke – or his wife – had slipped valuable military information to the Nazis before the shooting war began.[31]

The one-time King of Britain – and Australia – who had all the privileges and protection of being a member of the royal family, donned the mantle of the Nazis while his country and its dominions, including Australia, were fighting a desperate war against Nazi Germany. Churchill had railed to his staff that he would have the former king stand before a court martial if he did not take the plum post of governor of the Bahamas for the duration of the war. The former monarch escaped being tried for treason and, despite his Nazi sympathies, was fêted by European and American society until he died in Paris in 1972.

•

Eton-educated William Francis Forbes-Sempill, the nineteenth Lord Sempill, was a decorated naval pilot in World War I, rising to the rank of squadron commander. The dashing young Scottish aristocrat had it all. After the war, Sempill got a plum job testing planes for the Ministry of Munitions. He broke flying speed records in a new de Havilland DH.60 Moth seaplane.

In 1920, Sempill led a British delegation of Air Ministry and former naval airmen to Japan. Britain was willing to sell its expertise on aircraft carriers and navy flying to Japan. Sempill impressed the Japanese hosts, and the Imperial Japanese Navy thanked him for his assistance. With him was Royal Navy flying ace Frederick Rutland, who gave the Japanese advice on how to take off and land from aircraft carriers. The Japanese admiralty was ecstatic about the results.

When the twenty-year-old Anglo–Japanese Alliance was terminated in 1923 out of concern for the growing aggressive militancy in Japan, Sempill should have immediately ceased all military contacts with Japan, but he didn't. Throughout the 1920s and 1930s he kept up secret contact with the Japanese embassy in London. Abusing his Air Ministry position for cash, Sempill passed on top-secret information about new British naval planes to the Japanese military attaché. Sempill was also vehemently anti-Semitic. In this, he wasn't alone in the British Establishment.

By 1925 British intelligence had cracked the codes for Japanese transmissions from its London embassy, and in so doing discovered that Sempill was selling Japan confidential information. MI5 tapped Sempill's phone at his home and office. They discovered that his servant was an undercover Japanese naval rating. Finally, Sempill was overheard on a train chatting to foreign air officials about a secret new British seaplane.

British intelligence had Sempill cold. The aristocrat was asked to come in for a chat. There were no electric prods; he wasn't tied to a chair in a dank cellar and beaten till he told the truth. Instead it was cups of tea in leather armchairs, as a gentleman is wont to be treated. MI5 couldn't admit to Sempill that they had intercepted top-secret information he'd sold to the Japanese embassy as it would reveal they had cracked the Japanese code. Over tea, Sempill did what a decent chap ought to and conceded he had breached the Official Secrets Act on the train. Sorry about that.

What was the government to do with him? There were severe penalties for breaching the Official Secrets Act. By law, Sempill should have been thrown in jail. If he had been a working-class snitch there is no doubt he would have been dumped in the smallest cell. Or shot. But Sempill was an aristocrat, one of the young lords of high society, an Eton boy. Good heavens, his father was even aide-de-camp to King George V.

The question of what to do with Sempill went all the way to the top of the government. A meeting chaired by Foreign Secretary Sir Austen Chamberlain decided not to prosecute Sempill. It would be too embarrassing for the British Establishment, and a trial might reveal the interception of Japanese diplomatic cables. That alone would cause a huge diplomatic stink, and the flow of valuable information would stop until they could crack it again. Sempill was allowed to quietly leave the ministry to pursue other interests.

No one knew about Sempill's naughty bit of spying, and he flourished. He was made president of the prestigious Royal Aeronautical Society, a post that allowed him to be a paid consultant to foreign navies around the world, including Australia. He sat in the House of Lords as a Conservative Peer, voting on defence matters. He joined The Link, a right-wing group promoting Anglo–German friendship. He was a top figure in the Right Club, a group that wanted to kick Jews out of the Conservative Party. In 1931, Sempill became a paid consultant to Mitsubishi, acting as the armament firm's representative in Europe at the same time as Japan invaded Manchuria and China. Sempill was back as a paid-up agent for Japan.[32]

In 1939, when Britain declared war on Germany, First Sea Lord Winston Churchill brought his old Eton chum Sempill back to the Admiralty. Sempill promised not to tell the Japanese anything, but in 1940 MI5 intercepted messages from Mitsubishi concerning payments to Sempill for his work for Japan's military and naval attachés in London. Britain's attorney-general advised against prosecution, and Sempill got off again with only a caution. He'd claimed payments from Mitsubishi had stopped at the outbreak of war with Germany and that this payment was just catch-up money. It was a lie. MI5 tapped Sempill's phone throughout 1940 and 1941 and found that he was in frequent contact with Japanese embassy military attachés. In August 1941, MI5 intercepted cables from Japan's embassy that included accurate notes from a secret meeting held between Churchill and President Roosevelt. Sempill was the obvious source of the leak. Churchill was told of the 'undesirable contacts of Lord Sempill's'[33] but decided not to prosecute. It would have exposed treachery at the very top of the British Establishment and embarrassed Churchill, who had given Sempill the job despite knowing his links with Japan. Churchill ordered Sempill be posted to an isolated office somewhere in northern Scotland.

But Sempill's spying for Japan didn't stop. Just weeks before Japan's attack on Pearl Harbor, Sempill intervened to spring Mitsubishi's London manager out of jail after he was arrested on suspicion of espionage. On 13 December, six days after Japan's surprise attack on Pearl Harbour, Malaya, Hong Kong and Singapore, MI5 raided Sempill's office and home. They found secret Admiralty documents that shouldn't have been there. Two days later, Sempill was discovered making phone calls to the Japanese Embassy, even though war had been declared on Japan a week earlier.[34] Despite the overwhelming evidence of treason in wartime, Churchill again failed to act against his Eton chum, and Sempill simply retired from public office. It was all covered up and his reputation remained intact.

Sempill continued to sit in the House of Lords and was honoured with posts such as president of the British Gliding Association and the Institute of Advanced Motorists. He died in 1965. It wasn't until 1998, when some of his files were finally opened in the UK National Archives, that the truth emerged of the aristocrat spy and how Churchill had covered up for his chum. In an introduction to the files, the National Archivist at Kew noted that 'on the evidence of these files, Sempill's activities on behalf of the militaristic Japanese and Fascist contacts were less from any desire to help the enemy but more motivated by his own impetuous character, obstinacy, and flawed judgement.' Apparently even the archivists couldn't bring themselves to condemn a pillar of the British Establishment and a Churchill chum as anything more than a misguided, eccentric aristocrat.

This was nonsense. Lord Sempill was a traitor who passed on secrets that could have helped enable Japan to launch the deadly aircraft-carrier attacks on Pearl Harbour, and to develop highly effective warplanes that killed Australian, British and American sailors and troops. Sempill was allowed to live a long and respected life. Other traitors were shot.

Sempill's fellow spy for Japan, naval flying ace Frederick Rutland, resigned from the RAF in 1922 to work full-time for the Japanese, training Japanese pilots. He also gave valuable advice on developing new aircraft carriers, naval attack planes and bombers. Japan paid Rutland to spy on US naval install-ations in Pearl Harbor – information that was invaluable as Japan planned its surprise aircraft carrier attack for December 1941. US counterintelligence was suspicious of Rutland, and in October 1941 he returned to Britain where he was interned as soon as Japan attacked Pearl Harbor and Malaya. Rutland committed suicide in 1949.

Diana Mitford, one of London high society's glamorous Mitford sisters, was a Nazi who in 1936 married the leader of the British Union of Fascists, Sir Oswald Mosley, 6th Baronet of Ancoats. The wedding took place in Germany at the home of Joseph Goebbels, with Hitler as guest of honour. Diana was interned during the war, along with Mosley. Her sister Unity Valkyrie Mitford was a fanatical devotee of Hitler and was by his side for five years. At the outbreak of war, Unity tried to commit suicide in Munich. A 2007 documentary suggested that she was brought back to Britain pregnant with Hitler's baby. Unity was unrepentant, telling reporters she was glad to be back in England but that she wouldn't be on England's side in the war. Despite calls for her to be interned during the war like her sister, Unity remained free. All intelligence records relating to Unity were mysteriously missing when the official archives were eventually opened. She remained in seclusion until she died in 1948.[36]

New Zealand-born Captain Patrick Stanley Vaughan Heenan wasn't in the same league as other high-society spies. Considered to be a low-born bastard with family links to Irish republicans, Heenan couldn't get a commission in any British army regiment. He ended up in the British Indian Army in Malaya. When war broke out in Malaya, Heenan was caught transmitting radio signals to Japanese forces, giving them call signs and directions that helped them get through defences. He was court-martialled in Singapore and executed by his guards as Japanese troops advanced into the city. His body was dumped in the harbour.[37]

•

Few Australian TV viewers in the late 1950s could have known that the trustworthy man reading the nightly news on Channel 7 was the man behind the notorious wartime Tokyo Rose broadcasts. Allied soldiers gave the name Tokyo Rose to a woman who broadcast Japanese propaganda in stilted English during the war. Before the war, Charles Cousens was a popular radio announcer on Sydney's Radio 2GB. He'd been a British army officer in India serving on the North-West Frontier before making his way to Australia in 1927. When war broke out, Cousens joined up and was made captain in the Australian 19th Battalion. He was promoted to major just before the fall of Singapore. The Japanese discovered he'd been a radio announcer before the war and ordered him to broadcast propaganda on a radio station for Changi POW camp. Cousens refused. He was shipped to Japan and in Tokyo was threatened with torture unless he cooperated in writing propaganda for Radio Tokyo.

In Tokyo, Cousens coached English-speaking Japanese announcers to broadcast short-wave radio propaganda to Allied troops across South East Asia and the Pacific. The notorious 'Tokyo Rose' was in fact a string of Japanese women. Cousens also spoke his own material. After the war he insisted to Australian war crime investigators that he had been threatened with torture if he did not comply. He claimed the broadcasts he was involved in were of little use to the Japanese and that he had frequently sabotaged them with subtle ridicule and by inserting information useful to the Allies.[38]

Australian military authorities weren't convinced. Cousens was brought back to Sydney under arrest, facing charges of treason. Some saw him as the Japanese version of Lord Haw Haw who'd broadcast Nazi propaganda from Berlin. However, the attorney-general dropped the charge of treason. Had Cousens done anything as a POW to survive any differently from the POWs who built the Burma–Thailand Railway? The military considered court-martialling Cousens, but rejected the plan because it 'would have the appearance of persecution and would thus be politically inexpedient.'[39] Instead he was stripped of his rank. In 1947, veterans of his 19th Battalion, who knew Cousens's performance in battle and were convinced he had done what he had to in order to avoid being executed, asked him to lead the battalion on the Anzac Day march.

In 1949 Cousens flew to Chicago to defend the American-born Japanese woman Iva Toguri who was on trial as being the one and only Tokyo Rose. Cousens told the court that there were many women who played the role, and Iva Toguri had secretly worked with him to sabotage the broadcasts. Two Japanese who'd worked at Radio Tokyo, however, said she was the real Tokyo Rose and was dedicated to luring Americans to their doom. She was convicted of treason and jailed for ten years. The two Japanese later said they had lied under pressure from the FBI. In 1977, President Gerald Ford pardoned her in his last act in office.

Cousens was welcomed back to 2GB and in 1957–58 read the news on the new Channel 7. However, suspicion of his POW role in the Japanese propaganda machine hung over his head until he died in 1964.

In 1999 Iva Toguri said she was writing a book that would clear the name of Charles Cousens, proving he had indeed written scripts for her that undermined Japan's military.[40] She died before it could be completed.

●

Australia had its share of enemy undercover spies. In the German community of South Australia in the late 1930s there was a solid corps of Nazis who worshipped Hitler and sought to spread his evil ideology around the nation. Starting in the Barossa Valley, the group staged swastika-flagged rallies in rural halls and sheds. The führer of this little group was Dr Johannes Heinrich Becker, a German veteran of World War I and ship's doctor who had migrated to Australia in 1927. Becker was upset that Australia would not recognise his German medical qualifications, and secretly practised as a doctor in the German community. He visited Germany in the 1930s to join the Nazi Party and was later appointed the Nazi State's trustee for Australia.

In 1936, Becker ran foul of the German consul-general in Sydney and was sacked by the Nazi Party as their chief in Australia. When war broke out he was detained as a Nazi sympathiser and kept in a detention camp. After the war, he was deported to Germany and barred from returning to Australia to see his family. He died in Germany in 1961. His son, Heinrich Becker, was elected to the South Australian parliament in 1970 for the Liberal Party. In 2007 Heinrich asked: 'They called him a spy but what did he ever do when he was in Australia to warrant this? All he did was relay some harmless information to the early settlers in the Barossa Valley about what was happening in Germany.'[41]

Johannes Becker's successor as Nazi trustee in Australia was Walter Karl Ladendorff, who had been sent to Australia in 1929 as the agent for UFA films. He fared much better. Military intelligence recorded that Ladendorff held several meetings with pro-Nazi groups. Just four months before Hitler invaded Poland, Ladendorff was recalled to Germany. He served in the German army until 1943 when he was transferred to a senior Nazi Party position.

Then there was the mysterious case of suspected Nazi spy Annette Wagner. Swiss-born and married to a Frenchman, she grew up in England before arriving in Australia in 1938. She was on her own, explaining to visa authorities that she needed the dry air to recover from a medical condition. She presented herself as an expert on fashion and, after writing for *Australian Women's Weekly*, landed a regular spot on Sydney ABC Radio giving fashion advice and travel tips. But there were a few things about her that didn't seem quite right. Why did she meet up with Nazi sympathisers? Why, as a fashion expert, did she take a tour of the Newcastle BHP steel works? Why did she hire a small plane and pilot to fly over Newcastle and Sydney harbours while she took pictures?

Author Greg Clancy was intrigued by the story, as his uncle had piloted the plane. That in itself wasn't illegal, as there was no war on. But Clancy suspects that Wagner inserted secret coded messages for a German spy network into her radio fashion talks. 'When she commenced her program she would read out phoney cables from Paris – in French,' Clancy told the ABC in 2015. 'This was a strange thing to do considering most people couldn't speak French, but it was suspected that she might have been slipping little messages into the French.'[42]

Australian intelligence services became suspicious when they spotted her meeting Nazi sympathisers that they had under surveillance. They monitored her talking to German men on the phone and noted 'she does not make requests, she orders'. Their file on her described her as 'about 30, clever, smart, attractive, good talker and game, makings generally of a good spy'.[43] When war broke out, Wagner was barred from radio because she was a foreigner. She protested that she was Swiss and therefore neutral. It didn't help. In January 1940 she left Australia bound for Batavia (today's Jakarta). Clancy found that she had then worked for German intelligence in France during the war.[44] In 1946 she was taken to French police headquarters in Paris for questioning. She threw herself out a third-storey window, taking her spying secrets with her as she plummeted to her death.

12

THE HUNT NEVER ENDS

'If he can sit, hear and see, if he can eat,
he can also appear in a court.'

The 71-year-old woman stood up straight and proud in the German court and glared directly into the eyes of the crumpled old man in his wheelchair in the dock reserved for the accused.

Angela Orosz Richt-Bein had somehow survived being born inside Auschwitz concentration camp. The man in the wheelchair was former Auschwitz SS guard Reinhold Hanning, aged ninety-four. It all happened so long ago, but on 27 February 2016 in the courtroom of the German town of Detmold, the preceding seven decades simply evaporated. For the Auschwitz survivors it was as though the horrors of the Holocaust occurred only yesterday.

'People like you, Mr Hanning, made the hell of Auschwitz possible,' Orosz Richt-Bein thundered at him.

'People who looked on and assisted without asking questions,' she said in a strong voice that echoed around the courtroom.

'You know what happened to all the people. You enabled their murder. Tell us! Tell us!'[1]

The old man in the wheelchair heard every word. He didn't look up at his accuser. He stayed silent. What could he say? He had been a guard at Auschwitz. The court had his name in the camp records and a photo of him as a young man in SS uniform. Hanning was on trial for his complicity in 170,000 murders carried out at the Auschwitz camp during the one month he served there as a guard. Angela Orosz Richt-Bein's mother, Vera Bein, was four months pregnant when she was deported from Hungary to Auschwitz. She gave birth to Angela in the horror of the camp shortly before Christmas 1944.

Orosz Richt-Bein told the court the notorious SS doctor Josef Mengele had experimented with sterilisation drugs on her pregnant mother, injecting an acidic substance straight into her uterus. Records showed that the foetus shrank away from the injection.[2] Angela's birth in the camp months later went unnoticed because fellow prisoners provided protection by putting her mother on the top bunk at the back of the barracks for the birth. Baby Angela weighed just one kilogram. When Vera Bein had to leave the barracks for the roll call, tiny baby Angela was left behind, covered by blankets. Despite Vera's fear that guards would find the baby when she was left alone, she didn't cry out or make any noise. She was too weak to cry. Her malnourishment saved her life. Her mother managed to hide the tiny baby from guards and the evil clutches of Mengele for weeks. Five weeks after little Angela was born, Soviet troops liberated the camp. Doctors gave the baby little chance of survival. A year later, with good food to eat, Angela still weighed only three kilos – the size of a normal baby at birth. Decades later

Angela's mother told her of another mother who gave birth in Auschwitz. Mengele had bound the mother's breasts to see how long the baby could live without being fed. Mengele took notes, then had the mother and starving baby murdered.

In 2016 it was very difficult for Angela Orosz Richt-Bein to come face to face with the Auschwitz guard. This old man hadn't done anything himself to her, but he had been one of those who helped perpetrate the mass murder in the concentration camps. Angela Orosz Richt-Bein told reporters outside the court that she felt she had to give testimony 'on behalf of the six million Jews who cannot be here because they were murdered. It was more than the six million. Just think of all those children who didn't grow up and have children, not to mention the many women who survived Auschwitz but were never able to have children.'[3]

She told journalist Kate Connolly the fact Hanning was ninety-four didn't matter. 'So what if it's a death sentence for him? With ninety-four, you have no life expectancy anyway. If he can sit, hear and see, if he can eat, he can also appear in a court. He was part of the killing machine.'

She said it didn't matter how long Hanning served in prison. He had already lived a long life, while people like her father were killed at an early age. She felt it was more important that Hanning admitted what he did in Auschwitz so the Holocaust can't be denied, that people hear 'from the mouth of a Nazi what happened'.[4]

Hanning didn't deny he'd been a guard at Auschwitz. His photo and military record clearly showed he had been there. But he claimed he'd only served at Auschwitz Camp I, not the extermination Camp II at Auschwitz-Birkenau.

The chief judge involved in the Hanning trial, Anke Grudda, said prosecutors would have to prove Hanning was personally guilty of war crimes. 'We want to find out whether the defendant was in Auschwitz, in which period, and which activities he carried out.'[5] Prosecutors said Hanning was a guard at Auschwitz railway station when Jewish prisoners arrived and may have escorted some to the gas chambers.

When Hanning did speak to the court it was to express his shame. 'I want to say that it disturbs me deeply that I was part of such a criminal organisation. I am ashamed that I saw injustice and never did anything about it and I apologise for my actions. I am very, very sorry.'[6] His lawyer read a 22-page declaration from Hanning admitting that he knew mass murders were going on at the camp. 'People were shot, gassed and burned. I could see how corpses were taken back and forth or moved out. I could smell the burning bodies; I knew corpses were being burned,' the statement said. But he didn't admit he was part of the systemic murders.

In June 2016 Hanning was found guilty of being an accessory to the murder of at least 170,000 people while he was a guard at Auschwitz, and sentenced to five years in jail. He did not look up as the survivors of Auschwitz present in the court cried and embraced each other. Auschwitz survivor William Glied said the sentence wasn't important. 'What matters is that he is convicted by a German court for what he did.'[7] Hanning never went to jail. He died on 30 May 2017, waiting for his appeal to be heard, still a free man.

A year earlier, Oskar Gröning, the so-called 'book-keeper of Auschwitz', was sentenced in a German court to four years in prison.[8] He was responsible for counting belongings confiscated from prisoners and was accused of being complicit in the murder of 400,000 people while he served at Auschwitz. His lawyers argued that the ninety-four year old didn't commit genocide, but prosecutors argued he had helped Auschwitz run smoothly. Gröning admitted to the court that he had a 'moral guilt'.[9] Auschwitz survivor Leon Schwarzbaum told reporters after the verdict that he could never forgive Gröning. 'I lost 30 members of my family in Auschwitz,' he said.[10] Another survivor, Eva Kor, shook Gröning's hand in court and told reporters she forgave him. Delivering the verdict, Judge Franz Kompisch said Gröning had willingly taken a safe desk job in a system that was 'inhumane and all but unbearable for the human psyche'.[11]

The rush to have these ageing former concentration camp guards face trial in Germany began after the 2011 conviction of John Demjanjuk. The German judge had concluded that Demjanjuk's activities as a camp guard in Nazi-occupied Poland amounted to complicity in mass murder. Demjanjuk, aged ninety-one, was found guilty of being an accessory to the murder of 28,060 Jews while he served as a guard at Sobibor extermination camp.

German courts seem to have decided to bring war criminals to a final account, but it may be too late. Auschwitz guard Ernst Tremmel, aged ninety-three, died just days before he was due to go on trial for the murder of 1000 prisoners. A 92-year-old woman named under German law as Helma M was due to face trial in 2017, accused of being an accessory to the murder of 260,000 prisoners while she worked as a radio operator at Auschwitz. The 2016 trial of Hubert Zafke got bogged down in legal argument about his health and the judges' willingness to try him for being an accessory to the murder of 3681 prisoners while he was a medical orderly at Auschwitz. Zafke was charged with being a guard in one month in 1944, when fourteen trains arrived at Auschwitz carrying prisoners – including teenage diarist Anne Frank.

●

Some good has come from Germany putting these very old concentration camp guards on trial seventy years after the war. Before his trial, Gröning wrote a series of public statements about the atrocities he had personally witnessed at Auschwitz to counter German Holocaust deniers. 'I would like you to believe me,' he wrote, addressing the deniers. 'I saw the gas chambers. I saw the crematoria. I saw the open fires. I would like you to believe that these atrocities happened because I was there.'[12]

These people could not have been charged before 2011 when the judge's ruling in the Demjanjuk case made it easier to prosecute accused war criminals. Prosecutors no longer had to prove the accused actually pulled the trigger at a massacre or pushed the victim into the gas chamber. Now they just had to prove that the accused was present at the time, and was part of the group of perpetrators who committed these war crimes. The change came after decades of campaigning by Holocaust survivors, German lawyers, journalists and Nazi hunters. They had lists of more than a hundred suspected war criminals they wanted to prosecute, but there had been no chance of a conviction if they could not prove personal involvement in the war crime.

In 1958 Germany set up the Central Office of the State Justice Administrations for the Investigation of National Socialist Crimes. Still in operation, the Central Office claims to have helped track down and prosecute almost 7000 war criminals. They were urged on by Nazi hunters such as Simon Wiesenthal and married couple Serge and Beate Klarsfeld. Most Germans wanted the issue dead and buried. Wartime Nazis had found post-war jobs in all fields. The few cases that reached German courts received remarkedly light sentences. Judges often had their own Nazi past, and jurors displayed little sympathy for the victims. In October 1945 the Americans conducted an opinion poll in their sector of Allied-occupied Germany and found that thirty-nine per cent agreed with Hitler on the treatment of the Jews. Most Germans saw themselves as victims of Hitler – Hitler was the only bad man, and he had got them all to do these terrible things. German Nazi prosecutor Fritz Bauer, a former concentration camp inmate, said Germans regarded themselves as 'raped terrorised followers or depersonalised and dehumanized creatures compelled to do things that were completely alien to their nature.'[13]

In 1963, Bauer led a landmark trial of Auschwitz guards and staff in Frankfurt. The horrific stories told by the 350 Auschwitz witnesses brought home to Germans the terror of the camps. Bauer and his legal team suffered death threats and graffiti attacks on their homes. Most of the accused were acquitted and the others received lenient sentences. For decades after that, cases brought to court collapsed due to judicial resistance and the supposed confusion of ageing witnesses.

In 1974, SS camp leader Willi Sawatzki was accused of throwing 400 Hungarian children alive into a burning pit. He'd already served nine years in a Soviet prison for his part in the murder of 80,000 Jews. Witnesses told the German court that when the children tried to escape, the SS men kicked them back into the flames.[14] One witness said the children turned into tiny balls of fire who crawled over dead bodies trying to escape. After a two-year trial Sawatzki was acquitted, because the key witness for the prosecution – the person who could have identified Sawatzki – was no longer fit to be questioned. Sawatzki, aged fifty-four, walked away a free man.

In 2005 an Auschwitz staff member whose job it was to assess the value of the possessions of exterminated prisoners was ruled by a German court as carrying out a 'welcome byproduct for the war economy'.[15] Case closed.

After the 2011 Demjanjuk case eased the criterion for prosecution, the Central Office announced it would seek to prosecute another fifty low-level concentration camp staff. Only a handful will be physically able to face trial, if their cases get that far. Even if they do, the percentage of Auschwitz guards convicted for the horrors of that place will rise to just 0.48 per cent.[16]

The hunt continues. Each year the Simon Wiesenthal Center lists its most-wanted Nazi war criminals to face prosecution. The 2016 list includes six individuals living in Germany, and one in each of Canada, the US, Denmark and Sweden. Dr Efraim Zuroff, Jerusalem director of the centre, says there are many more. 'The passage of time in no way diminishes the guilt of the killers, old age should not afford protection to those who committed such heinous crimes . . .' Zuroff said.[17]

Certainly those still living who took a willing part in the terrible war crimes of World War II should be brought to trial and finally face justice. But we should not ignore the crimes of those who let so many of the worst war criminals go free or receive mockingly light punishments. We should never forget it was the Allies who embraced many of the worst murderers and torturers after the war in the belief that they could help the West in the new war against the East – a Cold War, an ideological war of capitalist versus communist. This was the greatest betrayal of those who died fighting to defeat Nazi Germany and cruel Imperialist Japan. It was the great betrayal of those who survived the war. The perpetrators of this treachery to their own people never faced justice.

They should have.

POSTSCRIPT

Australians are not innocent in the shocking litany of treachery and vile acts committed during World War II. Australia had its own human guinea pigs – servicemen who were ordered to walk into contaminated zones where chemical weapons were being tested.

In June 1939, two months before war began against Germany, the Australian government approved the import of a million chemical weapons, mostly mustard gas, from the UK and US.[1] Thousands of barrels were stored in disused railway tunnels and isolated outback depots.

Official policy was that the chemical weapons would only be used in retaliation if the enemy used chemical weapons on our troops, because to be the first to use chemical weapons in battle would breach the Geneva Protocol of 1925. This was an international agreement to prohibit the use of chemical weapons in war. It was signed after the horrors of gas used in the trenches of World War I.

Australia was a signatory, but Japan was not. Australia's military leaders noted that Italy, a signatory to the Geneva Protocol, had used chemical weapons against the Abyssinians in 1935, and thought the agreement was breaking down. The Military Board considered it essential, if Australia was invaded, to have the capacity to drop chemical weapons on advancing Japanese to contaminate food and other enemy supplies.[2]

The chemical weapons had to be tested in tropical conditions. In 1944 the Army called for volunteers to join experiments conducted on remote North Brook Island, 120 kilometres north of Townsville. Most volunteers were soldiers just returned from the Middle East, keen on the extra three shillings a day they would receive for putting their hands up to be part of the experiment. It also kept them away from the frontline in Papua New Guinea for a few precious weeks.

They were first tested wearing protective clothing and breathing apparatus, then the experiments became more extreme. Volunteers from the 9th Division, the heroes of Tobruk and El Alamein, were ordered to walk through the jungle as it was being bombed with mustard gas. All they had on were jungle uniforms, short shirt sleeves and a respirator. Members of the chemical weapons unit who tried to warn the seasoned soldiers of the dangers of the gas said that many ignored the safety precautions, taking off their respirators and brushing against the foliage dripping with the oily chemical substance. Sometimes the scientists covered the men's arms and legs in different protective creams that they were testing.

Royal Australian Air Force armourers, members of a top-secret unit who had been given rudimentary training in handling the chemicals, said the volunteers had no idea what they were walking into. Unit member Noel Stoneman told Geoff Plunkett, who later wrote an official military history on the unit, that many of the volunteers broke out in excruciatingly painful blisters after the tests. 'They screamed and screamed the whole night,' Stoneman recalled.[3] Unit Member John Crawford said many of the 'human guinea pigs' were badly burnt, their skin coming up in huge, pus-filled blisters, particularly around the groin and armpits where they sweated and the mustard gas stuck to them.[4] Some were deliberately exposed to the gas and then ordered to run an obstacle course as the blisters erupted over their skin. Unit member Bob Langsford said the scientists wanted to know how long the soldiers could keep on fighting after they had been struck with chemical weapons. After the experiments, there would be twenty to thirty volunteers recovering in a guarded, restricted ward at Innisfail Hospital, kept secret from the public and other military. Langsford said word went around, but was never confirmed, that one volunteer was in such agony he jumped out of a third-floor window to end the pain.[5]

Unit member Les Johnson said they were in Cairns when they were ordered to set up a gas chamber experiment in which they were to spray volunteers with mustard gas. But when they found that the 'volunteers' were from a nearby detention centre – men who had supposedly been promised pardons and prison reductions if they took part – the unit members refused to do it. 'Believing it unethical, three of us armourers refused to get involved,' Johnson said.[6] Their commanding officer agreed, and said they wouldn't be court-martialled as they were in a secret unit. The army couldn't let news of the chemical weapons testing on Aussie diggers get out to the public. Johnson said Americans later conducted the experiment on the inmates.

The chemical weapons were never used in battle, and after the war tens of thousands of barrels of chemicals were dumped at sea or burned in the outback. But that wasn't the end of the story. Medical records of the volunteers and unit members didn't reveal what happened to them. It was hushed up. The records didn't say what they had been exposed to, nor the long-lasting health effects. Despite having access to secret army files on the experiments, military historian Geoff Plunkett could find evidence of only two men killed from exposure to the mustard gas. The members of the unit were convinced there were many more.

The long-term consequences for the health of the unit members who spent years around the chemical weapons were disastrous. Geoff Burn saw his mates from the unit die from terrible cancers. But doctors didn't believe them when they said they worked with mustard gas during the war. The secrecy had been too effective. 'We were just fodder,' Burn said when he visited the storage site at Glenbrook at the foot of the Blue Mountains, west of Sydney, the first time he'd been there in sixty years. 'When the war was over they didn't want to know about us. They just wiped our war records. Mine said I had been attached to headquarters but I was never there.'[7]

The men of the top-secret RAAF chemical weapons unit didn't want to be part of chemical warfare. Burn and others said they joined the RAAF to fight the Japanese and defend Australia. But they suffered for the rest of their lives and were denied pensions for decades because their unit was still deemed secret. It was yet another instance of the betrayal of Anzac troops by their leaders, who failed to fight for them once the war was over.

Australians didn't need to be conscripted to fight. They stepped forward, with almost a million volunteering to take up arms and fight the evil of Nazi Germany and fanatical militaristic Japan. Forty thousand Australians gave their lives. Sure, there were tactical mistakes that cost lives. Certainly, Anzacs expected the enemy, particularly the Japanese, to disregard the supposed 'civilised rules' of warfare, such as the humane treatment of prisoners. But they did not fight so that Allied leaders on their own side could betray them after the war and allow enemy war criminals to escape justice.

Those who sought out enemy war criminals to serve in a new Cold War were traitors to all those who had fought for freedom against tyranny.

ENDNOTES

Introduction

1 Moscow Declaration on Atrocities, October 1943. Full text at: www.ibiblio.org/pha/policy/1943/431000a.html

Chapter 1

1 Len Deighton, *Blood Tears and Folly – An Objective Look at World War II*, Pimlico Random House, London, 1993, p. 590.
2 Graham Freudenberg, *Churchill and Australia*, Macmillan, Sydney, 2008, p. 261.
3 Antony Beevor, *Crete: The Battle and the Resistance*, John Murray, London, 2015, p. xv.
4 Correlli Barnett, *The Desert Generals*, Allen & Unwin, London 1960, p. 46.
5 Freudenberg, op. cit., p. 265.
6 Australian Government Department of Veterans' Affairs, *Australians in World War II: Greece and Crete*, 'Biography – Here you bloody well stay', http://anzac-portal.dva.gov.au
7 Freudenberg, op. cit., p. 265.
8 Gavin Long, *Official War History Volume 1, Greece, Crete and Syria*, Australian War Memorial, Canberra, 1953.
9 Freudenberg, op. cit., p. 271.
10 Peter Ewer, *Forgotten ANZACS – The Campaign in Greece 1941*, Scribe, Melbourne, 2008, p. 284.
11 Clement Semmler (ed.), *The War Diaries of Kenneth Slessor*, University of Queensland Press, 1985, p. 268.
12 ibid., p. 271.
13 Ewer, op. cit., p. 346.

14 George Savage statement to Australian Army staff in London, 10 April 1943. Marked Secret. File in National Archives of Australia NAA MP742/1, 255/1/79.

15 ibid., p. 2.

16 ibid.

17 ibid.

18 ibid.

19 For an excellent website of Stalag VIII-B, see www.lamsdorf.com

20 George Savage statement, loc. cit.

21 ibid.

22 ibid.

23 Weisz, G.M., 'Nazi Medical Experiments on Australian Prisoners of War – Commentary on the Testimony of an Australian soldier', *Journal of Law and Medicine*, vol. 23, no. 2, December 2015, pp. 457–59.

24 ibid.

25 ibid.

26 Konrad Kwiet, interview with author, June 2016.

Chapter 2

1 Lord Haw-Haw was a nickname given by the British to William Joyce, who broadcast propaganda for Germany during the war in an exaggerated English upper-class accent. His over-the-top performance made him a popular joke among the Allies, but he often hit home with detail of Allied losses. Born in America and raised in Ireland, he was hanged for treason after the war on the basis that he had acquired a British passport.

2 John Amery's proclamation, 20 April 1943, UK National Archives KV2/79–84.

3 Adrian Weale, *Renegades – Hitler's Englishmen*, Trafalgar Publishing, London, 1994, p. 147.

4 ibid.

5 UK Imperial War Museum K88/746.

6 National Archives of Australia NAA B883, WX1755.

7 Red Harrison, 'Diggers under the Reich', *The Weekend Australian*, 13 August 1994.

8 ibid.

9 Weale, op. cit., p. 158.

10 https://au.pinterest.com/pin/337840409516457898/

11 Harrison, loc cit.

12 Weale, op cit., 1994, pp 178–179.

13 ibid., p. 176.

14 UK National Archives KV 2/626–7.

15 'My Father the War Traitor', BBC News, 29 March 2002.

16 'Ex-Spy Prepares to be Prepared', *Canberra Times*, 25 April 1964.

17 'Man Fined for Claim to War Medals', *Canberra Times*, 11 March 1967.

18 'Campbelltown "Hero" Linked to Nazis', *Campbelltown MacArthur Advertiser*, 25 March 2009.

19 Harrison, loc. cit.

20 National Archives of Australia NAA B883, WX1839.

Chapter 3

1 Clifford Kinvig, *Churchill's Crusade – The British Invasion of Russia 1918–1920*, Hambledon Continuum, New York, 2006, p. 85.

2 Bruce Muirden, *The Diggers who Signed on for More*, Wakefield Press, Adelaide, 1990, p. 6.

3 Jonathan Walker, *Operation Unthinkable,* The History Press, Stroud, 2013, Loc 180 in ebook edition.

4 John Colville, *The Fringes of Power, Downing Street Diaries 1939–1955,* Hodder & Stoughton, London, 1985, p. 563.

5 Jonathan Walker, op. cit., Loc 623 ebook.

6 UK National Archives CAB 120/691.

7 UK National Archives CAB 120/691, 109040.

8 ibid.

9 General Lord Ismay, *The Memoirs of General Lord Ismay*, Heinemann, London, 1960, p. 392.

10 ibid., p. 393.

11 UK National Archives file CAB 120/691, 109040.

12 'Operation Unthinkable: "Russia: Threat to Western Civilization,"' British War Cabinet, Joint Planning Staff [Draft and Final Reports: 22 May, 8 June, and 11 July 1945], Public Record Office, CAB 120/691/109040/001.
   An online copy of the full report is available at https://web.archive.org/web/20101116152301/http://www.history.neu.edu/PRO2/

13 UK National Archives file CAB 120/691, 109040.

14 Report on Operation Unthinkable, chiefs of staff, 8 June 1945, UK National Archives CAB 120/691.

15 ibid.

16 Churchill memo to General Ismay, 10 June 1945, UK National Archives CAB 120/691.

17 ibid.

18 UK National Archives file CAB 120/691, 109040.

19 UK National Archives FO 954/20 #710.

20 Imperial War Museum, Montgomery Papers, BLM 162 reel 15.

21 Frank Walker, *The Tiger Man of Vietnam,* Hachette Australia, Sydney, 2009, p. 237.

22 Jonathan Walker, op. cit., Loc 2654.

23 Gian P Gentile, 'Planning for Preventative War 1945–1950', *Joint Force Quarterly*, Spring 2000.

24 US National Archives JPS PM – 44 CCS 381 5–31–45.

25 Truman, Harry S, *Memoirs of Harry S Truman 1946–1952, Years of Trial and Hope*, Smithmark, New York, 1954, p. 359.

26 Jonathan Walker, Loc 2792.

27 David Reynolds, *From World War to Cold War: Churchill, Roosevelt and the International History of the 1940s*, Oxford University Press, New York, 2006, p. 251.

28 Frank Walker, *Maralinga*, Hachette Australia, Sydney, 2014, p. 121.

Chapter 4

1 Moscow Declaration on Atrocities, op. cit.
2 John Cornwell, *Hitler's Pope*, Penguin, New York, 2008, p. xiii.
3 Alan Abrams, *Special Treatment*, Lyle Stuart, New York, 1985, p. 34.
4 Cornwell, op. cit., p. 296.
5 Katz, Robert, *Black Sabbath – The Politics of Annihilation*, Arthur Baker, London, 1969, p. 87.
6 Cornwell, op. cit., p. 304.
7 Katz, op. cit., p. 202.
8 ibid., p. 214.
9 ibid., p. 215.
10 Cornwell, op. cit., p. 309.
11 ibid., p. 313.
12 Dan Kurzman, *A Special Mission: Hitler's Secret Plot to Seize the Vatican and Kidnap Pope Pius XII*, Da Capo Press, New York, 2007, p. 12.
13 Cornwell, op. cit., p. 315.
14 Owen Chadwick, *Britain and the Vatican during the Second World War*, Cambridge University Press, Cambridge, 1986, p. 290.
15 Michael Phayer, *Pius XII, the Holocaust and the Cold War*, Indiana University Press, Indianapolis, 2008, p. 180.
16 Colonel-General Grigori Krivosheev, *Soviet Casualties and Combat Losses*, Greenhill Books, London, 1997, p. 276.
17 Gerald Posner and John Ware, *Mengele: The Complete Story*, McGraw-Hill, New York, p. 63.
18 ibid., p. 87.
19 ibid., p. 85.
20 Gerald Steinacher, *Nazis on the Run: How Hitler's Henchmen Fled Justice*, Oxford University Press, Oxford, 2012, p. 25.
21 Posner and Ware, op. cit., p. 113.
22 ibid., p. 279.
23 Ofer Aderet, 'Ultra-Orthodox Man Buys Diaries of Nazi Doctor Mengele for $245,000', *Haaretz*, 22 July 2011. http://www.haaretz.com
24 *Frankfurter Allgemeine Zeitung*, 26 September 2011, p. 4.
25 'How the Nazis Escaped Justice', *The Independent*, 28 January 2013.
26 'Wanted Nazi Walther Rauff "was West German spy"', BBC News, 27 September 2011.
27 Gitta Sereny, *Into that Darkness: From Mercy Killing to Mass Murder*, Vintage Digital, new edition 2013, p. 289.
28 ibid., pp. 289–290.
29 AS Rosenbaum, *Prosecuting Nazi War Criminals*, Westview Press, Boulder Colorado, 1993, p. 16.
30 US National Archives declassified secret file dispatch no. NGMA 32934.
31 Julian Borger, 'Why Israel's Capture of Eichmann Caused Panic at the CIA', *The Guardian*, 8 June 2006.
32 Tom Bower, *Blind Eye to Murder*, Andre Deutsch, London 1981, p. 379.
33 ibid., p. 380.

34 Borger, loc. cit.

35 John Loftus and Mark Aarons, *The Secret War Against the Jews – How Western Espionage Betrayed the Jewish People*, St Martin's Press, New York, 1994, p. 46.

36 Heinz Höhne and Hermann Zolling, *The General was a Spy – The Truth about General Gehlen and his Spy Ring*, Coward, McCann & Geoghegan Inc., New York, 1972, p. 31.

37 Magnus Linklater, Isabel Hilton and Neal Ascherson, *Klaus Barbie – The Fourth Reich*, Coronet Books, London, 1985, p. 169.

38 ibid.

39 US National Archives, 1967 memo for CIA deputy director, ZZ-16 box 4, Barbie Klaus.

40 Georg Bönisch and Klaus Wiegrefe, 'From Nazi Criminal to Postwar Spy: German Intelligence Hired Klaus Barbie as Agent', *Spiegel* magazine, 20 January 2011, http://www.spiegel.de/international/germany/from-nazi-criminal-to-postwar-spy-german-intelligence-hired-klaus-barbie-as-agent-a-740393.html

41 Linklater et al, p. 285; Damien Lewis, *The Nazi Hunters*, Quercus, London, 2016, p. 399.

42 Adam Chandler, 'Eichmann's Best Man Lived and Died in Syria', *The Atlantic* magazine, 1 December 2014.

43 Jodi Rudoren, 'A Long Sought Fugitive Died Four Years Ago in Syria, Nazi hunter says', *New York Times*, 1 December 2014.

44 Tim Weiner, *Legacy of Ashes – The History of the CIA*, Anchor Books, New York, 2008, p. 46.

45 Simon Wiesenthal Center, Vienna Documentation Center. http://www.wiesenthal.com/site/pp.asp?c=lsKWLbPJLnF&b=4441355

Chapter 5

1 Timothy Naftali, 'New Information on Cold War CIA Stay-Behind Operations in Germany and on the Adolf Eichmann Case', files available through http://www.fas.org/sgp/eprint/naftali.pdf

2 Calwell, A.A., *Be Just and Fear Not*, Lloyd O'Neil, Melbourne, 1972, p. 103.

3 Hansard, 2 December 1947, p. 2948.

4 Andrew Menzies, *Review of Material Relating to the Entry of Suspected War Criminals into Australia*, Australian Government Publishing Service, Canberra, 1987, p. 40.

5 Leslie Caplan, *The Road to the Menzies Inquiry – Suspected War Criminals in Australia*, Australian Jewish Historical Society, Sydney, 2012, p. 37.

6 Menzies, op. cit., p. 70.

7 Outward telegram from Commonwealth Relations Office, 13 July 1948.

8 *Truth,* 4 December 1949, p. 1.

9 Caplan, op. cit., p. 46.

10 Australian National Archives File No. A1842 item no. 1550/18.

11 Australian National Archives File A1838 item no. 1550/20.

12 Mark Aarons, *Sanctuary – Nazi Fugitives in Australia*, Octopus Publishing, Melbourne, 1990, p. 187.

13 Hansard, 22 March 1961, p. 451.

14 Mark Aarons, *War Criminals Welcome: Australia, A Sanctuary for Fugitive War Criminals Since 1945,* Black Inc., Melbourne, 2001, p. 449.
15 Mark Aarons, *The Family File,* Black Inc, Melbourne, 2010, p. xi.
16 Hansard, 23 August 1979, p. 555.
17 Aarons, *War Criminals Welcome,* op. cit., p. 460.
18 Aarons, *Sanctuary,* op. cit., p. 15.
19 *Sydney Morning Herald,* 29 August, 1979.
20 Kandell, Jonathan, 'Kurt Waldheim Dies at 88; ex-UN Chief Hid Nazi Past', *New York Times,* 14 June 2007.
21 Mark Aarons and John Loftus, 'Nazis in Australia', ABC Radio National, Background Briefing, 13 April, 20 April, 27 April 1986.
22 Mark Aarons and John Loftus, *Ratlines – How the Vatican's Nazi Networks Betrayed Western Intelligence to the Soviets,* Mandarin, London 1991, p. 82.
23 Caplan, op cit., p. 69.
24 Aarons and Loftus, 'Nazis in Australia', op. cit.
25 *Four Corners,* ABC television, 21 April 1986.
26 NSW Hansard 16 April 1986.
27 ibid.
28 Mark Aarons, *War Criminals Welcome,* op. cit., p. 530.
29 'Unit Failed to Nail War Criminals', *The Australian,* 2 January 2014.
30 Andrew Menzies, op. cit., pp. 113–115, 127–131.
31 Aarons, *War Criminals Welcome,* op. cit., p. 474.
32 ibid., p. 187.
33 ibid., p. 188.
34 National Archives Australia file A6119, 2723.
35 National Archives Australia file A6119/90.
36 Aarons, *War Criminals Welcome,* op. cit., p. 459.
37 Barkham, Patrick, *Konrad Kalejs obituary, The Guardian,* 12 November 2001.
38 Simon Mann, 'US Report Damns Australian Efforts to Convict War Criminals', *Sydney Morning Herald,* 16 November 2010.
39 Horner, Donald, *The Spy Catchers – The Official History of ASIO 1949–1963,* Allen & Unwin, Sydney, 2014. Loc 5262 in ebook format.
40 'Australian Migrants Denied Citizenship on Political Grounds Demand Recognition', *The Guardian, Australia,* 11 July 2016.
41 Horner, op. cit., Loc 5542.
42 ibid., Loc 5581.
43 ibid., Loc 5591.
44 ibid., Loc 5619.

Chapter 6

1 Dower, John, *War Without Mercy – Race and Power in the Pacific War,* Pantheon, New York, 1987, p. 22.
2 'The Tanaka Plan – Japan's Blueprint for World Conquest', Lloyd Wendt, *Chicago Tribune,* 15 February 1942; Dower, John W, *War Without Mercy – Race and Power in the Pacific War,* Pantheon, New York, 1987, p. 22.

3   Maritime Union of Australia website, 'The Dog Collar Act',
    www.mua.org.au
4   Isaac Isaacs, 'Australian Democracy and our Constitutional System', 1939,
    quoted in 'Echo of Dalfram Dispute', *Illawarra Mercury*, 14 April 1939, p. 6.
5   'Menzies and Pig Iron for Japan', *Sydney Morning Herald*, 17 July 1993.
6   Menzies weekly radio broadcast, 3 April 1942, transcript published in *The
    Forgotten People*, Chapter 11, 'Scrap Iron for Japan', Menzies Foundation,
    www.menziesvirtualmuseum.org.au
7   Bank for International Settlements, 'BIS history – the BIS and the Second
    World War', http://www.bis.org/about/history_2ww2.htm
8   Adam Lebor, 'Never Mind the Czech Gold the Nazis Stole', *The Telegraph*
    (UK), 31 July 2013.
9   Michael Hirsh, 'Nazi Gold – The Untold Story', *Newsweek*, 4 November 1996.
10 Charles Higham, *Trading with the Enemy*, Robert Hale, London, 1983,
    pp. 17–19, citing Nuremberg trial evidence.
11 Beth Piskora, 'Chase Apologises for Doing Biz with Nazis', *New York Post*, 23
    February 2000.
12 'Barclays to Compensate Jews', BBC News, 17 December 1998.
13 Ben Aris and Duncan Campbell, 'How Bush's Grandfather Helped Hitler's Rise
    to Power', *The Guardian*, 26 September 2004.
14 ibid.
15 Edwin Black, *IBM and the Holocaust*, Crown, New York, 2001, p. 8.
16 ibid., p. 9.
17 ibid., p. 43.
18 Edwin Black, 'IBM's Role in the Holocaust – What the New Documents
    Reveal', *Huffington Post*, 27 February 2012, updated 17 March 2015.
19 ibid.
20 ibid.
21 ibid. A photo of the machine is available at http://www.jewishvirtuallibrary.org/
    jsource/images/Holocaust/hollerith.jpg
22 ibid.
23 Edwin Black, *IBM and the Holocaust*, op. cit., p. 279.
24 ibid., p. 276.
25 ibid., p. 344.
26 'Watson Tells of Orders', *New York Times,* 15 March 1942.
27 Edwin Black, *IBM and the Holocaust*, op. cit., p. 345.
28 ibid., p. 348.
29 ibid., p. 398.
30 ibid., pp. 406–7.
31 'IBM Statement on Nazi-era Book and Lawsuit', 14 Feb 2001 http://www-03.
    ibm.com/press/us/en/pressrelease/1388.wss
32 'Addendum to IBM Statement on Nazi-era Book and Lawsuit', 29 March 2002,
    http://www-03.ibm.com/press/us/en/pressrelease/828.wss
33 *Scientific and Technical Mobilization: Hearings Before a Subcommittee of the
    Committee on Military Affairs*, United States Senate, 78th Congress, 1st session,
    S. 702, Part 16, Washington: Government Printing Office, 1944, p. 939.
34 Higham, op. cit., p. 34.

35 ibid.
36 Chesly Manly, 'Truman Accuses Standard Oil of Rubber "Treason"', *Chicago Tribune*, 27 March 1942, p. 12.
37 Higham, op. cit., p. 36.
38 Chesly Manly, loc. cit.
39 David McCullough, *Truman*, Simon & Schuster, New York, 1992, p. 267.
40 Glen Yeadon, *The Nazi Hydra in America*, Progressive Press, Joshua Tree California, p. 141.
41 Higham, op. cit., pp. 93–95.
42 ibid., p. 115.
43 Peter Handel, 'Another Big Story the Mainstream Media Missed: GE-Krupp Conspiracy Trial of '47', Truthout, http://www.truth-out.org/news/item/15892-another-one-the-msm-missed-ge-krupp-conspiracy-trial-of-47
44 United States v. General Electric Co., 80 F. Supp. 989 (S.D.N.Y. 1948), 8 October 1948, http://law.justia.com/cases/federal/district-courts/FSupp/80/989/1869204/
45 Higham, op. cit., pp. 116–117.
46 ibid., p. 121.
47 *News Chronicle*, London, 19 October 1943.
48 Higham, op. cit., p. 123.
49 ibid.
50 ibid., p. 126.
51 ibid., p. 127.
52 Henry Ford, *The International Jew – Jewish Influences in American Life*, four volumes first printed 1921, reprinted by University Press of the Pacific, Honolulu, 2003.
53 'Ford and GM Scrutinized for Alleged Nazi Collaboration', Michael Dobbs, *Washington Post*, 30 November 1998.
54 US National Archives document 862.00S/6 report, 'Money Sources of Hitler', from US embassy in Berlin.
55 Josiah E Dubois, *Generals in Grey Suits*, The Bodley Head, London 1958, p. 249.
56 Higham, op. cit., p. 161.
57 Michael Dobbs, 'Ford and GM Scrutinized for Alleged Nazi Collaboration', *Washington Post,* 30 November 1998, p. 1.
58 Higham, op. cit., p. 162.
59 ibid.
60 You can watch the video here: https://www.youtube.com/watch?v=qAJXHPaWUWw)
61 'Coca Cola pulls "Nazi" Fanta advertisement which referred to the 1940s as "the good old times"', Zoe Szathmary, *Daily Mail*, 5 March 2015.

Chapter 7

1 Peter Monteith, *P.O.W. – Australian Prisoners of War in Hitler's Reich*, Pan Macmillan, Sydney, 2011 loc4844 in ebook format. The nine Australians interned in Buchenwald are named in Monteith's book as Mervyn Fairclough,

James Gwilliam, Eric Johnston, Kevin Light, Thomas Malcolm, Keith Mills, Robert Mills, Raymond Perry and Les Whellum. After four terrible months they were moved to POW camp Stalag Luft III – site of the famous Great Escape.

2 Sabine and Harry Stein, *Buchenwald Memorial Guide Book,* Buchenwald Memorial, 1983, p. 47.
3 Knigge, Volkhard, *The Engineers of the Final Solution – Topf & Sons, Builders of the Auschwitz Ovens*, Buchenwald and Mittelbau-Dora Memorials Foundation, Weimar, 2005, p. 6.
4 ibid.
5 ibid., p. 7.
6 ibid., p. 73.
7 ibid., p. 74.
8 Topf & Sons – Builders of the Auschwitz Ovens Place of Remembrance, http://www.topfundsoehne.de/cms-www/index.php?id=75&l=1
9 'Nokia Hastily Pulls Ad using Nazi slogan', *Advertising Age,* 18 June 1998.
10 David Wroe, 'Petrol Station used Nazi Slogan on Posters', *The Telegraph* (UK), 14 January 2009.
11 UK National Archives FO 371 57587, Nuremberg Trials Deposition no. 313.
12 William Manchester, *The Arms of Krupp*, Bantam Books, New York, 1970, p. 576.
13 ibid., p. 625.
14 Tom Bower, *Blind Eye to Murder: Britain, America and the Purging of Nazi Germany – A Pledge Betrayed*, Andre Deutsch, London, 1981, p. 338.
15 ibid., p. 339.
16 Joseph Borkin, *The Crime and Punishment of I.G. Farben*, The Free Press, New York, 1978, p. 123.
17 ibid., p. 113.
18 US National Archives collection of World War II War Crimes Records, file VIII, NI-151148, p.375.
19 ibid., p. 405.
20 Josiah DuBois, *The Devil's Chemists*, Beacon Press, Boston, 1952, p. 229.
21 US National Archives collection of World War II War Crimes Records, NI-4830.
22 US National Archives collection of World War II War Crimes Records, VIII NI-10040, pp. 532–535.
23 DuBois, op. cit., p.220. This toll estimate was taken from a 1947 affidavit to the Nuremberg Trial of prisoner Ervin Schulhof, who worked as a labour deployment clerk.
24 UK National Archives file FO 371 39007/C15544.
25 UK National Archives files FO 371 57583/U2996 and 57583/U2439.
26 Borkin, op. cit., pp. 139–140.
27 US National Archives collection of World War II War Crimes Records, VIII, NI-12388, p. 621.
28 US National Archives collection of World War II War Crimes Records, VIII NI-11696.
29 Borkin, op. cit., p. 154.

30 Wollheim Memorial, 'Otto Ambros (1901–1990)', http://www.wollheim-memorial.de/en/otto_ambros_19011990. The online research centre is named for Norbert Wollheim, a survivor of IG Farben's Auschwitz forced labour factory who sought compensation from the firm.
31 Wollheim Memorial, ' Walther Dürrfeld (1899–1967)' http://www.wollheim-memorial.de/en/walther_duerrfeld_18991967
32 Bower, op. cit., p. 364.
33 ibid., p. 17, citing a report of the Office of the Military Government, United States, p. 160, kept at the US National Archive.
34 Jonathan Wiesen, *West German Industry and the Challenge of the Nazi Past 1945–1955*, University of North Carolina Press, Chapel Hill NC, 2001, p. 28.
35 Office of the Military Government, United States, p. 160, kept at the US National Archive, p.164.
36 'Hugo Boss Apology for Nazi Past as Book is Published', BBC, 21 September 2011.
37 Edmund L Andrews, 'Germany Accepts $5.1 Billion Accord to End Claims of Nazi Slave Workers', *New York Times*, 18 December 1999.
38 'Germany to Pay 772 million Euros to Survivors', *Der Spiegel*, 29 May 2013.

Chapter 8

1 Tom Bower, *Blind Eye to Murder: Britain, America and the Purging of Nazi Germany – A Pledge Betrayed*, Andre Deutsch, London, 1981, p. 111.
2 Annie Jacobsen, *Operation Paperclip – The Secret Intelligence Program that Brought Nazi Scientists to America*, Little Brown and Co., New York, 2014, ebook, Loc 34.
3 ibid., Loc 96.
4 ibid., Loc 107.
5 Bower, op. cit., p. 112.
6 US National Archives, FBI Counterintelligence file 105–10525.
7 Bower, op. cit., p. 112.
8 CG Lasby, *Project Paperclip*, Atheneum, New York, 1971, p. 38.
9 Bower, op. cit., p. 113.
10 Angela Fiedermann, Torsten Hess and Markus Jaeger, *Das KZ Mittelbau-Dora,* Westkreuz-Verlag, Berlin, 1993, p. 100.
11 'Aide Says von Braun wasn't Able to Stop Slave Horrors', *The Huntsville Times*, 26 October 2002.
12 Jacobsen, op. cit., loc 6733.
13 US National Archives collection of World War II War Crimes Records, RG 201–238.
14 Richard J Aldrich, *The Hidden Hand: Britain, America, and Cold War Secret Intelligence,* Overlook Press, New York, 2002, p. 187.
15 Australian National Archives NAA A367, C83656.
16 Gerard Ryle and Gary Hughes, 'How Australia Raided the Great Minds of Hitler's War Machine', *Sydney Morning Herald*, 16 August 1999.
17 Australian National Archives NAA A367, C83656.
18 Australian National Archives NAA A367, C83656, 1/6/1690.

19 'Professor Who Helped in Selection Praised Fuhrer', *Sydney Morning Herald*, 17 August 1999.
20 Australian National Archives NAA A367, C83656.
21 David Sadleir, 'Lloyd, Eric Edwin Longfield (1890–1957)', *Australian Dictionary of Biography*, Vol 15, MUP, 2000 http://adb.anu.edu.au/biography/lloyd-eric-edwin-longfield-10840.
22 Australian National Archives NAA A367, C83656.
23 Gerard Ryle and Gary Hughes, 'Rocket Science', *Sydney Morning Herald,* 21 August 1999.
24 Gretchen E Schafft and Gerhard Zeidler, *Commemorating Hell: The Public Memory of Mittelbau-Dora*, University of Illinois Press, Chicago, 2011, p. 26.
25 Australian National Archives NAA A367, C83656.
26 Fuchs, a communist, had fled to Britain in 1933 and was given UK citizenship. He was exposed by MI5 as a spy shortly after the Soviets exploded their first atom bomb. In January 1950, Fuchs admitted to MI5 he had supplied atomic secrets to the Soviets for years. Fuchs was sentenced in the UK to fifteen years jail, released after nine, and he moved to East Germany where he was welcomed as a hero.
27 Australian National Archives, 'Employment of Scientific and Technical Enemy Aliens – ESTEA 1947 to 1951', NAA A367, C83656.
28 Australian National Archives NAA A367, C83656.
29 Gerard Ryle and Gary Hughes, 'War Crimes Unit in the Dark on Scientists Says Adviser', *Sydney Morning Herald,* 17 August 1999.
30 'QC Suggests a Nazi Cover-up', *Sydney Morning Herald*, 18 August 1999.
31 Australian National Archives NAA A367, C83656.

Chapter 9

1 Hearing before the Committee on Veterans' Affairs, US House of Representatives, 17 September 1986, p. 17.
2 Peter Williams and David Wallace, *Unit 731 – The Japanese Army's Secret of Secrets*, Hodder & Stoughton, London, 1989, p. 56.
3 Australian War Memorial recorded interview with Desmond James Brennan https://www.awm.gov.au/collection/S02993/
4 Williams and Wallace, op. cit., p. 55.
5 Linda Goetz Holmes, *Guests of the Emperor*, Naval Institute Press, Annapolis Maryland, 2010, p. 22.
6 ibid., p. 22.
7 'POWs Claim Germ Warfare Coverup by US', *The Mercury News*, San Jose, California, 13 August 1995.
8 Holmes, op. cit., p. 21.
9 ibid., p. 27.
10 ibid., p. 20.
11 Fuyuko Nishisato, article in *Quarterly Report on Japan's War Responsibility*, summer 1996, cited in Holmes, op. cit., p. 19.
12 Sheldon Harris, *Factories of Death: Japanese Biological Warfare 1932–1945 and the American Cover-up*, Routledge, New York, 2002, p. 18.

13 ibid., p. 33.
14 ibid., p. 33.
15 ibid., p. 60.
16 Daniel Barenblatt, *A Plague upon Humanity, The Hidden History of Japan's Biological Warfare Program,* Perennial, New York, 2005, p. 77.
17 Figures gleaned from Unit 731 captives' testimony at the Khabarovsk War Crimes Trials in 1949 contained in the Soviet record – Otozo Yamada, *Materials on the Trial of Former Servicemen of the Japanese Army Charged with Manufacturing and Employing Bacteriological Weapons,* Foreign Languages Publishing House, Moscow, 1950 – held at New York Public Library.
18 Harris, op. cit., p. 101.
19 Barenblatt, op. cit., p. 190.
20 ibid., p. 192.
21 ibid., p. 197.
22 ibid., p. 218.
23 Justin McCurry, 'Japan Revisits its Darkest Moments where American POWs Became Human Experiments', *The Guardian,* 14 August 2015.
24 Gavan Daws, *Prisoners of the Japanese,* Scribe, Melbourne, 1994, p. 258.
25 ibid., pp. 258–259.
26 Australian National Archives MP375/14 WC51.
27 Testimony of 1st Lt. James A. McMurria regarding medical experiments and executions at Rabaul Tunnel Hill POW Camp, 21 July 1948. National Archives of Australia MP742/1, 336/1/1398, Parts 1, 2, 3.
28 Australian National Archives file cited in Rory Callinan, 'Commandos' Horrific End Kept Secret', *Sydney Morning Herald,* 5 October 2013, News Review section, p. 3.
29 Harris, p. 245.
30 ibid, p. 229.
31 US National Archives Record Group 107, biological warfare folder, Box 2
32 US National Archives Record Group 331, Box1434, 20 Case 330
33 'Virus Used on Captives', *New York Times,* 6 January 1946, p. 30.
34 Harris, op. cit., p. 244.
35 US National Archives Counterintelligence G2 file GHQ FEC APO 500 US – file No. 210 Book no. 1 Ishii.
36 US National Archives Record Group 331 Box 1772/330.
37 Barenblatt, op. cit., p. 207.
38 ibid., p. 212.
39 Harris, op. cit., p. 278.
40 US National Archives Record Group 153, Entry 145, Box 73, 000.5.
41 John Pritchard and Sonia Zaide (eds), *Proceedings of the International Military Tribunal of the Far East,* Garland, New York, 1981, Vol. 2, record for 29 August 1946, pp. 4546–4552.
42 Otozo Yamada, *Materials on the Trial of Former Servicemen of the Japanese Army Charged with Manufacturing and Employing Bacteriological Weapons,* Foreign Languages Publishing House, Moscow, 1950, p. 16.
43 ibid., p. 17.
44 ibid., p. 96.

45 Harris, op. cit., p. 320.
46 Barenblatt, op. cit., p. 227.
47 Harris, op. cit., p. 338.
48 ibid., p. 343.
49 Daws, op. cit., p. 375.
50 Barenblatt, op. cit., p. 227.
51 Phillip Knightley, *The First Casualty*, Harcourt Brace Jovanovich, New York, 1975, p. 355.
52 *New York Times* obituary, 17 December 2008.
53 Williams and Wallace, op. cit., *Unit 731*, p. 301.

Chapter 10

1 Dramatisation of the attack on *Vyner Brooke* reconstructed from accounts given by survivors, including Bullwinkel. For a longer depiction see Manners, Norman, *Bullwinkel*, Hesperian Press, Carlisle Western Australia, 1999, pp. 68–75.
2 Australian War Memorial, Vivian Bullwinkel collection, PRO1216
3 ibid.
4 AWM 54 1010/6/128
5 Bullwinkel's evidence to the Tokyo War Crimes Trial, 20 December 1946, held at the Australian War Memorial, Bullwinkel Papers Series 1, Folio 1/40.
6 Peter Thompson and Robert Macklin, *Kill the Tiger – Operation Rimau and the Battle for Southeast Asia*, Maverick House, Bangkok, 2007, p. 219.
7 ibid., pp. 233–234.
8 Frank Walker, *Commandos*, Hachette Australia, Sydney, 2015, p. 264.
9 ibid., p. 264.
10 Thompson and Macklin, op. cit., p. 241.
11 ibid., pp. 260–261.
12 National Archives of Australia MP742/1, 336/1/755.
13 Antony Beevor, *The Second World War*, Weidenfeld & Nicolson, London, 2012, p. 780.
14 Figures from National Archives of Australia MP742, A336/1/29.
15 Australian Archives MP742/1, 336/1/1444.
16 DCS Sissons, 'Australian War Crimes Trials and Investigations (1942–51)', published online by University of California, Berkeley, p. 54 https://www.ocf.berkeley.edu/~changmin/documents/Sissons%20Final%20War%20Crimes%20Text%2018-3-06.pdf
17 'Soldiers Warn Guilty Japs', *Daily Telegraph*, 22 February 1946.
18 Figures from Michael Carrel, *Australia's Prosecution of Japanese War Criminals – Stimuli and Constraints*, PhD thesis, University of Melbourne Law Faculty, August 2005, p. 101. Available at Australian War Memorial MSS1809.
19 National Archives of Australia A5954, Box 453, cable no. 209.
20 National Archives of Australia A5954, Box 453, cable no. 230.
21 National Archives of Australia A5954, Box 453, cable no. 303.
22 MacArthur to Chief-of-Staff US Army, cable, 25 January 1946 in John Reid and Herbert Fine (eds.), *Foreign Relations of the United States, 1946, Vol 8*

(The Far East), United States Government Printing Office, Washington, 1971, pp. 395–397.

23 BVA Röling and CF Ruter (eds.), *The Tokyo Judgment,* University Press, Amsterdam, 1977, Vol. 1, p. 478.

24 Cornelius Ryan, *Star Spangled Mikado*, McBride and Co, New York, 1947, p. 53.

25 Daws, op. cit., p. 369.

26 Schaller, Michael, 'America's Favorite War Criminal: Kishi Nobusuke and the Transformation of U.S.–Japan Relations', Japan Policy Research Institute, 11 July 1995.

27 Daws, op. cit., p. 374.

28 '"We must never repeat the horrors of war": Japanese PM Shinzo Abe offers condolences at Pearl Harbor', Jeff Mason, *Sydney Morning Herald*, 28 December 2016.

29 Justin McCurry, 'Anger as Japanese Minister Visits "War Crimes" Shrine After Pearl Harbor Trip', *The Guardian*, 29 December 2016.

Chapter 11

1 Higham, Charles, *Errol Flynn – The Untold Story*, Granada Publishing, London, 1980.

2 'A Scourge of Hollywood and Nazis', Philippe Mora, *Sydney Morning Herald*, 7 May 2012.

3 'Errol Flynn Spied for Allies, not Nazis', David Bamber and Chris Hastings, *The Telegraph*, 31 December 2000.

4 ibid., p. 84.

5 Higham, op. cit., pp. 108–116.

6 ibid., p. 114.

7 'Errol Flynn "Worked as a Nazi Spy and Met Adolf Hitler"', *The Telegraph*, 11 July 2009.

8 Higham, op. cit., p. 150.

9 ibid., p. 184.

10 ibid., pp. 162–163.

11 ibid., p. 165.

12 ibid., p. 173.

13 ibid., pp. 186–187.

14 http://filmstarfacts.com/2015/04/28/errol-flynn-1909–1959/

15 Ryan Kisiel and Neil Sears, 'Did Hitler Recruit Errol Flynn as a Spy for the Nazis?', *Daily Mail*, 11 July 2009.

16 Charles Higham, *Trading with the Enemy*, op. cit., p. 181.

17 Major-General Smedley D Butler, *War is a Racket*, Feral House, Los Angeles, 1935. Reprinted online by Aristeus Books, Chicago, 2014.

18 Jules Archer, *The Plot to Seize the White House*, Hawthorne Books, New York, 1973, p. 26.

19 ibid., p. 29.

20 ibid., p. 136.

21 'Gen. Butler Bares "Fascist Plot to Seize Government by Force"', *New York Times*, 21 November 1934, p. 1.

22 Archer, op. cit., p. 186.
23 ibid., p. 192.
24 ibid., p. 198.
25 'Dodd Resigns Post as Envoy to Reich', *New York Times*, 8 December 1937.
26 'Dodd Back, Bitter on Dictatorships', *New York Times*, 7 January 1938.
27 Higham, op. cit., *Trading with the Enemy*, p. 181.
28 ibid., p. 182.
29 Andrew Morton, *17 Carnations – The Windsors, The Nazis and the Cover-Up*, Michael O'Mara Books Ltd, London, 2015, ebook, p. 205.
30 ibid., p. 212.
31 ibid., p. 216.
32 UK National Archives PF1153 Volumes 1, 2, 3.
33 Paul Lashmar and Andrew Mullins, 'Churchill Protected Scottish Peer Suspected of Spying for Japan', *The Independent*, 24 August 1998.
34 Paul Elston, *The Fall of Singapore – The Great Betrayal*, BBC documentary, 2012. https://www.youtube.com/watch?v=hPwil1SaAW8
35 The National Archives UK, KV 2/871.
36 *Hitler's British Girl*, Channel 4 documentary, 2007, https://www.youtube.com/watch?v=Z9kBH47Ohlg
37 Peter Elphic, 'Cover-ups and the Singapore Traitor Affair', *www.abc.net.au*, 28 November 2001 http://www.abc.net.au/4corners/specials/noprisoners/view-points/elphick.htm
38 Ivan Chapman, 'Cousens, Charles Hughes (1903–1964)', *Australian Dictionary of Biography*, Vol. 13, MUP, 1993 http://adb.anu.edu.au/biography/cousens-charles-hughes-9842
39 ibid.
40 Terry Smyth, 'Tokyo Rose: I Can Clear Aussie Traitor', *Sun-Herald*, 6 June 1999.
41 'How Hitler's Man in Australia Could Have Changed the Course Of Politics', *Herald-Sun*, 29 November 2016.
42 Matthew Bevan, 'Annette Wagner – The Nazi Spy Who May Have Used ABC Radio to Send Encoded Messages Before WWII', ABC Radio, 11 August 2015.
43 Greg Clancy, *Hitler's Lost Spy*, Sunda Publications, Sydney, 2014, p. 176.
44 ibid., pp. 177–180.

Chapter 12

1 Philip Oltermann, 'Auschwitz Trial: Former Guard "Made Hell Possible" Says Witness Born Inside Camp', *The Guardian*, 27 February 2016.
2 Kate Connolly, '"Your Whole Life is the Holocaust!" The Woman who was Born in Auschwitz', *The Guardian*, 5 March 2016.
3 ibid.
4 ibid.
5 Oltermann, loc. cit.
6 'Auschwitz Trial: Ex-Guard Reinhold Hanning "Ashamed"', BBC, 29 April 2016.
7 'Former Auschwitz Guard Rheinhold Hanning Convicted', BBC, 17 June 2016.

8 Coralie Febvre, 'Ex-Nazi "Bookkeeper of Auschwitz" Asks For Forgiveness', *Agence France Press*, 22 April 2015.
9 Kate Connolly, '"Bookkeeper of Auschwitz" admits moral guilt', *The Guardian*, 22 April 2015.
10 'Auschwitz Book-Keeper Sentenced to Four Years', BBC, 15 July 2015.
11 Kate Connolly, 'Accountant of Auschwitz Jailed for the Murder of 300,000 Jews', *The Guardian*, 16 July 2015.
12 Matthias Geyer, 'An SS Officer Remembers – The Bookkeeper from Auschwitz', *Der Spiegel*, 9 May 2005.
13 Klaus Wiegrefe, 'Why the Last SS Guards Will Go Unpunished', *Der Spiegel*, 28 August 2014.
14 ibid.
15 ibid.
16 ibid.
17 Simon Wiesenthal Center Annual Report 2016 http://www.wiesenthal.com/site/apps/nlnet/content2.aspx?c=lsKWLbPJLnF&b=9356941&ct=14848993#.V1kyQU1JmbM

Postscript

1 Geoff, Plunkett *Chemical Warfare in Australia*, Australian Military History Publications, Canberra, 2007, p. 12.
2 ibid., p. 11
3 ibid., p. 248
4 ibid., p. 263
5 ibid., page 267
6 ibid., p. 273
7 Frank Walker, 'Deadly Chemicals Hidden in War Cache', *Sun-Herald*, 20 January 2008.

BIBLIOGRAPHY

Aarons, Mark, *The Family File*, Black Inc., Melbourne, 2010.

Aarons, Mark, *Sanctuary: Nazi Fugitives in Australia*, Mandarin, Melbourne, 1990.

Aarons, Mark, *War Criminals Welcome: Australia, a Sanctuary for Fugitive War Criminals Since 1945*, Black Inc., Melbourne, 2001.

Aarons, Mark, and Loftus, John, *Ratlines: How the Vatican's Nazi Networks Betrayed Western Intelligence to the Soviets*, Mandarin, London, 1991.

Aarons, Mark, and Loftus, John, *Unholy Trinity: The Vatican, the Nazis and Soviet Intelligence*, St Martin's Press, New York, 1991.

Abrams, Alan, *Special Treatment*, Lyle Stuart Inc., New York, 1985.

Aldrich, Richard J, *The Hidden Hand: Britain, America, and Cold War Secret Intelligence*, Overlook Press, New York, 2002.

Archer, Jules, *The Plot to Seize the White House*, Hawthorne Books, New York, 1973.

Armstrong, Stephen, *War PLC*, faber & faber, London, 2008.

BBC Radio, *The White House Coup – Prescott Bush Led Nazi Coup Attempt in 1933*, 28 September, 2008.

Barenblatt, Daniel, *A Plague upon Humanity: The Hidden History of Japan's Biological Warfare Program*, Perennial, New York, 2005.

Correlli Barnett, *The Desert Generals*, Allen & Unwin, London, 1960.

Beevor, Antony, *Crete: The Battle and the Resistance*, John Murray, London, 2015.

Beevor, Antony, *The Second World War*, Weidenfeld & Nicolson, London, 2012.

Black, Edwin, *IBM and the Holocaust: The Strategic Alliance Between Nazi Germany and America's Most Powerful Corporation*, Crown Publishers, New York, 2001.

Borkin, Joseph, *The Crime and Punishment of I.G. Farben*, The Free Press, New York, 1978.

Bower, Tom, *Blind Eye to Murder: Britain, America and the Purging Of Nazi Germany – A Pledge Betrayed*, Andre Deutsch, London, 1981.

Breitman, Richard and Goda, Norman JW, *Hitler's Shadow – Nazi War Criminals, US Intelligence, and the Cold War,* Published by the US National Archives and Records Administration, Washington DC, 2009.

Butler, Major-General Smedley, *War is a Racket*, Feral House, Los Angeles, 1935. Reprinted online by Aristeus Books, Chicago, 2014.

Calwell, Arthur, *Be Just and Fear Not*, Lloyd O'Neil, Melbourne, 1972.

Caplan, Leslie, *The Road to the Menzies Inquiry – Suspected War Criminals in Australia,* Australian Jewish Historical Society, Sydney, 2012.

Carrel, Michael, *Australia's Prosecution of Japanese War Criminals – Stimuli and Constraints*, PhD thesis, University of Melbourne Law Faculty, August 2005.

Chadwick, Owen, *Britain and the Vatican during the Second World War*, Cambridge University Press, Cambridge, 1986.

Clancy, Greg, *Hitler's Lost Spy,* Sunda Publications, Sydney, 2014.

Colville, John, *The Fringes of Power – Downing Street Diaries 1939–1955*, Hodder & Stoughton, London, 1985.

Cornwell, John, *Hitler's Pope – The Secret History of Pius XII*, Penguin, New York, 2008.

Daws, Gavan, *Prisoners of the Japanese*, Scribe, Melbourne, 2004.

Day, David, *The Politics of War – Australia at War 1939–45 from Churchill to Macarthur*, HarperCollins, Sydney, 2003.

Deighton, Len, *Blood, Tears and Folly – An Objective Look at World War II*, Pimlico Random House, London, 1993.

Dower, John, *War Without Mercy – Race and Power in the Pacific War*, Pantheon, New York, 1987.

Dubois, Josiah E, *The Devil's Chemists*, Beacon Press, Boston, 1952.

Dubois, Josiah E, *Generals in Grey Suits*, The Bodley Head, London, 1958.

Ewer, Peter, *Forgotten ANZACS – The Campaign in Greece 1941*, Scribe, Melbourne, 2008.

Freudenberg, Graham, *Churchill and Australia*, Macmillan, Sydney, 2008.

Gentile, Gian P, *Planning for Preventative War 1945–1950*, Joint Force Quarterly, Spring, 2000.

Gold, Hal, *Unit 731 Testimony*, Tuttle Publishing, North Clarendon Vermont, 1996.

Gutman, Roy, and Reiff, David (eds.), *Crimes of War*, Norton & Co., New York, 1999.

Harris, Robert and Paxman, Jeremy, *A Higher Form of Killing: The Secret History of Gas and Germ Warfare*, Chatto & Windus, London, 1982.

Harris, Sheldon H, *Factories of Death: Japanese Biological Warfare 1932–1945 and the American Cover-up*, Routledge, New York, 2002.

Higham, Charles, *Errol Flynn – The Untold Story*, Granada Publishing, London, 1980.

Higham, Charles, *Trading with the Enemy: How the Allied Multinationals Supplied Nazi Germany throughout World War Two*, Robert Hale, London, 1983.

Höhne, Heinz and Zolling, Hermann, *The General was a Spy – The Truth About General Gehlen and his Spy Ring*, Coward, McCann & Geoghegan, New York, 1972.

Holmes, Linda Goetz, *Guests of the Emperor: The Secret History of Japan's Mukden POW Camp*, Naval Institute Press, Annapolis Maryland, 2010.

Horner, Donald, *The Spy Catchers – The Official History of ASIO 1949–1963*, Allen & Unwin, Sydney, 2014.

Ismay, General Lord, *The Memoirs of General Lord Ismay*, Heinemann, London, 1960.

Jacobsen, Annie, *Operation Paperclip – The Secret Intelligence Program that Brought Nazi Scientists to America*, Little Brown and Co., New York, 2014.

Katz, Robert, *Black Sabbath – The Politics of Annihilation*, Arthur Baker, London 1969.

Kinvig, Clifford, *Churchill's Crusade – The British Invasion of Russia 1918–1920*, Hambledon Continuum, New York, 2006.

Knigge, Volkhard, *The Engineers of the Final Solution – Topf & Sons, Builders of the Auschwitz Ovens*, Buchenwald and Mittelbau-Dora Memorials Foundation, Weimar, 2005.

Knightley, Phillip, *The First Casualty*, Harcourt Brace Jovanovich, New York, 1975.

Krivosheev, Colonel-General Grigori, *Soviet Casualties and Combat Losses*, Greenhill Books, London, 1997.

Kurzman, Dan, *A Special Mission: Hitler's Secret Plot to Seize the Vatican and Kidnap Pope Pius XII*, Da Capo Press, New York, 2007.

Lasby, CG, *Project Paperclip*, Atheneum, New York, 1971.

Lewis, Damien, *The Nazi Hunters: The Ultra-secret SAS unit and the Hunt for Hitler's Worst War Criminals*, Quercus, London, 2015.

Linklater, Magnus; Hilton, Isabel; Ascherson, Neal, *Klaus Barbie – the Fourth Reich*, Coronet Books, London, 1985.

Loftus, John, *The Belarus Secret*, Penguin, New York, 1982.

Manchester, William, *The Arms of Krupp*, Bantam Books, New York, 1970.

McCullough, David, *Truman*, Simon & Schuster, New York, 1992.

McKale, Donald M, *Nazis after Hitler: How Perpetrators of the Holocaust Cheated Justice and Truth*, Rowman & Littlefield, Lanham Maryland, 2012.

Manners, Norman, *Bullwinkel*, Hesperian Press, Carlisle Western Australia, 1999.

Menzies, Andrew, *Review of Material Relating to the Entry of Suspected War Criminals into Australia*, Australian Government Publishing Service, Canberra, 1987.

Minear, Richard H, *Victors' Justice – The Tokyo War Crimes Trial*, Princeton University Press, Princeton New Jersey, 1971.

Monteith, Peter, *P.O.W. – Australian Prisoners of War in Hitler's Reich*, Pan Macmillan, Sydney, 2011.

Morton, Andrew, *17 Carnations – The Windsors, the Nazis and the Cover-Up*, Michael O'Mara Books Ltd, London, 2015.

Muirden, Bruce, *The Diggers who Signed on for More*, Wakefield Press, Adelaide, 1990.

Nagorski, Andrew, *In Pursuit – The Men and Women Who Hunted the Nazis*, Simon & Schuster, London, 2016.

Phayer, Michael, *Pius XII, the Holocaust and the Cold War*, Indiana University Press, Indianapolis, 2008.

Plunkett, Geoff, *Chemical warfare in Australia*, Australian Military History Publications, Canberra, 2007.

Posner, Gerald and Ware, John, *Mengele: The Complete Story*, McGraw-Hill, New York, 1986.

Pritchard, John and Zaide, Sonia, (eds.), *Proceedings of the International Military Tribunal of the Far East, Vol. 1 and 2*. Garland Publishing, New York, 1981.

Reynolds, David, *From World War to Cold War: Churchill, Roosevelt and the International History of the 1940s*, Oxford University Press, New York, 2006.
Röling, BVA and Ruter, CF (eds.), *The Tokyo Judgment,* University Press, Amsterdam, 1977.
Rosenbaum, AS, *Prosecuting Nazi War Criminals*, Boulder Colorado, Westview Press, 1993.
Sampson, Anthony, *The Arms Bazaar*, Coronet Books, 1977.
Semmler, Clement (ed.), *The War Diaries of Kenneth Slessor*, University of Queensland Press, Brisbane, 1985.
Sereny, Gitta, *Into that Darkness: From Mercy Killing to Mass Murder*, Vintage Digital, new edition, 2013.
Soviet Union report, *Kharbarovsk War Crimes Trial – Materials on the Trial of Former Servicemen of the Japanese Army Charged with Manufacturing and Employing Bacteriological Weapons*, Foreign Languages Publishing House, Moscow, 1950.
Stahl, Daniel, *Nazi-Jagd: Südamerikas Diktaturen und die Ahndung von NS-Verbrechen,* Wallstein Verlag, Göttingen, 2013.
Stein, Sabine and Harry, *Buchenwald Guide Book*, Buchenwald Memorial, 1993.
Steinacher, Gerald, *Nazis on the Run: How Hitler's Henchmen Fled Justice*, Oxford University Press, Oxford, 2012.
Taylor, Telford, *The Anatomy of the Nuremberg Trials: A Personal Memoir*, Alfred A Knopf, New York, 1992.
Taylor, Telford, *Sword and Swastika – Generals and Nazis in the Third Reich*, Barnes & Noble reprint, New York, 1995.
Thompson, Peter and Macklin, Robert, *Kill the Tiger – Operation Rimau and the Battle for Southeast Asia*, Maverick House, Bangkok, 2007.
Truman, Harry S., *Memoirs of Harry S Truman 1946–1952: Years of Trial and Hope*, Smithmark, New York, 1954.
United States Congress Committee on Veterans Affairs, *Treatment of American Prisoners of War in Manchuria*, US Government Printing Office, Washington DC, 1986.
Walker, Frank, *Commandos*, Hachette Australia, Sydney, 2015.
Walker, Frank, *Maralinga*, Hachette Australia, Sydney, 2014.
Walker, Frank, *The Tiger Man of Vietnam*, Hachette Australia, Sydney, 2009.
Walker, Jonathan, *Operation Unthinkable*, The History Press, Stroud UK, 2013.
Weale, Adrian, *Renegades: Hitler's Englishmen*, Trafalgar Publishing, London, 1994.
Weiner, Tim, *Legacy of Ashes – The History of the CIA*, Anchor Books, New York, 2008.
Whittman, Rebecca, *Beyond Justice – The Auschwitz Trial*, Harvard University Press, 2005.
Wiesen, Jonathan, *West German Industry and the Challenge of the Nazi Past 1945–1955*, University of North Carolina Press, Chapel Hill NC, 2001.
Williams, Peter and Wallace, David, *Unit 731 – The Japanese Army's Secret of Secrets*, Hodder & Stoughton, London, 1989.

ACKNOWLEDGEMENTS

No book seeking to cover as vast a topic as war crimes committed during World War II could be written today without drawing on the work of others who have gone down this path. The victims and perpetrators of the crimes of the war are now dead or in their late nineties, so it is nigh impossible to get original first-hand accounts. However, many gave interviews to writers, historians and investigators in the past, and that history was invaluable.

Official archives and records mostly give the bare details, and often the details are decidedly one-sided and don't reveal the full picture. Sometimes there are gems to be found in letters, memoirs or reports written at the time that give vivid accounts of events all those years ago.

For those gems and the keeping of the records, I thank archivists in Australia and around the world. They toil away unseen and unheralded, but their work is extremely appreciated by authors such as myself who come seeking details of what happened at some long-forgotten event. My thanks to the archivists at the

Australian War Memorial and the Australian National Archives, especially to those who perform the never-ending task of putting archived documents online. It is very much appreciated.

I thank Eric Van Slander and his colleagues at the US National Archives in Maryland, who were extremely helpful in directing me to the right documents in their vast facility. Librarians at New York Public Library and Columbia University went out of their way to assist. Archivists at the UK National Archives and Imperial War Museum in London helped direct me to documents that I could access online.

Archivists at Buchenwald Concentration Camp work in a horrendous place, but the work they do is so very important. Dr Michael Loeffelsender, in particular, was very helpful in providing historical details of the camp as it is preserved today, and provided me with photographs of some of their exhibits. For others, they help find records of family or lost loved ones among the entries for hundreds of thousands of prisoners.

I thank two very good friends, Connie Czymoch and David Arkless, who volunteered to accompany me on my mission to Buchenwald. It wasn't easy for them or for me to walk the cold paths in that terrible place, and I am grateful that they were there with me.

I thank others who have assisted me in the United States, including Linda Goetz Holmes, Gale Epstein, Betsy and Steve Bush in New York, and my long-time journo mate Maggie Hall in Washington. Thanks to Ruth Blank in Germany. Also to Mike Weekes in Sydney for his many computer rescues. Thanks also to old journo mate Bronwyn Watson for her help in Canberra. Another old journo mate, Terry Smyth, provided valuable information in passing on his earlier research into Australian traitors.

Writing a book puts enormous strain on an author's family and I thank Esther and Hannah for putting up with me as I brought this to fruition. My brother and former journo Peter was once again a great help in checking my copy, giving birth to many commas and full stops and sage advice. And big thanks to Bella for keeping my feet warm under the desk.

Finally, thanks for the fifth time to my publisher at Hachette, Vanessa Radnidge, without whom there wouldn't be a book. Many thanks also to editors Deonie Fiford and Jacquie Brown who did a superb job in picking up my inconsistencies and pointing out where I could improve the book for the reader. They beat this tangled web into shape, and any mistakes that slipped past their eagle eyes are my own.

Readers are welcome to contact me through my website www.frankwalker.com.au.

Frank Walker
Sydney 2017

INDEX

TRAITORS

Milne Bay massacre 230
Mitford, Diana 263
Mitford, Unity Valkyrie
   263–4
Mitomo Kazuo 208
Mitsubishi 261, 262
Montgomery, Field Marshal
   Bernard 50, 54
Morotai 231
Morrow, Colonel Thomas
   203–4
Moscow xii, xiii, 37, 50
Moscow Declaration on
   Atrocities (1943) xiii,
   57, 63
Mosley, Sir Oswald (6th
   Baronet of Ancoats)
   263
Mossad 69, 73
Mukden prisoner-of-war
   camp (Shenyang)
   184–6, 190, 209
munitions manufacture 168
   IBM 121
   Krupp 150
Munitions Manufacturing
   Corporation (IBM) 121
Murmansk 38
Murphy, Captain John J
   198–9
Mushu Island 200
Mussolini, Benito 3, 42,
   59, 258
Mutually Assured
   Destruction (MAD) 54

Nagasaki 51, 169, 227
Nanjing (Nanking) 195
   massacre 108, 195, 224,
   241
Napier 8
NASA 174
National Archives of
   Australia 16, 27–8, 99,
   100, 176
Navicert clearance for ship-
   ping 133, 134
Nazi Germany xii, 57–8
   British and dominion
      sympathisers 20
   political parties 57–8

surrender 35, 43, 44
Nazi money, shifting
   112–14
Nazi scientists
   Australia, in 176–83
   medical experiments on
      POWs 1–2, 10–13,
      16–19, 170–1
   recruitment by Allies
      168–74
Netherlands 75 see also
   Holland
New Guinea 202, 222, 230,
   233, 247, 280
New Mexico 50
New Zealand
   Expeditionary Force
   Greece, in 6–8
   POWs 142
Nishi Toshihide 207
Nixon, Richard M 79
Nizam 8
Nobusuke Kishi 'Showa
   Monster' 240
Nokia 150
Norman, Montagu 113
North Africa 3–5, 8, 23
North Brook Island 280
North Korea 209, 210, 211
Nuremberg
   Doctors' Trials 174
   Industrialists' trial
      158–64
   Nuremberg Race Laws 74
   War Crimes Trials xiii,
      61, 64, 65–6, 68, 73,
      79, 154, 160

Office of Special
   Investigations (OSI) 90
Office of Strategic Services
   (OSS) 71
oil for German war effort
   128
O'Neil, Tom 253
Operation Jaywick 224
Operation Paperclip 167–8,
   172, 175
Operation Pincher 53
Operation Rimau 224–8

Operation Unthinkable
   45–9, 53, 54
Orita, Major 222, 223–4
Orosz Richt-Bein, Angela
   269–71
Otsuka, Major-General 228
Oursler, Fulton 257–8
Outram Road Jail 225, 228

Pacelli, Cardinal Eugenio
   see Pius XII, Pope
Pacific War 40, 43, 44, 46,
   47, 229
Palestine 2, 29
Panama 133
Papua New Guinea 200,
   280
Paraguay 68, 69
partisans
   Cretan resistance 7–8, 14
   execution of 70, 91, 100
   Vietnamese 51
   Yugoslav 49–50
Patton, General George
   S 48
Pavelic, Ante 93
Pavlov, Nikolai see
   Alferchik, Nikolai
Pearl Harbor 122, 129, 237,
   238, 247, 262–3
   memorial 241
Peenemunde 172, 180
Peiper, Colonel Joachim
   164
Pershing missile 175
Philippines 185
pig iron dispute 107–12
Ping Fan 190, 191–3, 201,
   205
Pinochet, Augusto 70
Pius XII, Pope 58–62
plague 191, 193, 194–5,
   202, 203, 208, 210, 211
Pokorny, Dr Adolf 66–7
Poland 15, 39, 45, 49, 91,
   99, 147
   German invasion 126,
      138, 150, 155, 267
   labour from 151
   non-German SS divisions
      21

316